adapted
physical
education

adapted physical education

GENE A. LOGAN
University of Southern California

WM. C. BROWN COMPANY PUBLISHERS

PHYSICAL EDUCATION

Consulting Editor
Aileene Lockhart
University of Southern California

PARKS AND RECREATION

Consulting Editor
David Gray
California State College, Long Beach

HEALTH

Consulting Editor
Robert Kaplan
Ohio State University

Copyright © 1972 by Wm. C. Brown Company Publishers

Library of Congress Catalog Card Number: 74—163053

ISBN 0—697—07202—9

Printed in the United States of America

contents

Preface   vii

1. Adapted Physical Education   1

2. Growth and Development   11

3. Musculoskeletal Interrelationships   19

4. Postural Adaptations   63

5. Congenital and Pathological Conditions   101

6. Musculoskeletal Injuries   120

7. Principles of Exercise   138

8. Exercise Programs   155

9. Sports in the Adapted Physical Education Program   223

10. Organization and Administration of the Adapted
    Physical Education Program   227

Index   245

preface

Adapted physical education is a program of physical activity intended for individuals with physical limitations who may not safely or successfully participate in regular, unrestricted physical education. This book is designed to serve as a text for adapted physical education theory courses for college students majoring in physical education.

The orientation for adapted physical education lies in the physiological effects of physical activity. These positive effects of exercise or physical activity are strength, cardiovascular endurance, muscular endurance, flexibility, and skill. Although the text is primarily concerned with these potential outcomes of physical activity, it is understood that adapted physical education also has the potential of making positive contributions to help eliminate emotional, sociological, and psychological problems of students. These are seen as concomitant consequences resulting from the individual's participation in physical activity; therefore, discussions of these factors are integrated into the text where appropriate.

Physical education includes adapted physical education. Adapted physical education with its objectives, specialized subject matter, professional skills for physical educators, and implications for programming is discussed in detail.

A physiological orientation in physical education is primarily concerned with the concept of man in motion. The physical educator must know the physiological effects and outcomes of physical activity for normal individuals before he can adapt physical activity to meet the requirements of atypical students. This means that the future physical educator must have a basic knowledge of anatomy, physiology, physiology of exercise, and kinesiology. In addition, knowledge of certain laws of physical growth and development is necessary. Once principles from these areas are understood, the physical educator can undertake a study of adapted physical education. This book relates knowledge and principles from the above areas to individuals with physical limitations.

Principles of physical development and characteristics of growth are discussed. It is stressed that there are different phases of posture development. Although there are variations in these different phases, it is pointed out that they are not necessarily abnormalities. Apparent deviations at one level may be outgrown at a subsequent level.

Musculoskeletal structures constantly subjected to the environmental forces which positively or negatively affect man's motion are presented. Illustrated and discussed are the fundamental mechanisms of the musculoskeletal system involving the major joints and their supporting musculature.

Three chapters are devoted to a discussion of the specific forces which often cause physical deviations. Extensive consideration is given to *postural adaptations* resulting from the effect of gravity on the feet and total body posture. *Congenital and pathological conditions* involving the musculoskeletal system are presented along with implications for physical activity. *Musculoskeletal injuries* resulting from trauma of the type most frequently encountered in physical education and athletics are described, as well as the mechanisms of these injuries. Recommendations for the rehabilitation of athletic injuries are included.

One chapter is devoted to the *principles of exercise* as used in adapted physical education, including the objectives, purposes, and recommended dosages of such exercise.

Exercise programs for common disabling conditions and divergencies are illustrated and described. The "exercise-routine method" of administering exercise to a class on the basis of subgroups for individuals with similar disabilities is included. Therapeutic exercise for most of the musculature surrounding the major joints of the body is presented in this manner. In addition, there is a comprehensive general conditioning program for those students requiring overall physical development in the adapted physical education program.

The bases of sports programming for these students are discussed. Criteria are presented for the selection of sports and other activities for the individual with physical limitations.

Organization and administration of the adapted physical education program are presented, in addition to selected classification systems, methods of keeping records, and class scheduling.

In applying the physiological approach to adapted physical education, it is believed that the teacher's function is to (1) utilize existing knowledge of man in motion, (2) understand the effects of external and internal forces which affect motion, and (3) determine the demands of various physical activities on the organism. By judiciously applying principles of exercise, the professionally prepared physical educator should be able to provide physical activities which will aid in the alleviation or amelioration of negative adaptation of the body resulting from the forces of gravity, congenital defects, injury, illness, or disease. This is the major aim of adapted physical education.

I wish to express my appreciation to Dr. James G. Dunkelberg and Dr. Wayne C. McKinney for their contributions to the manuscript. Appreciation is also expressed to Janice Stevenson for her contribution to the section on neurological integration and for preparing the manuscript. Thanks are offered to Lorenzo J. Rossi, Jr., for providing some of the photographs.

Gratitude is expressed to the following individuals who served as models for the illustrations: Gareth Burk, Linda Graham, Henry Jackson, Donna Noguchi, Janice Stevenson, and Leonora Webb.

GENE A. LOGAN

adapted
physical education

Adapted physical education is physical education for individuals with physical limitations. It offers the individual the opportunity for optimum development and the maintenance of physical fitness. It provides opportunities for facilitating normal growth of the child. It helps to develop, as well as to prevent the reversal of, such factors as strength, cardiovascular endurance, muscular endurance, flexibility, and skill. Some of the satisfactions that are gained from participation in physical activity are a sense of achievement, creativity, tension release, and the joy of creation. The school should offer experiences in activities to provide a basis for the development of an interest that will result in the use of physical activity for avocational pursuits or as a way of spending leisure time. Physical activity in the form of exercise, sports (fig. 1.1), and dance can provide a setting in which recreational activity may be learned or enjoyed. Schools must provide the opportunity for students to experience the satisfactions that can be derived from participation in a variety of physical activities.

Activities offered in physical education are the vehicles through which voluntary activity of a recreational nature can be provided. Recreation possesses certain characteristics which distinguish it from other types of activities offered in an educational program. Any form of leisure-time experience or activity through which the individual receives enjoyment or satisfaction can be termed recreation. The individual engages in activity because he chooses that activity without any external compulsion. Immediate and direct satisfaction that the individual experiences is one of the main characteristics of participation in recreation.

Physical education is generally considered indispensable in meeting the developmental requirements of the child. The responsibility

Figure 1.1. Adapted physical education class—sports phase. (Photo courtesy Robert A. Millikan High School, Long Beach Unified School District, Long Beach, California.)

for providing the child with experiences and physical activity that will afford a more complete education must be assumed by the school. Physical activities must play an integral part in the total educational process of the student.

Opportunities for medically supervised play must be provided for the physically handicapped child to help him develop desirable traits of character. Children who are physically handicapped are often limited in their opportunity to safely experience the world around them, their own emotions, and the benefits that come through their participation in physical activity. Physically handicapped children have a greater requirement for physical activity than the "average" child because their normal growth behavior is often restricted due to their disability.

It is frequently observed that physically handicapped children also have an accompanying emotional problem. Emotional problems often arise from the individual's inability to function in a manner similar to his peers. Emphasis is usually placed upon the physical aspect of the condition with little attention being paid to the prevention of a potential emotional maladjustment. The physically handicapped individual has an intensified sociological and psychological requirement as well. Obviously there is no special psychology of the physically handicapped individual compared to the individual without physical impairment. However, physical limitations can present obstacles to the individual which intensify the problems experienced by all human beings. The intensity of the emotional involvement of the physically handicapped individual is usually in direct proportion to his personal reaction and the reaction of others with whom he is associated.

Selection of activities and the provision of these activities in adapted physical education must be based on principles which utilize developmental characteristics. These characteristics are the physical status, readiness, requirements, and interest of the students. Further, a thorough knowledge of the activities in the program is required to achieve the objectives of the program. Because the physically handicapped individual who participates in adapted physical education is usually homogeneously grouped with other individuals having similar problems, he may find ways to achieve social adjustments with his associates. Socialization and group interaction can be attained in the adapted physical education class, although the major emphasis is upon dealing with the physically handicapped. Experience has shown that coeducational classes in adapted physical education offer these kinds of opportunities to many students.

Adapted physical education, through games, sports, and rhythms, affords the student an opportunity through which he may limit the degree and severity of his adaptation to demands imposed by gravity, trauma, injury, congenital defect, illness, or disease. The ultimate objective should be improvement of the physiological factors necessary for skill performance which is essential for effective and efficient daily living.

PHYSICALLY HANDICAPPING CONDITIONS

The student's participation in regular physical education is most frequently prohibited by the following physically handicapping conditions: (1) orthopedic handicaps, (2) poor body mechanics, (3) cardiovascular conditions, (4) visual handicaps, (5) auditory handicaps, and (6) other traumatic, pathological, and congenital conditions.

Disability Grouping

Due to the repetitive incidence of certain physically handicapping conditions, it becomes possible to generalize about the requirements of students who will be recommended for adapted physical education. Students with physical restrictions tend to fall into one or more of the following groups: (1) those seeking to adapt themselves to a permanent condition, (2) those desiring to rehabilitate a physical disability, (3) those requiring limited physical activity, and (4) those recommended for a developmental program.

Adapted Physical Education Defined

Classes which are provided for students with physical restrictions who may not safely or successfully participate in the regular physical education program have a number of different titles. These include adapted physical education, corrective physical education, developmental physical education, individual physical education, medical gymnastics, remedial gymnastics, remedial physical education, corrective therapy, prescribed exercise, and exercise therapy. Because of the great variation of titles which describe this particular area of endeavor, the American Association for Health, Physical Education and Recreation conducted a survey to determine the title most acceptable. This survey, conducted in 1947, indicated that the term *adapted physical education* best described these classes. This committee defined adapted physical education as—

A diversified program of developmental activities, games, sports, and rhythms, suited to the interests, capacities and limitations of students with disabilities who may not safely or successfully engage in unrestricted participation in the general physical education program.[1]

It should be noted that if this definition were to be read just through the word *students,* one would have a functional definition of physical education. When the concept of students with disabilities is included with the definition of physical education, this definition becomes applicable to adapted physical education. Of course, the key words in the definition are *safely* and *successfully.*

Objectives of Adapted Physical Education

A general objective of adapted physical education which is applicable to all students is to provide opportunities for the student to acquire the maximum physiological, psychological, and sociological development of which he is capable, through participation in properly selected and controlled physical activities.

Specific objectives for those students who have physical limitations necessitating their assignment to adapted physical education classes are essential. The nature and scope of adapted physical education may be guided by the following objectives:

1. To protect each student's condition from further aggravation by arranging a program of activities within his limitations.
2. To assist the student in understanding and accepting his own limitations.
3. To correct or alleviate the student's remediable weaknesses or malalignments.
4. To develop the best possible organic vigor or condition in view of the individual's limitations.
5. To develop skill and knowledge of recreational sports and games suitable or adaptable to the individual's limitations.
6. To develop the student's knowledge and appreciation of good body mechanics and efficiency.
7. To help students make satisfactory social and emotional adjustments to problems imposed by their disabilities.
8. To help students gain security through improved function and increased ability to meet the physical demands of daily living.

1. "Guiding Principles for Adapted Physical Education," *Journal of the American Association for Health, Physical Education and Recreation* 23, no. 4 (April 1952): 15.

Bases for Adapted Physical Education

Two factors influence development of the curriculum and program planning in the regular physical education program: (1) the requirements and interests of the students and (2) the philosophy of the physical education department and/or school. In addition, the student should have a physical examination before participating in physical education. He should have medical approval for unrestricted participation in the regular physical education program. A well-rounded program should include a wide variety of team sports, dual and individual sports, games, aquatics, rhythmic activities, and exercises that are appropriate for students at various developmental levels.

As a result of the physical examination, the physician determines whether or not the student may safely or successfully participate in the regular physical education program. If the physician feels that the student cannot do this, the student is then assigned to the adapted physical education program. The major factor that should have the most influence on the nature of this program and which is the basis for the program is the *medical diagnosis and recommendation of the physician.*

The bases for both the regular physical education program and the adapted physical education program are almost identical. The difference lies in the emphasis placed upon the student's requirements and the results of the physical examination.

The relationship between the regular physical education and adapted physical education programs is illustrated in figure 1.2. Boxes formed by the solid lines indicate the structure of the regular physical education program. Boxes formed by the broken lines indicate individualization of the regular physical education program. This individual emphasis then indicates the structure of the adapted physical education program. Adapted physical education has as its primary concern the individual requirements of students. Regular physical education, on the other hand, is based primarily upon group characteristics and requirements of students.

Because of the nature of the handicapping conditions of those students who may benefit through adapted physical education, the four major phases of regular physical education, (1) developmental activities, (2) games, (3) sports, and (4) rhythms, are grouped into two major sections. This grouping for adapted physical education is discussed in terms of organization and administration in chapter ten.

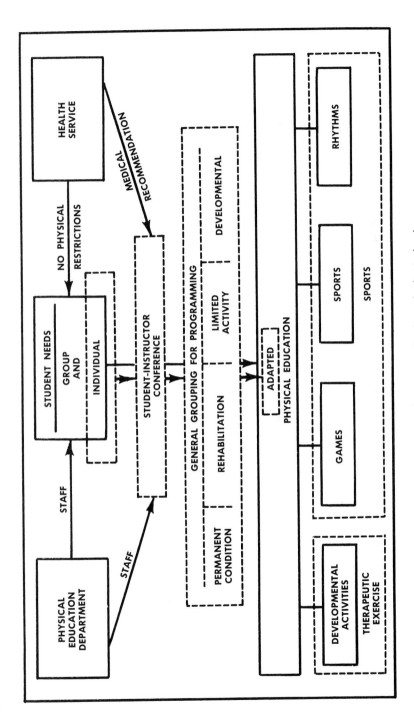

Figure 1.2. Relationship between general physical education and adapted physical education.

7

PROGRAMMING FOR ADAPTED PHYSICAL EDUCATION

Because students assigned to adapted physical education tend to fall into one or more of four general groups, certain implications for programming become obvious. In order to meet the requirements of students composing these groups, it becomes necessary to provide therapeutic exercise and sports within the adapted physical education program. Those students with such limitations as postural defects, remediable physical disabilities, or those with low physical fitness may benefit from participation in the therapeutic exercise phase of the program. This phase is designed primarily to improve strength, cardiovascular endurance, muscular endurance, and flexibility. The sports phase of the program includes sports, games, rhythms, and aquatics. Students with permanent disabilities, such as congenital amputations, cerebral palsy, or visual or aural handicaps, may benefit from participation in this phase. Students with asthma, diabetes, and cardiovascular divergencies may also receive benefits from participation in the sports phase of the adapted physical education program. In many instances, the students may receive additional benefits from participation in both aspects of the program. For example, a student who has received maximum benefit from the therapeutic exercise phase may then become involved in the sports phase. Here his medical recommendation may indicate the requirement for a low energy output to prevent him from participating in the regular physical education program.

Children require activity, recognition, status, self-direction, self-expression, group acceptance, and new and interesting experiences. The major task in adapted physical education is the adaptation of normal activities to meet the specific requirements of individual students. This involves thoughtful combining of the individual interests, aptitudes, abilities, previous experiences, and physical limitations to satisfy the student's particular requirements.

The primary purpose of the adapted physical education program should be to help prepare the student with physical disabilities to live a full and satisfying life in a society of non-handicapped individuals. The student should, therefore, be provided with the opportunity to learn sports and other activities which are enjoyed by his non-handicapped peers. The selection of activities for the adapted physical education program should include mainly those sports activities which do not require extensive adaptations of the rules or the nature of the activity. When the sport is so modified that it loses its identity, the student in adapted physical education may react negatively because the teacher is "letting him win."

Return to Regular Physical Education

It might be said that the function of the adapted physical education teacher is to work himself out of a job. The teacher's purpose should be to make every effort to return the student to the regular physical education program when his condition permits. In such instances where the student may be returned to the regular physical education program, it may be necessary for the adapted physical education program instructor to inform the regular physical education teacher of the student's condition. Because students are assigned to adapted physical education for rehabilitation of such limitations as joint injuries, they are frequently able to be reassigned to the regular physical education program. It is necessary, therefore, that the regular physical education instructor be aware of the situation. It is possible for that teacher to provide certain activities that would not be detrimental to the student who may still have some minor physical limitations. A close relationship between the adapted physical education teacher and the regular physical education teacher is necessary in dealing with students who have been returned to the regular physical education program.

The adapted physical education teacher should make every effort to encourage the student to return to the regular physical education program whenever possible. Ideally, all students ought to have the opportunity to participate in regular physical education with their peers. If class size would permit, students with physical limitations could participate with their non-handicapped peers in many instances. However, with the high ratio of students to the individual teacher in the public school situation, it becomes necessary, primarily from an administrative standpoint, to provide the smaller adapted physical education class which tends to segregate the handicapped individual. Although the segregation of the handicapped individual may tend to heighten his awareness of his handicap, the adapted physical education class does provide him with an opportunity to improve his physical status and/or give him an opportunity to learn physical skills in a setting which will not aggravate his condition.

SELECTED REFERENCES

1. AAHPER COMMITTEE ON ADAPTED PHYSICAL EDUCATION. "Guiding Principles for Adapted Physical Education." *Journal of the American Association for Health, Physical Education and Recreation* 23, no. 4 April 1952):15, 28.
2. ARNHEIM, DANIEL D.; AUXTER, DAVID; and CROWE, WALTER C. *Principles and Methods of Adapted Physical Education.* St. Louis: The C. V. Mosby Company, 1969.

3. CLARKE, H. HARRISON, and CLARKE, DAVID H. *Developmental and Adapted Physical Education*. Englewood Cliffs, N. J.: Prentice-Hall, Inc., 1963.

4. DANIELS, ARTHUR S., and DAVIES, EVELYN A. *Adapted Physical Education*. New York: Harper & Row, Publishers, 1965.

5. DE VRIES, HERBERT A. *Physiology of Exercise for Physical Education and Athletics*. Dubuque, Ia.: Wm. C. Brown Company Publishers, 1966.

6. DUNKELBERG, JAMES G., and LOGAN, GENE A. "New Directions in the Professional Preparation of Teachers of Adapted Physical Education." Paper presented to the Joint Meeting of the Professional Preparation and Adapted Physical Education Sections, Southwest District Convention, American Association for Health, Physical Education and Recreation, Albuquerque, New Mexico, 1961.

7. FAIT, HOLLIS F. *Special Physical Education*. Philadelphia: W. B. Saunders Company, 1966.

8. FALLS, HAROLD B., ed. *Exercise Physiology*. New York: Academic Press, Inc., 1968.

9. FLINT, M. MARILYN. "Current Trends in Adapted Physical Education on the College Level." *Journal of the Association for Health, Physical Education and Recreation* 38 (September 1967):63-66.

10. FULTON, JOHN F., ed. *A Textbook of Physiology*. 17th ed. Philadelphia: W. B. Saunders Company, 1955.

11. KESSLER, J. W. "The Impact of Disability on the Child." *Journal of the American Physical Therapy Association* 46 (1966):153-159.

12. LOGAN, GENE A. *Adaptations of Muscular Activity*. Belmont, Calif.: Wadsworth Publishing Co., Inc., 1964.

13. ———, and McKINNEY, WAYNE C. *Kinesiology*. Dubuque, Ia.: Wm. C. Brown Company Publishers, 1970.

14. MATHEWS, DONALD, K.; KRUSE, ROBERT; and SHAW, VIRGINIA. *The Science of Physical Education for Handicapped Children*. New York: Harper & Row, Publishers, 1962.

15. METHENY, ELEANOR, and LOGAN, GENE A. *The Dentist's Daily Seven: A Series of Exercises for Dentists*. Human Factors Research Division, University of Southern California School of Dentistry, Los Angeles, 1964.

16. MOORE, C. A. "The Handicapped Can Succeed." *The Physical Educator* 24 (1967):163-164.

17. MOREHOUSE, LAURENCE E., and MILLER, AUGUSTUS T. *Physiology of Exercise*. 5th ed. St. Louis: C. V. Mosby Company, 1967.

18. RASCH, PHILIP J., and BURKE, ROGER K. *Kinesiology and Applied Anatomy*. 3rd ed. Philadelphia: Lea & Febiger, 1967.

19. SEAMAN, JANET A. "Attitudes of Physically Handicapped Children Toward Physical Education." *Research Quarterly* 41 (October 1970): 439-445.

growth
and
development

It is essential that the physical education teacher have a thorough background of knowledge of a child's physical growth and development. This is particularly important because of the influence that physical activity has on growth and development of the body. Guiding the growth and development of the child is a major responsibility of the physical education teacher in the school program. Through his knowledge of the principles and the laws of physical processes, the teacher selects those physical activities which are most appropriate at various developmental levels.

Growth signifies those changes which indicate an increase in size and proportion. Exercise plays a vital role in the growth process of children. Vigorous physical activity which stresses the body tends to cause the organism to adapt to greater demands, thereby providing optimum growth of the bones, muscles, and other tissues.

Development is the process through which the child achieves maturity. This process is influenced by or is dependent upon factors of maturation and learning.

Maturation indicates the appearance or unfolding of innate hereditary traits. The emergence of a trait through maturation is characterized by its involuntary appearance, whereas the evolution of a change in behavior of an individual as a result of volition is due to the process of learning. Maturation is an important factor in determining one's ability to learn. It provides the raw material for learning and influences the patterned sequence of learning. Learning must wait until maturation has occurred. An individual cannot learn new skills until he has achieved the necessary physical and mental development; these factors provide the foundation for learning.

PRINCIPLES OF PHYSICAL DEVELOPMENT

Complex natural laws guide and control the developmental process that takes the individual through infancy, childhood and adolescence, to physical maturity. The unfolding of specific characteristics at a given age level has led to the following statement of principles pertaining to human development. These guiding principles are the consensus of those found in the literature.

Changes are quantitative and qualitative in nature. The term *development* involves changes in size, proportion, function, and structure of the body. Development, however, is one aspect of the growth process which involves changes in function or structure. Growth, as indicated previously, involves an increase in size or proportion.

Development follows a pattern that is orderly, continuous, and predictable. Each phase of development is the outcome of the preceding phase, and each phase is prerequisite to the next. Development continues from the time of conception to maturity. Pace is slow and regular—though, of course, not always the same for everyone. However, the general pattern is not altered by the speed of development: All children pass through the same phases or steps at approximately the same time. Since the pattern is so fixed in its sequence, and appears so consistently in a majority of children, it is possible to establish certain standards of expectation at various age levels. This consistency has led to the establishment of height-weight tables, tests of mental and social age, and similar measurement tools and standards. Nonetheless, though age-correlated developmental levels are useful for developing norms, they should be applied to individuals only with the greatest caution and professional judgment.

Development occurs at different rates for different parts of the body. Not all parts of the body develop at the same rate, but each proceeds at its own rate and reaches maturity at different times. For example, the brain attains maximum physical size at approximately six years of age. The hands and feet reach adult size early in adolescence; this may account for the apparent awkwardness of adolescent children. Skeletal growth and ossification continue into the early twenties.

Development proceeds from general to specific responses. In learning a new physical skill, the individual first attempts general or total-body responses that are not required for the efficient performance of the skill. Such irrelevant or even detrimental movements may include exaggerated actions of the body, head, or limbs. Through practice, however, the individual eventually learns to decrease or eliminate the generality and to increase the specificity of the responses. The elimination of undesired movement is possibly the predominant factor in the acquisition of skilled movement.

Rate of development is influenced by individual differences. All children normally pass through each major stage of development, though they do not do so necessarily at the same age. Each child grows at his own rate. Individual differences in overall growth rate generally remain constant. The accelerated (or the retarded) developer at an early age is likely to be accelerated (or retarded) at a late age also. Significant factors in a child's experience (amount and kind of instruction, opportunity, practice, motivation, and interests) as well as certain environmental factors (improper diet, lack of exercise, injury, or disease) could greatly accelerate or retard a child's performance capabilities or his motor development. The resultant positive or negative modifications in the developmental timetable are much more significant than the innate influences. Development, however, must wait for prerequisite maturation to occur. A child who is retarded in his physical performance according to developmental norm tables could make unusual progress. If, for example, retardation is the result of poor environmental influences, the removal or reversal of such influences in order to capitalize completely upon the degree of maturation that is already present could significantly change the rate of development. However, early gaps or losses in the process of maturation and development can never be entirely recovered.

SKELETAL GROWTH

Wolff's law and the *carpal index* must be included in any discussion of the characteristics of skeletal growth. Wolff's law accounts for the skeletal development of the bones of the body. This law states: "Every change in the form and function of the bone, or of the function alone, is followed by certain definite changes in their internal architecture, and equally definite secondary alteration in their external conformation, in accordance with mathematical laws" (Wolff, 1892). The phrase "in accordance with mathematical laws" has been attacked continuously since its proposal. Steindler has modified Wolff's statement to indicate that the *external shape and the internal structure of bone are changed according to the stress involved* (Steindler, 1970). In terms of the effect of pressure on bone growth, it has been concluded (Mainland, 1945), as a result of an extensive review of research, that constant pressure, even though slight in magnitude, usually causes atrophy, but that *intermittent* pressure, even though great, seems to result in bone growth. Thus, the small gravitational torques resulting from postural deviations may be debilitating to the bone, although the tremendous stresses of sports participation, if less than traumatic in magnitude, may result in desirable growth and strengthening of bone. A recent review of the literature on the relationship between exercise and bone growth and metabolism further substantiates the favorable effects of physical activity on bone growth (Lamb, 1968). The carpal index utilizing X rays of the carpal bones of the wrist is used to determine skeletal age as it relates to the chronological age of the individual. This index indicates the amount of ossification that has occurred at a given age.

The growth of bones is accomplished by adding new bone tissue to their width at their outer edge beneath the periosteum. This growth process is analogous to tree growth. Long bones of the arms and legs grow near their ends, where a narrow strip of cartilage remains throughout the growing years. The long bones, as well as the new bones, grow rapidly during puberty and do not become firmly united until several years later. A description of the bone segments involved in long-bone growth includes (1) the shaft of the long bone called the *diaphysis*; (2) at either end of the shaft, the area of bone growth called the *metaphysis*; (3) immediately beyond the ends of the metaphyses, a cartilage called the *epiphyseal plate*; and (4) a bony structure separated from the shaft by the cartilage and called the *epiphysis*. Bone growth occurs at the epiphysis and at the metaphysis. When the epiphysis and diaphysis unite or become ossified into a single unit, growth in length ceases.

As indicated previously, development occurs at different rates for different parts of the body. It also occurs at different rates for the ages at which the various bones reach maturity. Some examples of the differences in skeletal maturity may help to clarify this principle. At birth, the human being has no epiphyses in the hand and has no carpals. At about two years of age, two or three wrist bones appear. During the preschool years, epiphyses and most of the carpals appear. Not until adolescence, however, does the last carpal bone appear. Union of the epiphyses and carpals of the hand is not completed until approximately eighteen years of age. The hip bones do not unite until around twelve or fourteen years of age, whereas the sacral bones unite at about eighteen years. The spine at birth is soft, pliable, and easily distorted, since it is basically cartilaginous in structure. Approximately one-half to two-thirds of the entire growth of the vertebrae occurs during the first three years, although the vertebrae continue to grow until the early twenties. A further example may be illustrated in the development of the adult curves of the spine. At birth, the spine has a single posterior flexion curve. This initial flexion curve remains in the thoracic and sacrococcygeal portions of the spinal column. The hyperextension curve of the cervical spine appears when the child becomes able to raise his head from a prone position. The hyperextension curve of the lumbar spine begins to form when the child uses the spinal extensors for kicking and walking. The thoracic curve becomes more pronounced when the child is able to manipulate his arms and hands in front of him.

POSTURAL PATTERNS AT DIFFERENT LEVELS OF DEVELOPMENT

Specific traits are evident at each developmental level. The relationship of various developmental levels of postural patterns is of particular interest to the physical education teacher. It is readily obvious that children at different age levels display different standing postural and walking patterns. Unfortunately, the postural patterns of young children are often evaluated by standards that are based on the adult structure. Because of this, it is essential that the physical educator have a thorough understanding of the postural characteristics of children at the various growth and developmental stages through which they will pass on their way to maturity. Too often the characteristics of a particular developmental period are mistaken for postural defects. In reality, they are simply normal characteristics of the particular developmental level. However, these postural characteristics at another level may be considered postural defects. The majority of children are born with supinated feet (soles of the feet turned inward), bowlegs, internal tibial torsion (longitudinal twisting of the tibia), and muscular imbalance of the knees, hips, and trunk. The nature of the fetal position is the probable cause of such characteristics. In the fetal position, thighs are flexed upon the trunk and are rotated outward with the knees flexed. The soles of the feet are facing inward. The flexors of the joints involving these body segments may be shorter in relation to the joint extensors due to the intrauterine pressure. As the child begins to bear weight in the standing position in the early stages of walking, he will evidence some degree of pronation (weight-bearing on the medial border of the feet) and knock-knees. In the standing position, greater pressure as the result of gravity is applied to the lateral borders of the feet as well as to the knees. In accordance with Wolff's law, this pressure stimulates bone growth on the lateral borders of the feet, resulting in a normal growth pattern. The developmental process continues until about the age of three. There is a gradual decrease until about six years of age at which time the lateral deviation of the knees and the internal torsion of the tibia have practically disappeared. The degree of pronation has also lessened. The preschool child's posture is characterized by a prominent abdomen, an exaggerated lumbar curve, a relatively straight thoracic area, and prominent or projecting scapulae (winged scapulae). The downward pull upon the abdominal viscera is usually a result of the pull of gravity. The weak abdominal musculature is usually seen at this age level. Because of the weak abdominals and the anterior tilting of the superior aspect of the pelvis, there is an associated increased lumbar curvature. The scapulae are prominent because of weakness of the serratus anterior muscles which serve to hold the scapulae to the rib cage. This weakness is probably due to a lack of activities such as crawling or climbing. Contributing to this condition is a rounded rib cage which is inclined downward from gravitational pull on the abdominal viscera. As a result, the ribs present a surface which is not well suited to maintain a properly positioned scapula.

Knock-knees have usually disappeared by the time the average child enters school. Pronation of the feet has practically disappeared. A somewhat prominent abdomen will be evident, along with an increased lumbar curve. The child may assume an extended position of the knees while standing, but in walking or running he will still be unable to fully extend his knees and hips and will evidence the tendency to flex the knees and hips slightly. This tendency toward hip and knee flexion persists because hip flexors are stronger than the hip extensors. His head, neck, and shoulders will be in good alignment, but he may appear to have an increase in the thoracic curve. This apparent increase is caused by the sunken appearance of the chest due to the downward displacement of the ribs.

Preadolescent postural patterns are somewhat different from those of the earlier developmental phases. These patterns are characterized by a straight upper back, straight neck, aligned shoulders, and depression of the chest. The abdominal area may be prominent, but the degree of increase in the lumbar curve is much less than in earlier periods. At this point, the preadolescent is beginning to approach the adult standard. Evidence of specific body type is more pronounced. His extreme activity at this time may account in part for his "good" posture.

Describing the adolescent posture is difficult. It includes a period from twelve to twenty years of age. However, from fourteen to seventeen years of age, body type becomes firmly established. At this time, the adolescent's posture is characteristic of his adult life. It should be remembered, however, that this is a period of rapid growth, and the individual often assumes positions that may cause temporary postural deviations. These positions may lead to permanent postural habits. An example of such an adaptation is the tall adolescent who assumes a slouch position to conform more closely to the height of his peers. This, in turn, may increase his thoracic curve.

In order to plan and conduct a scientifically sound program of physical education and, more specifically, of adapted physical education, the teacher must continually observe the factors affecting growth and development of the child. The physical educator can use his knowledge to determine which students need referral to appropriate medical personnel. The physician should provide a diagnosis and recommendation upon which the adapted physical education program can effectively meet the requirements of the student.

SELECTED REFERENCES

1. BRECKENRIDGE, MARIAN E., and MURPHY, MARGARET N. *Growth and Development of the Young Child.* 8th ed. Philadelphia: W. B. Saunders Company, 1969.
2. BRITTEN, SAMUEL D. "A Unit of Work in Growth and Development and Early Detection of Physical Divergencies of the Elementary School Child." Paper presented to the Joint Conference of the Southwest District, American Association for Health, Physical Education and Recreation, Long Beach, California, 1963.
3. CURRICULUM COMMITTEE FOR HEALTH, PHYSICAL EDUCATION, and SAFETY IN THE ELEMENTARY SCHOOLS. "Child Growth and Development, Characteristics and Needs." *Journal of the American Association for Health, Physical Education and Recreation* 20 (April 1949):223-224, 278-282.
4. DAVIES, EVELYN A. *The Elementary School Child and His Posture Patterns.* New York: Appleton-Century-Crofts, Inc., 1958.
5. GARRISON, KARL C. *Growth and Development.* New York: Longmans, Green, 1959.
6. HURLOCK, ELIZABETH B. *Adolescent Development.* 3rd ed. New York: McGraw-Hill Book Co., Inc., 1967.
7. LAMB, D. R. "Influence of Exercise on Bone Growth and Metabolism." In *Kinesiology Review—1968.* Washington: American Association for Health, Physical Education and Recreation, 1968, pp. 43-48.
8. LEE, J. MURRAY, and LEE, DORRIS MAY. *The Child and His Development.* New York: Appleton-Century-Crofts, Inc., 1958.
9. LOGAN, GENE A. *Adaptations of Muscular Activity.* Belmont, Calif.: Wadsworth Publishing Co., Inc., 1964.
10. MAINLAND, D. *Anatomy as a Basis for Medical and Dental Practice.* New York: Harper & Row, Publishers, 1945.

11. MATHEWS, DONALD K.; KRUSE, ROBERT; and SHAW, VIRGINIA. *The Science of Physical Education for Handicapped Children.* New York: Harper & Row, Publishers, 1962.
12. RARICK, G. LAWRENCE. "Exercise and Growth." In *Science and Medicine of Exercise and Sports,* edited by W. R. Johnson. New York: Harper & Row, Publishers, 1960.
13. STEINDLER, ARTHUR. *Kinesiology of the Human Body.* Springfield, Ill.: Charles C Thomas, Publisher, 1970.
14. THORPE, LOUIS P., and CRUZE, WENDELL W. *Developmental Psychology.* New York: Ronald Press Co., 1956.
15. WOLFF, JULIUS. *Das Gesetz der Transformation der Knochen.* Berlin, Germany: Hirschwald, 1892.

musculoskeletal
interrelationships

Human motion is a result of complex interrelationships within the musculoskeletal system. To provide a basis on which adapted physical education can be established, this chapter discusses, from a general viewpoint, the fundamental functions of the muscles and bones. Specific attention is paid to selected anatomical structures and to functional components that are considered important in the study of adapted physical education.

MUSCULOSKELETAL SYSTEM

Joint Structure

Motion of the body takes place at the articulations of the bones of the skeleton. The joint, which is a result of the articulation between two bones, may be classified in three ways: (a) immovable (synarthrodial), (b) slightly movable (amphiarthrodial), (c) freely movable (diarthrodial). An example of an immovable joint is the junction at the sutures of the skull. An example of a slightly movable joint exists at the symphysis pubis. The large joints of the limbs are freely movable joints.

Emphasis here is placed upon a knowledge of freely movable joints because of the frequency of injury to the limbs. Joints are held together by ligaments, variously arranged fibrous tissues, tendons, and muscles. In a freely movable joint, a ligamentous structure surrounds the articulation and is known as the *articular capsule*. This capsule, or "housing," is lined with a synovial membrane which secretes a lubricant known as *synovial fluid*. At the ends of the surfaces where

19

the bones come together and make contact with each other a cartilage is located to provide a smooth surface. It is called the articular cartilage and is composed of *hyaline cartilage.* In some joints—the knee, for example—an additional piece of cartilage lies between the articular cartilages of the tibia and the femur. Some other joints also have these *interarticular discs.* Freely movable joints are further described as (1) gliding (arthrodial), (2) hinge (ginglymus), (3) pivot (trochoid), (4) biaxial ball-and-socket (elipsoid), (5) knuckle (condyloid), (6) triaxial ball-and-socket (enarthrodial), and (7) a unique, triaxial joint, the saddle joint of the thumb.

There is a functional distinction between ligaments and tendons. Although their basic composition is similar from a microscopic standpoint, the arrangement of fibers and other factors cause them to differ. Basically, ligaments attach bone to bone, whereas tendons serve to attach muscle to bone and muscle to skin. Tendons may also have other anatomical relationships. However, in order to make functional distinction between ligaments and tendons, a tendon should be regarded as a functional extension of a muscle—as a fibrous structure that connects the muscle to other structures, particularly to bone. The tendon often provides a narrowed attachment for the muscle, thereby preventing large, bulky masses from having to function at joints. For example, if the muscle belly instead of the tendon were to cross the wrist joint, it is unlikely that such a highly skilled mechanism as the hand would exist. Tendons provide certain pulley actions that allow efficiency of movement, especially where fine motions are desired. In addition to these functional differences, ligaments are nonelastic and do not shorten adaptively. *Muscle tissue will adapt in length to habitually shortened positions* if enough time is allowed for it to do so. In a case of poliomyelitis, where the muscles most involved (agonists) have lost their innervation, the tendons of the contralateral muscles (antagonists)—because of their ability to shorten by active contraction—will eventually adapt to their shortest length if proper therapeutic exercise is not employed to maintain an adequate range of motion. It is is important that the physical educator understand the differences between ligaments and tendons.

Joint integrity, especially within the limbs, is maintained by the surrounding structures. Ligaments serve as limiting structures to extremes and directions of motion of the bone. The articular capsule functions as a support, and the tendons and their associated muscles provide movement as well as support and stability of the joint. These structures, the muscles and their tendinous attachments, are the major stabilizing components of the joint. One of the most important functions of therapeutic exercise is to aid in the restabilization of joints after injury.

Not only do ligaments function as limiting components for extremes in range of motion, but also the location of the ligaments at each joint largely determines the type of movement that the muscle is able to provide. In addition, factors such as the shape of the articulating bone help to determine the potential for movement at each joint. For example, in the elbow joint, the humerus articulates with the ulna in a hingelike fashion. At the extreme of elbow extension, the olecranon process contacts the posterior surface of the distal end of the humerus in an action similar to that of a doorstop. Thus, acting in connection with ligaments, this structure limits hyperextension of the elbow in the normal individual. The ligaments along the lateral aspects of the joint prevent medial and lateral movement of the distal end of the ulna. Along with the ligaments, any formation at the joints is considered in relation to the movements that are possible at the joints. The hingelike relationship of the humerus and the ulna at the elbow predetermines the potential movement at that joint.

Spatial Relationships of Muscles to Joints

In order to understand the movement at joints from a functional standpoint, it it necessary to know the location or position of the ligaments and muscles in relation to the joints. Knowing the spatial relationship of muscles and ligaments to joints provides the student with information through which he can deduce the action of muscles. In order to do this, he must have a knowledge of the bones to determine the proximal and distal muscle attachments, the line of pull of the muscle as it crosses the joint, the movements which are possible at the particular joint, and the planes of motion through which the part moves. If the limiting ligaments are on the medial or lateral sides of the joint and a muscle is attached anteriorly to the joint, then one should expect, for example, only *flexion* of the elbow and only *extension* of the knee.

The spatial relationship of muscles to joints aids the student in determining muscle action. If a particular joint allows only flexion and extension, then the muscles that cross that joint will in turn perform flexion or extension at that joint, depending on the anatomical location of the muscles. There are a few rare exceptions to this concept. One is the abductor pollicis brevis muscle and its relationship to the metacarpophalangeal joint of the thumb. This muscle crosses the carpometacarpal joint *and* the metacarpophalangeal joint of the thumb. But despite this muscle's being in a position to abduct the metacarpophalangeal joint, it cannot abduct because the ligaments of the joint permit only flexion and extension. Along with some other minor movements, the major action of that muscle is abduction of the carpometacarpal joint of the thumb. If the student knows the movements that are possible at a particular joint, and the spatial relationship of the muscle to that joint, the action of the muscles will be obvious.

MUSCULATURE

The three basic types of muscle are (1) *involuntary,* or smooth; (2) *cardiac,* or heart; (3) *voluntary,* or skeletal. There are histological differences among the three types, but the concern here is mainly with the voluntary, or skeletal, muscle. Muscles perform various functions through their ability to contract, to relax, and to stretch. Alternations between contraction and relaxation of skeletal muscles as they span joints and act upon the articulations of the bone result in motion.

Muscular Contraction

The contraction of muscle is characterized by the development of *tension.* The tension, after being applied to a system of levers, can either overcome a resistance and result in shortening of a muscle or be overcome by a resistance and result in the lengthening of a muscle. In either case, the muscle is regarded as "contracting" or developing tension.

Muscles which are contracting in a static state are in *isometric* contraction. When they are changing length or acting in phase with each other and performing *phasic* actions, they are in *isotonic* contraction. Since a movement that is phasic involves shortening or lengthening (isotonic contractions of muscles), a further description of the action is necessary. Therefore, the shortening of a muscle during isotonic contraction is called *concentric* contraction. The lengthening of a muscle during isotonic contraction is called *eccentric* contraction.

Joint and Muscle Interrelationships

When determining the optimum point at which muscles can exert the greatest force at a given joint, at least three elements are involved:

(1) the angle of the joint, (2) the angle of pull of the muscle to the bony levers, and (3) the length of the muscle at the time the force is being exerted. Because of limitations in our present knowledge, however, it is not possible to indicate, for instance, the specific point at which such a factor as strength development might be best attained. Although investigators have made determinations of the points at which strength is maximum on groups of experimental subjects, it is known that individuals who partake in specific kinds of activities other than those participated in by the general population have greater strength at other points in the range of motion than those indicated in the research literature.

Neurological Integration

Volitional muscular movements result from a highly complex interrelationship between the muscular and central nervous systems. Only those neurophysiologic functions that pertain to disabilities and divergencies frequently seen in the adapted physical education class will be discussed. Additional detailed information may be found in neurophysiology textbooks.

Various centers of the brain ultimately initiate and control voluntary muscle action. Impulses for such movement originate in the cerebral cortex. Three areas of the cortex are especially important: (1) The *sensory* (somesthetic) area is the primary receiving area for information from the eyes, ears, nose, skin, joints, and muscles; (2) The *motor* area originates impulses for specific muscular actions; and (3) The *premotor* area originates impulses for generalized patterns of movement. The motor and premotor divisions may be referred to collectively as the motor cortex (de Vries, 1966). Other areas of the brain such as the thalamus, brain stem, basal ganglia, and cerebellum function in coordination of the motor act that arises in the motor cortex. Of these, the cerebellum acts as the integrating mechanism of the activity. It also functions in error control which is an important aspect of skilled movement. That is to say, if muscular performance does not match the movement that was "intended" upon initiation in the motor cortex, then the cerebellum has the ability to make adjustments to correct such errors.

While the body or body segment is in motion, sensory data from the sense organs, muscles, and joints are constantly fed back to the central nervous system. The data concern information about tension of muscle fibers, joint angles, and body position in space. Through feedback the body has the capacity to regulate volitional movements. This servomechanism is referred to as autoregulation.

In performance of physical skills, the proprioceptors within the muscle and joint play a vital role in autoregulation. Of the proprioceptors, an understanding of the function of the muscle spindle is important when dealing with various physical disabilities.

Muscle spindles are specialized muscle fibers (intrafusal) that may be found between the contractile fibers of the skeletal muscles. As the contractile fibers stretch, a concomitant stretching of the intrafusal fibers results. An impulse is relayed to the spinal cord, synapses with a motor neuron, which in turn fires. Firing results in contraction of the muscle fiber to oppose the stretch. At the same time, firing of a different motor neuron results in contraction of the intrafusal fiber and resets the spindle. Its length now coincides with that of the new length of the contracted skeletal muscle fibers. This reflex is known as the *stretch* or *myotatic reflex.*

Reflexes are defined as involuntary acts. Whereas in normal individuals basic reflexive actions are not exhibited, they may become quite apparent in individuals with neurological disorders. The overt reflexive action is the result of a synapse or connection between a sensory (afferent) neuron and a motor (efferent) neuron. Such a synapse is known as a *reflex arc* which is the basic functional unit of the nervous system. The simplest arc or loop consists of five parts: (1) receptor, a sensory nerve ending that receives information regarding the environment. Impulses are discharged and transmitted via (2) an *afferent neuron* to the spinal cord where a (3) *synapse* or connection occurs between the sensory and motor fibers. (4) The *efferent neuron* or motor neuron conducts the impulse from the spinal cord to the effector. (5) The *effector organ* is responsible for the response. The knee jerk is a classic example of a simple reflex arc. As illustrated in figure 3.1, striking of the patellar tendon of the quadriceps muscle results in stretching of the extrafusal muscle fibers and the specialized muscle spindles (Falls, Wallis, and Logan, 1970). An impulse is conducted to the spinal cord. The resulting motor neuron involvement causes a contraction of the quadriceps, i.e., knee jerk, to relieve the stretch.

In movement and in all static positions, another example of a stretch reflex may be illustrated. The *postural* or *spinal reflex* functions to maintain the body against the pull of gravity without conscious involvement. Gravity exerts a downward force on the body. In order to resist the gravitational pull, the body must constantly make slight adjustments. Bodily sway away from a balanced position

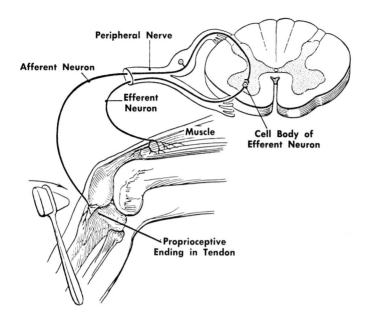

Figure 3.1. Simple reflex arc (knee jerk). (From Grollman, S. **The Human Body,** © 1964. By permission of The Macmillan Company, New York.)

puts stretch on the extensor muscles, which in turn stimulates the muscle spindles within the extensors. An impulse via the afferent neuron is relayed to the spinal cord where it synapses with a motor neuron. The impulse travels over the efferent nerve to the quadriceps muscle which contracts to maintain balance. The postural reflex may also be referred to as the *extensor* or *extensor thrust* reflex because of the involvement of the antigravity (extensor) muscles.

A muscle is said to respond on an all-or-none basis. That is to say, a motor nerve impulse causes all the muscle fibers with which it connects to contract maximally. A fiber either contracts maximally or not at all. In order to bring about a submaximal contraction of a whole muscle, only a few of the available motor units contract. Smooth or even contraction of a muscle is the result of asynchronous firing of motor units.

The *flexion* or *withdrawal* reflex also warrants discussion. This reflex is characterized by complete withdrawal of a body part. For example, an individual steps on a sharp object. The information is sent to the brain via the spinal cord, and the message for withdrawal is returned to the effector organ.

When the extensor and flexion reflexes function alternately with each other in the limbs, they are termed the *crossed extensor* reflex. The crossed extensor reflex constitutes the main basis of locomotion.

The phenomenon of muscle tonus was once thought to be the result of constant activity in a small number of muscle fibers. However, with development of electromyographic equipment (measures amount of electrical activity within a muscle), new evidence has been brought forth to indicate that muscle tonus is the result of passive and active components. The latter refers to the neuromuscular activity. It may or may not be present. Pressure and elasticity of muscle and connective tissue make up the passive component. It is always present. In the resting state, the muscle may be electrically silent. In an erect standing posture, on the other hand, both components are believed to be present (de Vries, 1966).

Musculoskeletal Motion

The starting point for utilizing descriptive terminology that is based on planes and axes of motion is the *anatomic position*. This is a position with the body erect, the arms at the sides, and the palms of the hands facing forward. Originally, this position was probably one in which cadavers were placed so that anatomists could work most effectively when dissecting. It has subsequently become standardized, and all anatomic movements are derived from this basic position.

The anatomic position serves as the standard reference for defining and naming joint action. Once a given joint action has been named and defined, then the joint action terminology suffices even if the body position is changed and other joints have been moved out of the anatomic position. Difficulty arises in attempting to apply this formalized terminology when one begins to desribe basic movement patterns. The body very rarely moves in these planes that the anatomists employ for description. An analysis of most movements reveals that the human organism functions in diagonal patterns of motion, particularly when that motion is of a fast or ballistic nature. These planes of movement are diagonal to the longitudinal axis of the body. The joints most involved in which diagonal movements occur are the hip and shoulder. In addition to the three traditional planes, (1) anteroposterior, (2) lateral, and (3) transverse, three diagonal planes of motion have been introduced (Logan-McKinney, 1970). These planes are (1) *high diagonal* of the upper limbs, (2) *low diagonal* of the upper limbs, and (3) *low diagonal* of the lower limbs.

ANATOMIC MOVEMENTS

Spatial relationship of muscles to joints was discussed previously. According to that discussion, if the movements of flexion and extension, for example, are the only movements possible at a given joint, and the muscle or muscles spanning the joint attach in such a manner that flexion or extension will occur, then the function of the muscle can be deduced. With this in mind, very little mention of the action of muscles will be introduced here. What will be emphasized is a knowledge of (a) movements possible at joints, (b) bones and ligaments that make up these joints, and (c) the muscles with their tendons which cross the joints. These fundamentals are essential for the application of therapeutic exercise in the adapted physical education program.

In discussing anatomic movement, the assumption is made here that the body is in the anatomic position. The definitions of anatomic movement pertain only to the beginning of a movement in order to describe the *direction* of motion. For example, if in the anatomic position the upper limb is moved in the lateral plane away from the midline of the body, the action at the shoulder joint is called *abduction*. If this same movement continues for more than ninety degrees, the upper limb will then be moving back *toward* the midline of the body. But since this movement beyond ninety degrees is purely a continuation of the initial movement away from the center line of the body, it is still called abduction.

Anatomic movement and positions with their definitions are contained in the following list:

1. *Abduction:* Movement away from the midline of the body.
2. *Adduction:* Movement toward the midline of the body.
3. *Circumduction:* Movement of a limb in a manner that describes a cone.
4. *Depression:* Downward movement of a part.
5. *Diagonal abduction:* Movement by a limb through a diagonal plane across and away from the midline of the body.
6. *Diagonal adduction:* Movement by a limb through a diagonal plane toward and across the midline of the body.
7. *Diagonal extension:* A combination of rotation and extension of the vertebrae at the facets through a diagonal plane.
8. *Diagonal flexion:* A combination of rotation and flexion of the vertebrae at the facets through a diagonal plane.
9. *Dorsiflexion:* Bending foot upward (flexion of the ankle).

10. *Elevation:* Upward movement of a part.
11. *Eversion:* Movement of the sole of the foot outward.
12. *Extension:* Movement resulting in the increase of a joint angle.
13. *Flexion:* Movement resulting in a decrease of a joint angle.
14. *Horizontal abduction:* Movement of the upper limbs from a full front horizontal position to a side horizontal position.
15. *Horizontal adduction:* Movement of the upper limbs from a side horizontal position to a front horizontal position.
16. *Hyperextension:* Movement beyond the position of extension.
17. *Inversion:* Movement of the sole of the foot inward.
18. *Lateral flexion:* Movement of the trunk or head laterally away from the midline of the body.
19. *Opposition of the thumb:* Diagonal movement of the thumb across the palmar surface of the hand to make contact with one of the four fingers.
20. *Plantar flexion:* Bending of the foot downward (extension of the ankle).
21. *Pronation:* Turning the back of the hand forward.
22. *Prone position:* Lying in a face-down position.
23. *Radial flexion:* Movement at the wrist of the thumb side of the hand toward the forearm.
24. *Protraction:* Forward movement of a part (shoulder girdle).
25. *Retraction:* Backward movement of a part (shoulder girdle).
26. *Rotation downward:* Rotary movement of the scapula with the inferior angle moving medially and downward.
27. *Rotation laterally:* Movement around the axis of a bone away from the midline of the body.
28. *Rotation medially:* Movement around the axis of a bone toward the midline of the body.
29. *Rotation upward:* Rotary movement of the scapula with the inferior angle moving laterally and upward.
30. *Supination:* Turning the palm of the hand forward.
31. *Supine position:* Lying in a face-up position.
32. *Ulnar flexion:* Movement of the little finger side of the hand toward the forearm.

JOINTS AND THEIR MOVEMENTS

Presented together in the following chart are (1) the major joints, (2) the classification of the joints, (3) the bones by which the joints are formed, and (4) the anatomic movements that are possible at each joint.

Joint	Type	Bones Involved	Movements Possible
Ankle	Hinge	Tibia, fibula, talus	Dorsiflexion, plantar flexion
Knee	Modified hinge	Tibia, femur, patella	Flexion, extension, rotation (when knee is flexed)
Hip	Ball-and-Socket	Femur, pelvis	Flexion, extension, adduction, abduction, diagonal adduction, diagonal abduction, medial and lateral rotation, circumduction
Intervertebral (Spine)	Gliding	Vertebrae	Flexion, extension, rotation, lateral flexion, hyperextension
Shoulder	Ball-and-Socket	Humerus, scapula	Flexion, extension, adduction, abduction, diagonal adduction, diagonal abduction, medial and lateral rotation, circumduction, hyperextension, horizontal adduction, horizontal abduction
Sterno-clavicular (shoulder girdle)	Gliding	Clavicle, sternum, scapula	Elevation, depression, protraction, retraction, rotation, circumduction
Sterno-clavicular (scapula)	Gliding	Scapula (scapular movements)	Elevation, depression, adduction, abduction, upward and downward rotation
Elbow	Hinge	Humerus, radius, ulna	Flexion, extension
Radio-ulnar	Pivot	Radius, ulna	Pronation, supination
Wrist	Condyloid	Radius, navicular, lunate, triangular	Flexion, extension, adduction, abduction, circumduction (adduction and abduction also called ulnar and radial flexion respectively)
First carpo-metacarpal (thumb)	Saddle	Multiangular, first metacarpal	Flexion, extension, adduction, abduction, rotation, opposition

SELECTED ANATOMIC STRUCTURES
AND RELATIONSHIPS

Certain anatomic structures and functions are more vulnerable to negative adaptive changes than others. Some parts of the body seem to be especially susceptible to injury—perhaps because of weaknesses or because of undue stresses placed upon them in specific physical activity. Disabling conditions tend to have similar effects upon most individuals involved with those conditions. Therefore, certain recurring disabilities can be anticipated.

Since not all anatomic structures can be presented here, those structures that are most frequently involved in disabilities will receive the greatest consideration. Highlighted will be the anatomic structures and relationships that must be understood in order to adapt muscular

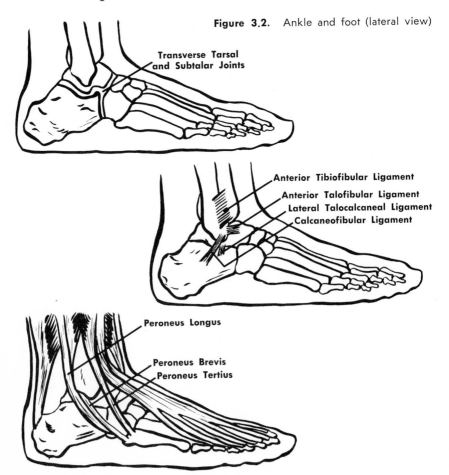

Figure 3.2. Ankle and foot (lateral view)

Transverse Tarsal
and Subtalar Joints

Anterior Tibiofibular Ligament
Anterior Talofibular Ligament
Lateral Talocalcaneal Ligament
Calcaneofibular Ligament

Peroneus Longus

Peroneus Brevis
Peroneus Tertius

activity to those individuals in adapted physical education. Due to the high incidence of injury to the joints of the limbs, maximum attention will be paid to their rehabilitation.

This section is intended as a source of basic material. Only a brief presentation is made of each illustration in the following anatomic discussion. Contained herein will be anatomic structures with kinesiologic considerations which have a specific application in adapted physical education for individuals with physical disabilities. The ankle, foot, knee, hip, trunk, shoulder, shoulder girdle, and elbow will be presented.

The motions of eversion and inversion of the foot take place at the transverse tarsal and subtalar joints. The double line in figure 3.2 indicates the articulations that form these joints. These joints are formed by the articulations between the talus and navicular bones as well as the calcaneus and cuboid bones. It should be noted that plantar flexion and dorsiflexion are the *only* motions that take place in the ankle joint. Lateral or side-to-side motion that appears to take place at the ankle joint actually occurs below and anterior to the talus bone. The ligaments of the ankle joint are shown from a lateral view: anterior tibiofibular, anterior talofibular, lateral talocalcaneal, and calcaneofibular. The lateral stabilizing muscles are indicated: peroneus longus, peroneus brevis, and peroneus tertius.

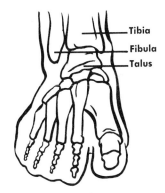

The structures of the ankle joint as viewed from the front are shown in figure 3.3. The ankle joint is composed of three

Figure 3.3. Ankle and foot (anterior view)

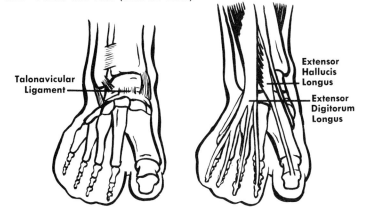

bones: fibula, tibia, and talus. Only one ligament is shown in this view: talonavicular. Anterior stabilizing muscles are shown: extensor digitorum longus and extensor hallucis longus.

Medial and posterior ligaments are shown in figure 3.4: deltoid, posterior talotibial, posterior talocalcaneal, and medial talocalcaneal. The deltoid is the strongest and most important of these ligaments. When extreme stresses are placed upon this ligament, a chip fracture of the tibia may occur because the ligament has such great tensile strength. Medial stabilizing muscles of the ankle are shown: tibialis posterior, flexor hallucis longus, tibialis anterior, and flexor digitorum longus.

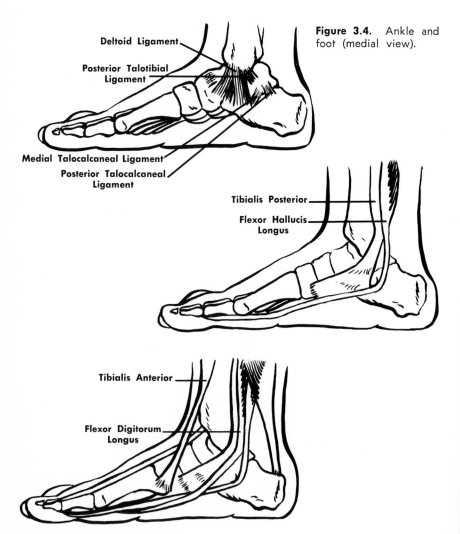

Deltoid Ligament

Posterior Talotibial
Ligament

Medial Talocalcaneal Ligament
Posterior Talocalcaneal
Ligament

Figure 3.4. Ankle and foot (medial view).

Tibialis Posterior
Flexor Hallucis
Longus

Tibialis Anterior

Flexor Digitorum
Longus

These muscles, in addition to their stabilizing components at the ankle on the medial side, also serve to help support the medial longitudinal arch.

Ligaments on the posterior aspect of the ankle are shown in figure 3.5: posterior tibiofibular and posterior talofibular. Medial stabilizing muscles of the ankle are shown from the rear: tibialis posterior, flexor hallucis longus, and flexor digitorum longus. Lateral stabilizing muscles are also shown from a posterior view: peroneus brevis and peroneus longus. The tendon of the gastrocnemius-soleus muscle group, sometimes called the triceps surae, is indicated: Achilles tendon.

Figure 3.5. Ankle and foot (posterior view).

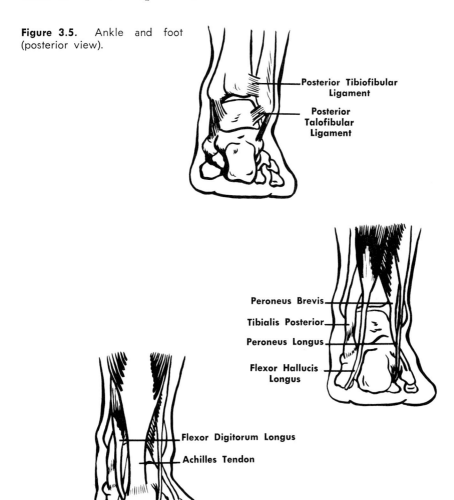

Posterior Tibiofibular Ligament

Posterior Talofibular Ligament

Peroneus Brevis

Tibialis Posterior

Peroneus Longus

Flexor Hallucis Longus

Flexor Digitorum Longus

Achilles Tendon

The bones of the foot are structured in such a manner that they form arches. The position of the bones is maintained primarily by the ligaments and secondarily by muscle. The weight of the body is borne on the inferior surface of the calcaneus and the metatarsal heads. Represented in figure 3.6 from a medial view are first metatarsal, second cuneiform, first cuneiform, navicular, sustentaculum tali of the calcaneus, talus, and calcaneus.

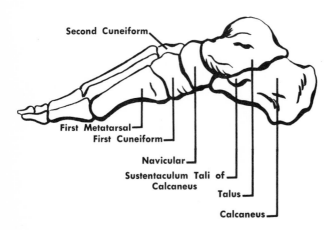

Figure 3.6.   Bones of the foot (medial view)

The bones of the feet are illustrated in figure 3.7 from a lateral view: tarsals, metatarsals, phalanges, cuboid, fifth metatarsal, and third cuneiform.

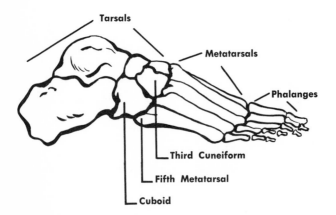

Figure 3.7.   Bones of the foot (lateral view)

Deep structures (fig. 3.8) aid in the maintenance of the medial longitudinal arch by the calcaneonavicular or "spring" ligament and the sustentaculum tali, which in turn is supported by the tendon of the flexor hallucis longus as shown. The "spring" ligament is one of the few ligaments in the body that contain elastic fibers. The head of the talus bone rests upon this ligament from above. The elasticity of this ligament allows for the absorption of shock as the sole of the foot strikes the ground. This is often the site of pain in the medial longitudinal arch when supporting muscles become weakened because

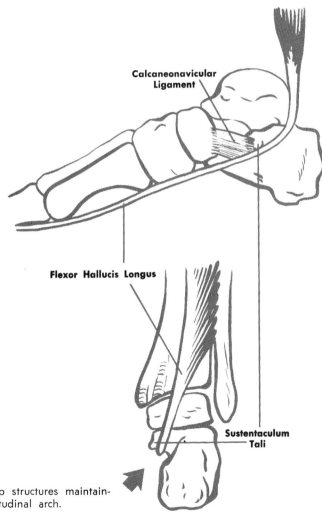

Figure 3.8. Deep structures maintaining medial longitudinal arch.

of disuse. Attention is directed to the line of pull of the tendon of the flexor hallucis longus muscle indicated by the arrow. This muscle helps to maintain the calcaneus in a normal upright position. It also helps to maintain normal position of the arch.

Beneath most of the muscles on the posterior plantar surface of the foot is the long plantar ligament (fig. 3.9). Some of the short (intrinsic) muscles of the foot which comprise the third layer are indicated: adductor hallucis, flexor hallucis brevis, and flexor digiti minimi. Note the large area (five bones) covered by the tendon of the tibialis posterior. The tendon of the peroneus longus is also indicated.

Muscles in the sole of the foot which often require strength-development exercises to help maintain a normal arch are indicated: flexor digitorum brevis, lumbricales, abductor hallucis, abductor digiti minimi, and flexor hallucis longus (fig. 3.10).

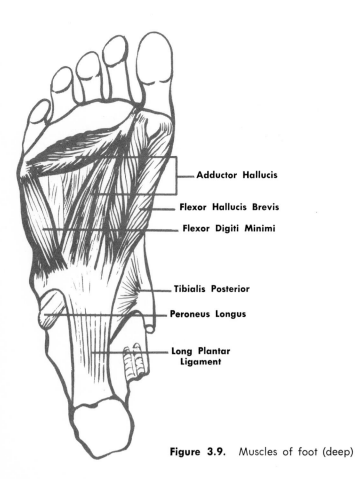

Adductor Hallucis

Flexor Hallucis Brevis

Flexor Digiti Minimi

Tibialis Posterior

Peroneus Longus

Long Plantar Ligament

Figure 3.9. Muscles of foot (deep)

Shown in figure 3.11 is a medial view indicating some of the long (extrinsic) muscles of the foot. Extrinsic muscles which help support the medial longitudinal arch are shown: tibialis anterior, tibialis posterior, flexor hallucis longus, and flexor digitorum longus. The Achilles tendon is also indicated.

Figure 3.10. Muscles of foot (superficial)

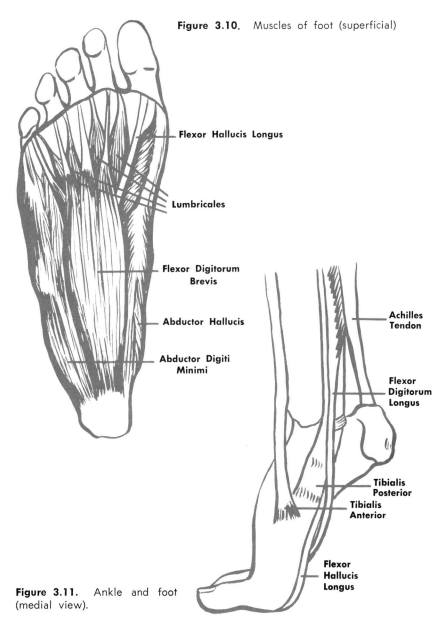

Flexor Hallucis Longus

Lumbricales

Flexor Digitorum Brevis

Abductor Hallucis

Abductor Digiti Minimi

Achilles Tendon

Flexor Digitorum Longus

Tibialis Posterior

Tibialis Anterior

Flexor Hallucis Longus

Figure 3.11. Ankle and foot (medial view).

The view of the foot shown in figure 3.12 includes the muscles noted in figure 3.11 with the addition of the tendons of the peroneus longus and peroneus brevis.

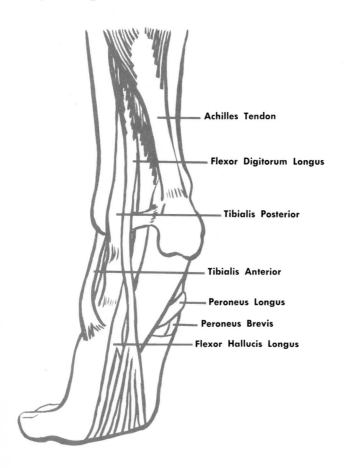

The knee joint (fig. 3.13) is composed of three bones: femur, tibia, and patella. The fibula does not articulate at the knee joint. The patellar ligament, running from the tibial tuberosity to the patella, is actually the tendon of the quadriceps muscle group that attaches to the tibial tuberosity.

The right knee joint flexed to ninety degrees and viewed anteriorly is shown in figure 3.14: lateral collateral ligament, meniscus, tendon of the biceps femoris, posterior cruciate ligament, anterior cruciate ligament, and medial collateral ligament. The major function of the anterior and posterior cruciate ligaments is to prevent excessive hyper-

Figure 3.13. Right knee (lateral view)

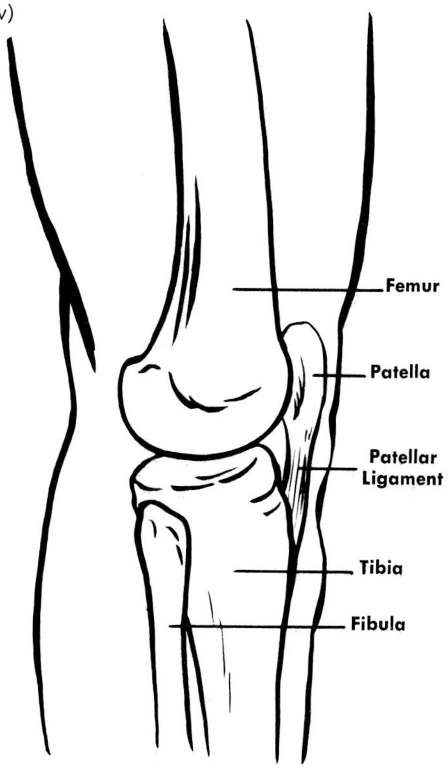

- Femur
- Patella
- Patellar Ligament
- Tibia
- Fibula

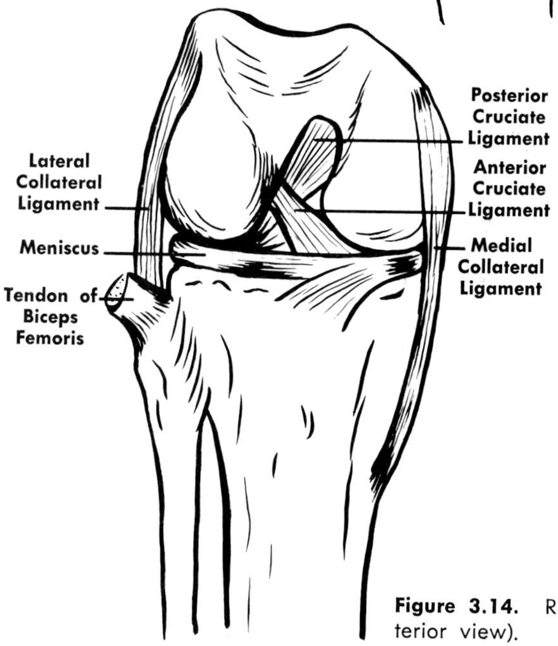

Lateral Collateral Ligament

Meniscus

Tendon of Biceps Femoris

Posterior Cruciate Ligament

Anterior Cruciate Ligament

Medial Collateral Ligament

Figure 3.14. Right knee flexed (anterior view).

extension and hyperflexion. All the ligaments involved in the knee joint help prevent rotation at the joint when the knee is extended.

The cruciate ligaments are indicated in figure 3.15: anterior cruciate and posterior cruciate. The femur has been sectioned anteroposteriorly so that the proximal attachments of the ligaments can be seen. An injury might occur to the anterior cruciate ligament when the tibia is forced anteriorly while the femur is in a fixed position. When the tibia is forced posteriorly on a fixed femur, the posterior cruciate ligament may be injured.

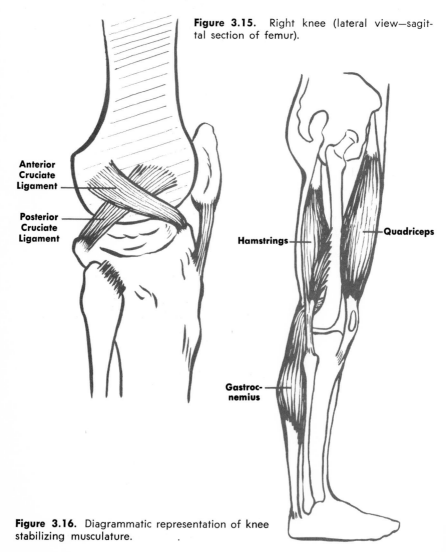

Figure 3.15. Right knee (lateral view—sagittal section of femur).

Anterior
Cruciate
Ligament

Posterior
Cruciate
Ligament

Hamstrings

Quadriceps

Gastroc-
nemius

Figure 3.16. Diagrammatic representation of knee stabilizing musculature.

Shown in the figure 3.16 are the three major muscles or muscle groups that act upon the knee joint: gastrocnemius, hamstrings, and quadriceps. These muscles are indicated diagrammatically so that the attachments may be visualized in terms of the functions of these muscles. Two of the major muscle groups attach below the knee joint, and one major muscle attaches above the joint. Strengthening the muscles for preventive or rehabilitative purposes is one of the primary uses of therapeutic exercise.

Anatomic structures of the hip are presented in figure 3.17. The hip joint is held intact anteriorly by the iliofemoral (Y-ligament) and the pubofemoral ligaments. Important structures are indicated: anterior superior iliac spine, anterior inferior iliac spine, iliofemoral ligament, pubofemoral ligament, greater trochanter, and lesser trochanter.

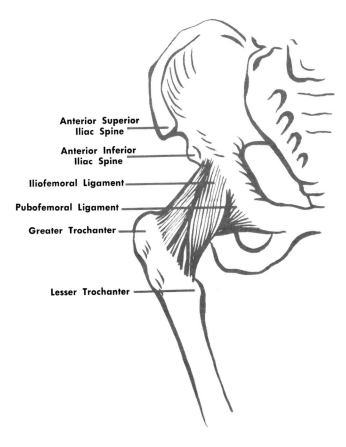

Figure 3.17. Right hip (anterior view)

Some of the anatomic structures which involve both the hip and knee are shown in figure 3.18: proximal attachment of the rectus femoris (anterior inferior iliac spine), rectus femoris, distal attachment of the rectus femoris on the tibial tuberosity, proximal attachment—anterior superior iliac spine—tensor fasciae latae muscle, tractus iliotibialis, and sartorius. It should be noted that the proximal attachment of the rectus femoris on the anterior inferior iliac spine is covered by the tensor fasciae latae and sartorius muscle and is not palpable.

The hip adductors and flexors are depicted in figure 3.19. Also indicated is the inguinal ligament. This ligament provides a type of pulley arrangement to maintain functional positioning of the hip flexors.

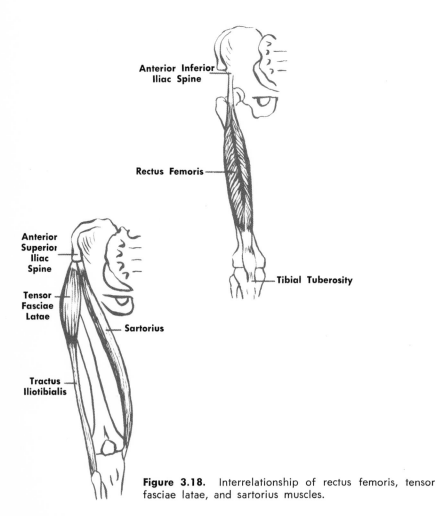

Figure 3.18. Interrelationship of rectus femoris, tensor fasciae latae, and sartorius muscles.

The adductor muscles of one hip are indicated on the right and left sides of the illustration. All of the muscles shown are actually located on one thigh and hip area only. They are separated here to illustrate their relative locations: psoas major, inguinal ligament, iliacus, distal attachment of the iliopsoas group on the lesser trochanter, pectineus, adductor longus, gracilis, adductor brevis, and adductor magnus. Of the adductors shown, the gracilis is the only muscle that acts upon the knee joint.

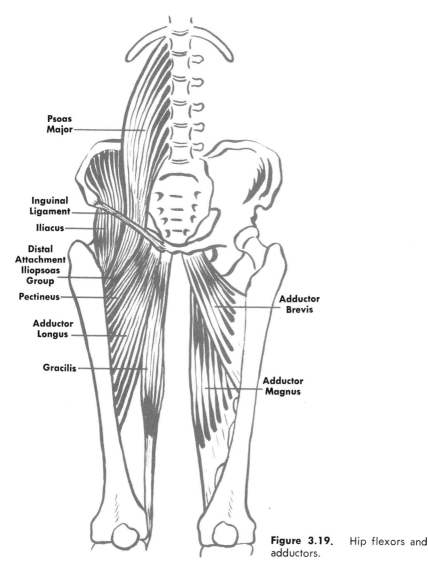

Figure 3.19. Hip flexors and adductors.

The hip is shown from the lateral side in figure 3.20: attachment of the gluteus medius on the greater trochanter; location of the gluteus medius between the tensor fasciae latae and the gluteus maximus, and the tractus iliotibialis. It is interesting to note that the gluteus maximus, gluteus medius, and tensor fasciae latae form a group which function similarly to the deltoid muscle of the shoulder.

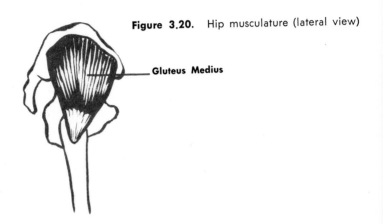

Figure 3.20. Hip musculature (lateral view)

Gluteus Medius

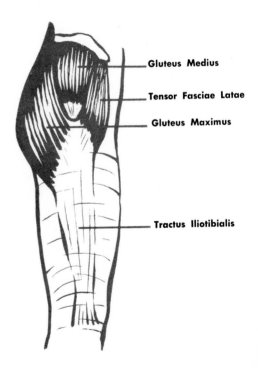

Gluteus Medius

Tensor Fasciae Latae

Gluteus Maximus

Tractus Iliotibialis

The hip area is shown (fig. 3.21) from a posterior view with the gluteus maximus removed: gluteus minimus, gemellus superior, obturator internus, gemellus inferior, obturator externus, gluteus medius, piriformis, gemellus superior, obturator internus, gemellus inferior, quadratus femoris (covering the obturator externus), and hamstring group.

Figure 3.21. Hip musculature (posterior deep)

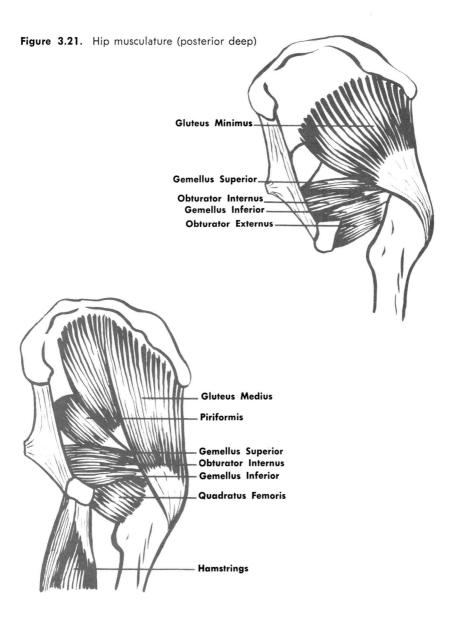

Gluteus Minimus

Gemellus Superior
Obturator Internus
Gemellus Inferior
Obturator Externus

Gluteus Medius

Piriformis

Gemellus Superior
Obturator Internus
Gemellus Inferior

Quadratus Femoris

Hamstrings

The rectus abdominis is shown in figure 3.22. This muscle, a trunk flexor, attaches to the rib cage and pubis. It is divided into separate segments by tendinous inscriptions. The muscle is also separated into a right and left rectus abdominis by the linea alba (white line). Curvature of this line is often an indication of a postural malalignment of the spine.

Muscles composing the abdominal region other than the rectus abdominis are indicated in figure 3.23: external oblique, internal oblique, and transverse abdominis. These muscles are in layers. The external oblique is the most superficial and the transverse abdominis is the deepest of the three abdominal muscles. The external oblique runs diagonally downward from lateral to medial (the same direction the fingers would run if the hands were placed in the pockets). The ex-

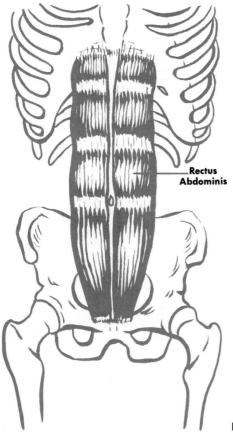

Rectus
Abdominis

Figure 3.22.   Rectus abdominis

ternal oblique on one side continues into the internal oblique on the opposite side forming a functional unit. The two pairs of muscles composed of the external oblique of one side and the internal oblique on the other side form the shape of an X. This design provides the muscles with the ability to work in conjunction with each other for spinal flexion and in opposition to each other for spinal rotation and lateral flexion. By opposition it is meant that one set of muscles is shortening while the other set of muscles is lengthening. At any one

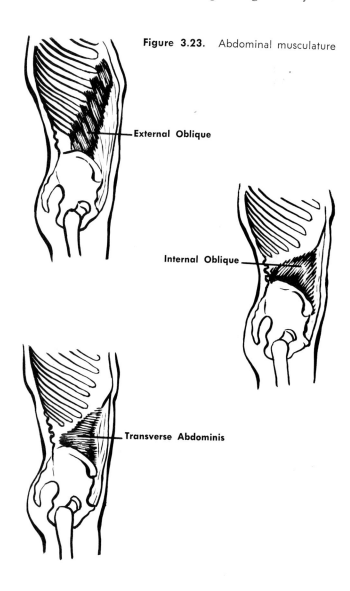

Figure 3.23. Abdominal musculature

External Oblique

Internal Oblique

Transverse Abdominis

point in the action, the interaction between shortening and lengthening provides a moving stabilization that has been termed *dynamic stabilization* (Logan and McKinney, 1970).

The spinal extensor group, which begins at its attachment on the sacrum and the pelvis and terminates in the superior nuchal line of the skull, is illustrated in figure 3.24. This muscle group has four subdivisions. Each of these subdivisions is again subdivided. The spinal

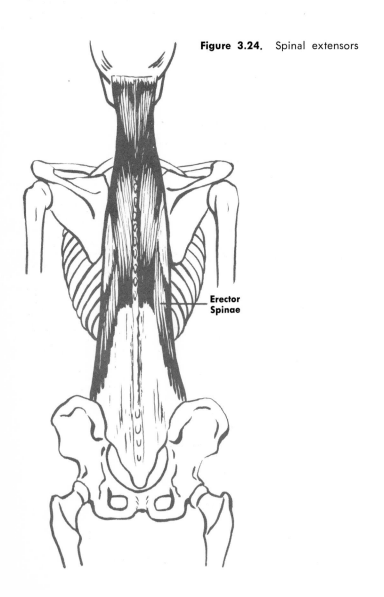

Figure 3.24.   Spinal extensors

Erector
Spinae

extensor group muscles (erector spinae) should be conceived as a total unit when its major functions, those of extension and hyperextension, are considered.

Represented in figure 3.25 is a cross section of the trunk through the lumbar region. The muscles passing through this level of the body are indicated: external oblique, internal oblique, transverse abdominis, rectus abdominis, erector spinae, psoas major, quadratus lumborum, and latissimus dorsi. Note should be made of the relationship of the erector spinae and psoas major to the lumbar vertebrae. A discussion of the

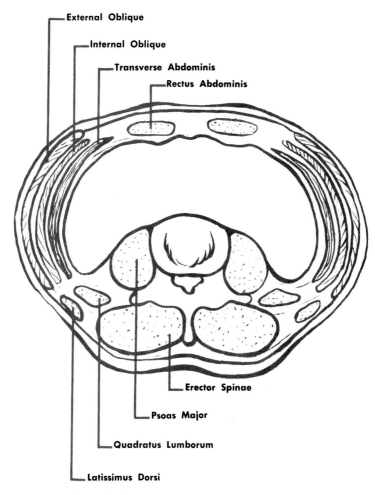

Figure 3.25. Trunk musculature (transverse section)

functions of these muscles as they relate to normal and abnormal lumbar curvature appears in chapter 4.

Shown in figure 3.26 are the scapula, clavicle, humerus, and deltoid muscle of the shoulder. This view is from the side and slightly above the shoulder.

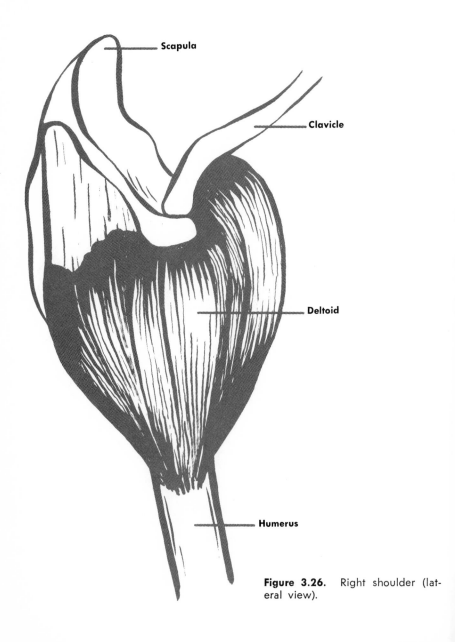

Scapula

Clavicle

Deltoid

Humerus

Figure 3.26. Right shoulder (lateral view).

In figure 3.27 the shoulder is viewed from above. The muscles and bones are shown with the trapezius and deltoid muscles removed. The deep muscles surrounding and attaching to the humerus are indicated: subscapularis, supraspinatus, spine of scapula, infraspinatus, humerus, clavicle, corocoid process, tendon of subscapularis, tendon of supraspinatus, tendon of infraspinatus, and tendon of teres minor. The four tendons of these muscles make up the "rotary cuff." These four muscles work together to maintain the head of the humerus at the shoulder joint. In addition, they function to prevent the head of the humerus from jamming into the structure composed of the acromion process and the clavicle just above the head of the humerus. This action occurs when the humerus is abducted or flexed.

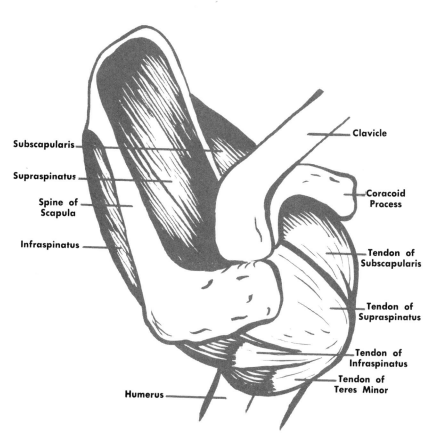

Figure 3.27. Right-shoulder musculature (superior view—deep).

In figure 3.28 the scapula and humerus are shown from an anterior view. The following structures are represented: subscapularis, supraspinatus, coracoid process, coracoacromial ligament, acromion process, "rotary cuff," tendon of the long head of biceps brachii, and humerus. Most of the stability of the shoulder joint is dependent upon the functional integrity and strength of the subscapularis muscle. Along with the "rotary cuff," the coracoacromial ligament serves as a pulley for the supraspinatus muscle which, in turn, helps to prevent the humerus from jamming into the bony roof above the shoulder joint. Attention is called to the coracoid process. Three muscles involved at the shoulder attach to this bony process: (1) coracobrachialis, (2) short head of the biceps brachii, and (3) pectoralis minor.

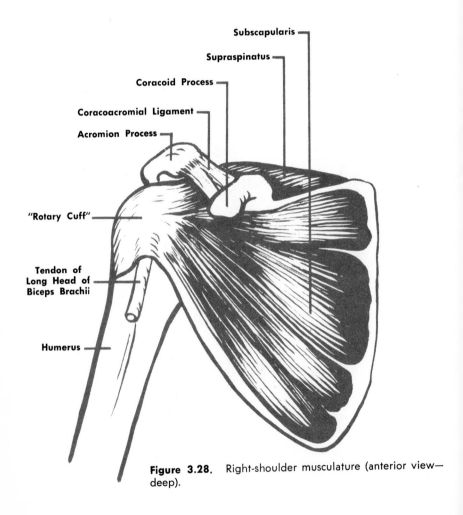

Figure 3.28. Right-shoulder musculature (anterior view—deep).

Muscles of the shoulder and upper arm are shown from the posterior view in figure 3.29. These muscular relationships are indicated: supraspinatus, infraspinatus, teres major, acromion process, "rotary cuff," teres minor, and triceps brachii (long head). The long head of the triceps brachii divides the teres major and teres minor on its way to its attachment on the scapula. It should be noted that the teres minor is on the posterior surface of the humerus, and the teres major is on the anterior surface. The long head of the triceps brachii is often neglected as one of the major muscles of the shoulder joint. It is particularly important in fine movements because of its action in controlling the limb after the throwing motion has been initiated. A lack of extensibility of this muscle is often a cause of muscle soreness in the early stages of conditioning.

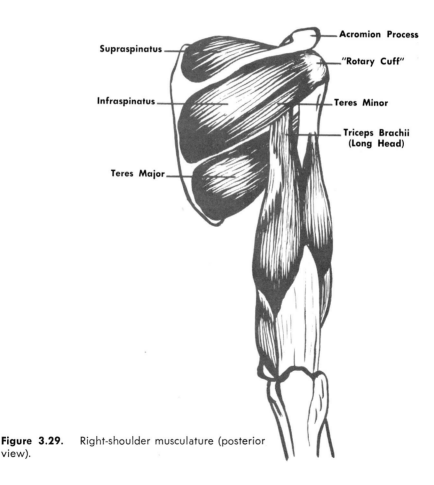

Figure 3.29.   Right-shoulder musculature (posterior view).

A superior and anterior view of the shoulder girdle is shown in figure 3.30. The shoulder girdle is not a complete bony girdle like that found in the pelvis. The girdle is completed with the addition of the rhomboid muscles which attach the vertebral border of the scapula to the spinal column. The scapula, clavicle, acromion process, coracoid process, and glenoid fossa are indicated.

Some of the muscles that produce movement of the scapula are indicated in figure 3.31. The important muscles are represented: rhomboid minor, rhomboid major, levator scapulae, serratus anterior, and

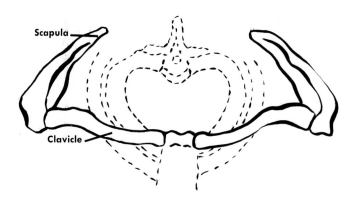

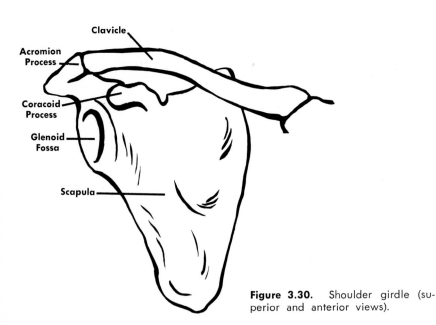

Figure 3.30. Shoulder girdle (superior and anterior views).

pectoralis minor. Concentric contraction of the rhomboids, levator scapulae, and the pectoralis minor muscles results in downward rotation of the scapula as indicated by the arrows. Downward and upward rotary movements of the scapula are not true rotary movements because the axis about which they revolve tends to move as the scapular movement is produced. Using the inferior angle of the scapula as a landmark, *medial* and upward movements of this axis occur in downward rotation; *lateral* and upward movements occur in upward rotation.

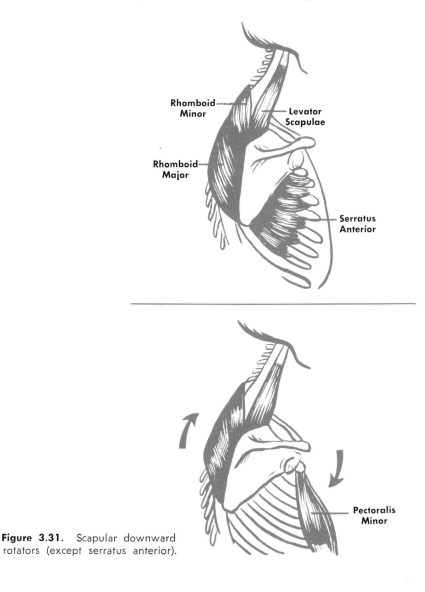

Figure 3.31. Scapular downward rotators (except serratus anterior).

The drawings in figure 3.32 show the relationship between the trapezius and serratus anterior muscles in performing the movement of upward rotation of the scapula. The muscles shown are trapezius and serratus anterior. The attachments of the trapezius along the spine of the scapula should be noted. Concentric contraction (shortening) of this muscle (indicated by the small arrows) when the scapula is *adducted* produces upward rotation of the scapula (large arrows). On the other hand, when the scapula is *abducted,* moved away from the

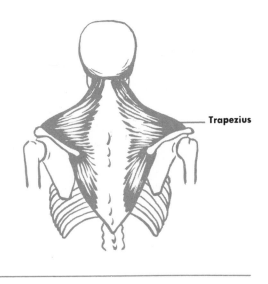

Trapezius

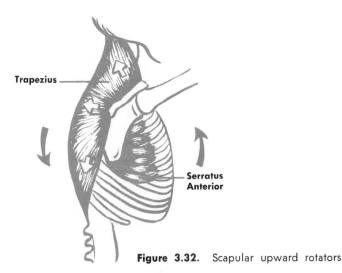

Trapezius

Serratus
Anterior

Figure 3.32. Scapular upward rotators

posterior midline of the body, upward rotation is performed primarily by the serratus anterior. The amount of movement performed by either one of these two muscles depends upon the condition of the scapula in relation to the posterior midline of the body.

Illustrated in figure 3.33 are two muscles of great importance to the disabled person who must rely upon his upper limbs to perform such activities as crutch-walking. These two muscles are pectoralis major and latissimus dorsi. The arrow suggests the action of the latis-

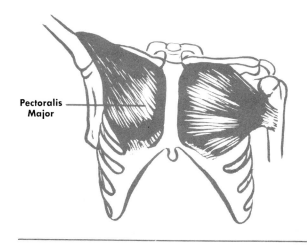

Pectoralis
Major

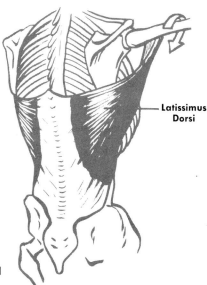

Latissimus
Dorsi

Figure 3.33.   Pectoralis major and latissimus dorsi muscles.

simus dorsi on the humerus. This muscle is an important medial ro-
tator, adductor, diagonal adductor, and extensor of the humerus. Since
the pectoralis major functions in a three-part relationship, several
movements are possible by contraction of that muscle. An understanding of the combined actions of these two muscles is important
in adapted physical education.

The bones of the elbow are shown in figure 3.34. The elbow joint
is formed by these articulating bones: humerus, radius, and ulna. The
radius is wider at its distal end than the ulna. The ulna forms the
hinge with the radius. When pronation (from a position of supination)
is performed, the radius moves to a position diagonal to the ulna.
When in the anatomic position, the radius lies parallel to the ulna.

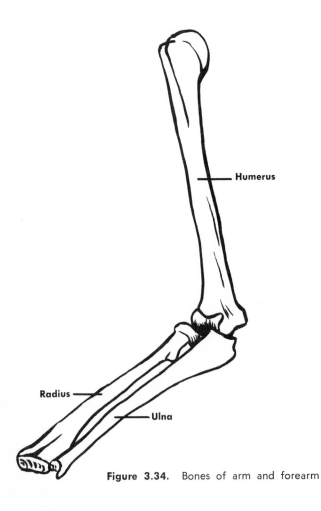

Figure 3.34. Bones of arm and forearm

Some of the muscles of the elbow joint are depicted in the figure 3.35. These include the brachialis and biceps brachii. Note that the distal tendon of the biceps brachii wraps around the radius in order for the biceps brachii to perform supination of the forearm. Flexion of the elbow is the major function of these two muscles.

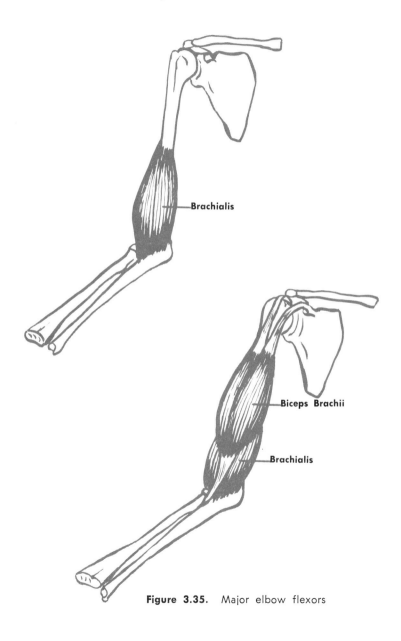

Figure 3.35. Major elbow flexors

Superficial muscles of the anterior aspect of the elbow joint are illustrated in figure 3.36: biceps brachii, distal tendon of the biceps brachii, brachioradialis, pronator teres, lacertus fibrosus (tendinous slip from the distal biceps brachii tendon), flexor carpi radialis, palmaris longus, and flexor carpi ulnaris.

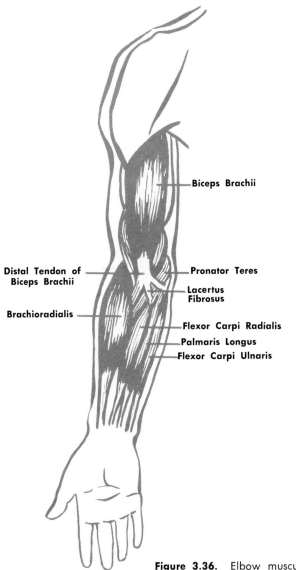

Figure 3.36. Elbow musculature (anterior)

Posterior muscles of the elbow joint are shown in figure 3.37: triceps brachii and anconeus. Note that the long head of the triceps brachii attaches to the scapula just below the glenoid fossa. This muscle serves as an adductor and extensor at the shoulder joint.

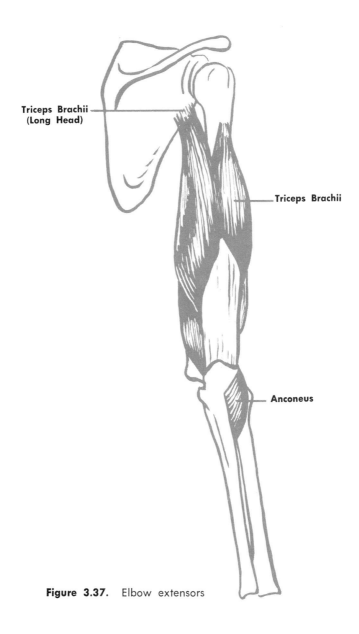

Figure 3.37. Elbow extensors

SELECTED REFERENCES

1. BARHAM, JERRY N., and THOMAS, WILLIAM L. *Anatomical Kinesiology: A Programmed Text.* New York: The Macmillan Company, 1969.
2. BASMAJIAN, J. V. *Primary Anatomy.* 5th ed. Baltimore: Williams & Wilkins Co., 1964.
3. COOPER, JOHN M., and GLASSOW, RUTH B. *Kinesiology.* St. Louis: The C. V. Mosby Co., 1963.
4. DAVIS, ELWOOD C.; LOGAN, GENE A.; and McKINNEY, WAYNE C. *Biophysical Values of Muscular Activity.* Dubuque, Ia.: Wm. C. Brown Company Publishers, 1965.
5. DE VRIES, HERBERT A. *Physiology of Exercise for Physical Education and Athletics.* Dubuque, Ia.: Wm. C. Brown Company Publishers, 1966.
6. FALLS, HAROLD B.; WALLIS, EARL L.; and LOGAN, GENE A. *Foundations of Conditioning.* New York: Academic Press, Inc., 1970.
7. GRANT, J. C. BOILEAU. *Grant's Dissector.* 6th ed. Baltimore: The Williams & Wilkins Co., 1967.
8. ――――, and BASMAJIAN, J. V., eds. *Grant's Method of Anatomy.* 7th ed. Baltimore: The Williams & Wilkins Co., 1965.
9. GRAY, HENRY. *Anatomy of the Human Body.* 28th ed. Edited by Charles M. Goss. Philadelphia: Lea & Febiger, 1966.
10. JENSEN, CLAYNE, and SCHULTZ, GORDON W. *Applied Kinesiology.* New York: McGraw-Hill Book Company, 1970.
11. LOGAN, GENE A. *Adaptations of Muscular Activity.* Belmont, Calif.: Wadsworth Publishing Co., Inc., 1964.
12. ――――, and McKINNEY, WAYNE C. *Kinesiology.* Dubuque, Ia.: Wm. C. Brown Company Publishers, 1970.
13. MOSELEY, H. F. "Disorders of the Shoulder," *Ciba Clinical Symposia* 11, no. 3 (1959):75-102.
14. RIEDMAN, SARAH R. *Physiology of Work and Play.* New York: Holt, Rinehart and Winston, Inc., 1950.
15. SCOTT, M. GLADYS. *Analysis of Human Motion.* New York: Appleton-Century-Crofts, 1963.
16. WELLS, KATHARINE F. *Kinesiology.* 4th ed. Philadelphia: W. B. Saunders Company, 1966.

postural
adaptations

Most physical deviations seen in adapted physical education are due to the pull of gravity, congenital or pathological conditions, and traumatic musculoskeletal injuries. It is the purpose here to discuss and explain the role of therapeutic exercise in aiding the organism to counteract or adjust to the adaptations which are made when one or more stresses or forces result in physical changes within the organism.

THE EFFECT OF GRAVITY

A concern for the prevention of adaptive changes in the elementary school child should be of primary importance. There should be a special emphasis on the prevention and/or familiarization of those adaptations which come about as a result of insufficient ability to counteract the force of gravity. During the elementary school years the bones assume the internal structure and the external shape that are determined by the direction of the external pressures placed upon them. If these pressures are not in the proper balance or alignment required for normal growth relationships, the bones will tend to become abnormally formed. They may adapt in such a way as to become permanently fixed. For example, downward pressures applied with greater intensity on one side of the body of the vertebrae than on the other side will impede the growth of that side. Vertebral growth activity will be greater where the pressure is less intense. Structural changes may result from these imbalanced pressures.

If imbalances or poor postural habits are allowed to persist, they may encourage adaptive shortening of connective tissues that bind the body together. Once such shortening has occurred, correcting the fault becomes much more difficult. Stretching will be required before strength and endurance activities can become effective for the resumption of good alignment.

Physical activity in its various forms can counteract the effect of gravity. It can also provide the strength, cardiovascular endurance, muscular endurance, flexibility, and skill, necessary for the maintenance of upright postures. The individual can make better use of his body as an instrument to perform the many tasks required of it in his daily living if he maintains it by exercising regularly. A well-conditioned body is not only more effective in counteracting the stresses of the pull of gravity, but it is also in a better state to perform efficient movements. A comprehensive consideration of the effects of gravity on the organism and the implications for programming in adapted physical education are contained herein.

A continuing battle is being waged by the human body against the force of gravity. Throughout man's waking hours, much of his energy is spent in the maintenance of his antigravity, dynamic postures. Even while he is asleep, changes in positions are numerous to avoid discomfort. This is largely caused by pressure between the bony structures and the supporting surfaces upon which the body is resting. Although a variety of positions help to relieve these pressures, the force of gravity is always present. Certain neurological mechanisms—spinal or postural reflexes, for example—are important in helping to sustain the body in antigravity postures. These reflexes, which operate involuntarily, provide the individual with the ability to maintain his antigravity positions without requiring his conscious attention. Other neurological mechanisms that help in man's orientation to his environment were presented in chapter 3.

Generally, the extensor muscles of the body perform the antigravity function, and the flexors are responsible for the execution of skilled acts. These two functions are not independent of each other. However, they may be more easily studied by approaching them separately. Complex interrelationships exist between antigravity functions and patterns of motion requiring a high level of skill. Not only must the muscle function to maintain the body in an upright position, but it must also serve to perform movements by the individual.

Antigravity Musculature

There are two major groups of antigravity muscles. These are the anteroposterior antigravity muscles and the lateral antigravity muscles. The anteroposterior muscles, because they are composed of the large extensors of the body, are the foundation upon which skilled movements are to be developed. If the antigravity muscles have insufficient strength and endurance, certain negative adaptation may result. For example, if the body is allowed to submit to the force of gravity, the connective tissues contralateral (antagonistic) to the extensor muscles will tend to shorten adaptively. This may produce a decrease in the range of motion or flexibility. Normal function may be inhibited, which may in turn encourage additional undesirable adaptations. Exercise plays a significant role in breaking the cycle for the reversal of undesirable adaptations. It also serves a preventive function against further negative adaptations.

Muscles which make up the anteroposterior antigravity mechanism are indicated in figure 4.1. Certain joints of the body tend to suc-

Figure 4.1. Anteroposterior antigravity muscles.

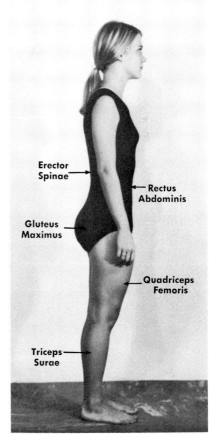

cumb to the pull of gravity. These joints are the ankle, knee, hip, and intervertebral joints of the spine. A minimum number of antero-posterior antigravity muscles must function at these joints to prevent flexion. These muscles are—at the ankle, the triceps surae; at the knee, the quadriceps femoris; at the hip, the gluteus maximus. Along with this group of antigravity muscles is the erector spinae group. This muscle group acts to prevent the trunk from falling forward. It runs between the sacrum and the base of the skull, being attached along the spinal column between these two points. The abdominal muscles serve a *reflex* antigravity function in holding the pelvis and rib cage together in a relatively constant position when the erector spinae muscle group acts to extend or hyperextend the spinal column. The erector spinae and the abdominal muscles work in a paired relationship to maintain the balance of the body segments.

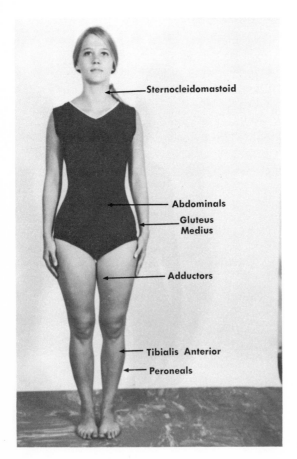

Figure 4.2. Lateral anti-gravity muscles.

Illustrated in figure 4.2 are the lateral antigravity muscles. These muscles, which function at the ankle, hip, lumbar, and cervical spinal regions, provide lateral stability in the upright position. They provide the movement of eversion and inversion at the subtalar and transverse tarsal joint. Providing a lateral stabilizing function at the hip are the adductors: adductor brevis, adductor longus, adductor magnus, and gracilis. Further stability is provided by the gluteus medius. Lateral stabilization of the lumbar and cervical spine is provided by the rectus abdominis and erector spinae muscles. Along with the erector spinae, the sternocleidomastoids serve as antigravity muscles in the cervical spine.

From a postural standpoint, a further antigravity function is provided by the trapezius and rhomboid muscles (fig. 4.3). Their function is to maintain the scapulae in their normal relationships, which

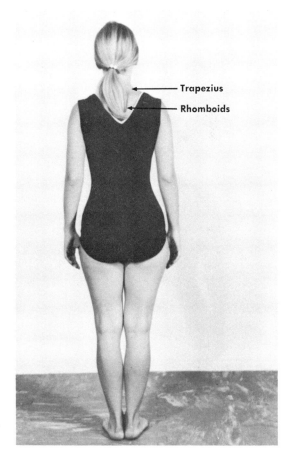

Figure 4.3. Scapular antigravity muscles.

in turn maintain the shoulder in balanced alignment upon the rib cage. Weakness of the scapular adductors tends to allow the shoulder to drop and project forward. Long-term maintenance of this position tends to develop an adaptive shortening of the pectoral muscles.

Effect of Gravity on Upright Posture

In the bipedal upright position, it is assumed the pull of gravity is capable of causing adaptations of various parts of the body. These adaptations initially affect the skeletal system. They alter the alignment of the bony levers at their articulations. Any change in the skeletal system would consequently cause changes within the muscular system as well. Such changes involve the impairment of muscular balance in those muscles that cross the affected joints. This alteration occurs through the lengthening or stretching of one group of muscles and the shortening of its contralateral (antagonistic) muscles.

A given posture is the result of the organism's adaptations to the stress of gravity upon its upright position. It is essential, therefore, to evaluate posture in order to ascertain the effectiveness with which the individual is able to cope with gravitational force. Effective adaptation may be characterized as facilitating normal growth and development in addition to providing the individual with a more efficient ability to perform the activities of daily living.

When one speaks of *posture,* the connotation is usually that of a static, erect standing position. It is more appropriate to accept the concept of *postures,* because it provides a basis for a *functional* approach to posture. *Effective and efficient function should be the key to "good posture."* Development of strength, cardiovascular endurance, muscular endurance, and flexibility is prerequisite to improved function.

Emphasis upon "good" standing posture has led to the practice of many physical education teachers applying a single, rigid standard for body alignment to all people of all ages. Unfortunately, current practice is not always consistent with present knowledge. The weight of authoritative opinion is against applying a single standard to everyone. It has been stressed that there is no standard form or shape for any aspect of the human body and that it is impossible to have postural standards (Morrison and Chenoweth, 1955). In an attempt to provide a standard that would take into consideration one's body type, orthograms of the anteroposterior standing positions of young adult white males have been presented in the literature (Goff, 1952). The orthograms consist of four body types which are the result of mean tracings of subjects in each group. This study proposes to set criteria for normal posture on a scientific basis. Nonetheless, authoritative opinion indicates "good" posture is largely an individual matter. This position was taken by Metheny when she commented that there is no one best posture for everyone. She stressed the point that each person has to make the best of what he has by balancing body segments with the most support and least strain (Metheny, 1952).

A dilemma faces the physical educator today. If one is not to make postural judgments based upon the static standing position, and if one must reject the use of a single standard and evaluate posture on an individual basis, what criteria are to be used?

In general, the justification for using the static upright position as a basis for postural evaluation is in the *aesthetic* value placed on "good" posture by our society. The *aesthetic* appeal of erect posture is not to be denied. Aesthetic and culturally determined standards cannot be ignored. "Good" posture is usually taken to indicate an optimistic outlook on one's life. Striving for the aesthetic value of good posture is an asset to the individual (Davis, Logan, and McKinney, 1965). Each adapted physical education teacher should strive to develop his own aesthetic judgment to the point where he is capable of judging what constitutes "good" posture. This quality of judgment can be acquired just as one can develop the ability to judge such events as gymnastics and ice skating.

Criteria to be used to evaluate postures may be drawn from the principles of *stability* and *balance* or *equilibrium*. The major principles that have been advanced concerning standing posture which might serve as a basis for evaluation may be stated as (1) a body is in equilibrium when its center of gravity falls within its base and (2) its most stable position is when its segments are vertically aligned. This position is one in which the center of gravity of each weight-bearing segment lies in a vertical line directly over the base of support or in which a deviation in one direction is exactly balanced in the opposite direction. Morrison and Chenoweth advocate that in order for posture to be classified as "good," it must be mechanically free, true to anatomical facts, and provide for better functioning of one or more organs (Morrison and Chenoweth, 1955).

Applying the principles of stability to a standing position that is balanced and free from muscular or ligamentous strain requires that the line of gravity of the center of the head, chest, trunk, and pelvis fall in a straight line. Any displacement of a body segment would disturb the equilibrium of the whole. Adjustments of other body segments would have to be made to regain and maintain balance. The acceptance of the line of gravity as a guide to balanced posture has resulted in acceptance of the line of gravity as a criterion for ideal posture. Unfortunately, the early works of Christian Wilhelm Braune and Otto Fischer, published in 1889 and concerned with the determination of the center of gravity of the various body segments, have been misinterpreted. It is now assumed erroneously by many physical educators that Braune and Fischer's findings represent a guide for the ideal posture. An account of their work, in which four frozen cadavers were nailed to a wall in attempt to determine the center of gravity and the line of gravity, is presented in the literature (Hirt, Fries, Hellebrandt, 1944).

Postural Screening

When screening for postural divergencies, the physical educator should be more concerned with marked deviations than with slight or minor malalignments. In discussing screening for postural adaptations, specific checkpoints are generally used for vertical and/or horizontal alignment. However, it must be clearly understood that these checkpoints are to serve only as general guides and are not presented as being absolute checks for "good" upright posture.

Postural adaptations made in response to the force of gravity may be grouped into two major classifications which serve as conceptual models. First, a *functional* divergency is one that involves only the soft tissues such as muscles or ligaments. A further qualification is that the divergency will disappear when the effect of gravity is eliminated. This tendency may be tested by (1) hanging or being suspended by the hands, (2) lying in a prone or supine position, (3) assuming a bent-forward position while standing. Second, a *structural* divergency is one in which the bones have changed their shape. It is a permanent condition which does not disappear when one of the previously mentioned positions is assumed.

One of the functions of the adapted physical education teacher is to identify whether or not the deviation is functional. After identification, remedial action should start as soon as possible. Attention is required since slight postural adaptations place unusual stresses on the soft tissue of the body surface. Consequently, a marked joint or segmental malalignment places unusual stress on some of the muscles and ligaments on one side and causes a shortening of the corresponding structures on the opposite side. The stretched muscles usually become weakened. The shortened muscles are stronger or more resistant to stretch, possibly as a result of the adaptive shortening of the connective tissue. Such soft tissue changes cause unusual muscular tensions to be exerted on the bone. This force may be of sufficient intensity and duration to cause changes in the external shape and internal structure of the bone in accordance with Wolff's law. Improper mechanical functioning of the joints and body segments can, and frequently does, have a similar effect. If movements requiring limited range of motion are used habitually, some of the muscles crossing the joint may begin to weaken. The contralateral (antagonistic) muscles, because they are relatively unopposed, tend to lose their extensibility, and the connective tissue may shorten to a fixed position. This adaptive shortening establishes muscular imbalance.

During the screening process for unilateral development and deviations, careful note should be made of their relationship to the total body structures. Individuals with marked deviations who evidence pain or who have limited range of motion should be immediately referred to a physician. An additional criterion for referral to a physician is the age of the subject. A very young child has pliable bones. This factor can make the condition more severe. Also, the age can be made to work for the correction of the condition. Therefore, remedial procedures should be undertaken as soon as possible.

Although much of the material in this chapter is concerned with screening for postural adaptations on the basis of standing position, it should be remembered that such assumed static positions are held only momentarily, if at all, in normal daily living. It is more logical to believe that all movement begins and ends with a posture.

THE FEET

The feet function as *locomotor* organs for propelling the body in motion and as a base of *support* for the body in a standing position.

When the feet are close to each other in the standing position, the seven tarsal and five metatarsal bones of the feet present an arched structure resembling a dome. Each foot, then, can be characterized as an architectural half-dome. The foot has a *longitudinal* arch that runs anteroposteriorly from the base of the calcaneus to the heads of the five metatarsals. In reality, the longitudinal arch is five arches in one, the highest of which is on the medial aspect of the foot and terminates at the distal head of the first metatarsal. The arches terminating at the second, third, and fourth metatarsals become progressively lower until the arch of the fifth metatarsal is almost nonexistent. In addition, the longitudinal arch gives the impression of a transverse arch extending from the head of the metatarsals to their proximal ends. This secondary arch, which exists noticeably across the more proximal end of the metatarsals, is referred to as the *transverse metatarsal* arch.

The weight of the body is transferred from the tibia directly to the talus, which in turn transfers half of the weight downward to the calcaneus. The other half is transferred to the navicular bone of the longitudinal arch. Through the navicular, the weight is distributed to the cuboid, the three cuneiforms, and through them to the metatarsals. The weight is then distributed equally to the heads of the second, third, fourth, and fifth metatarsals, and to each of the two sesamoid bones under the head of the first metatarsal (Morton and Fuller, 1952).

In the standing position, the line of gravity intersects the navicular and cuboid bones. The weight is born over these bones. Since the medial aspect of the longitudinal arch is higher than that of the lateral arch, it is not well adapted for weight-bearing. However, it provides the resiliency in the foot that prevents undue strain on the individual participating in vigorous activity.

Relationship of Foot Position to Weight-Bearing

Proper weight-bearing is essential for the normal growth and development of the feet. Conversely, improper weight-bearing can cause structural divergencies of the feet. Abramson and Delagi have indicated that weight-bearing brings about changes in the formation of bone. This concept corresponds to Wolff's law. Thus, as one adapts a weight-bearing position that varies the normal structural alignment of the foot, the muscles in the affected area are subjected to abnormal stresses. Abramson and Delagi believe that the added muscular stress is of greater importance in the alteration of bony growth than in weight-bearing *per se* (Abramson and Delagi, 1960). It is imperative that any alteration of one's posture take into account the weight-bearing of the feet.

Attention is called to the movements that occur at the subtalar and transverse tarsal joint, *eversion* and *inversion*. The movements of the sole of the foot outward (eversion) and inward (inversion) are voluntary movements. Because they are, they can be easily observed and described.

The movements and positions of *abduction* and *adduction* must be considered in detail when discussing the feet. Much confusion arises in the use of these terms as they apply to the foot. Abduction and adduction are defined as movements of a whole or part of a body segment toward (adduction) or away (abduction) from the midline of the body. Therefore, one must indicate whether the terms refer to the total foot or to the distal aspect, the forefoot. Abduction and adduction of the *whole foot* are concomitants of rotation of the leg at the knee when the knee is flexed, or rotation of the lower limb when the knee is extended. However, these movements in the fore-foot—with the action occurring at the metatarsophalangeal articulation —are so limited as to be almost nonexistent as voluntary movements. The confusion is compounded when one considers abduction and adduction in terms of foot position.

Functional definitions are used here for the terms *eversion, inversion, abduction,* and *adduction* to indicate anatomical movements or positions of the *total* foot. In reference to foot positions related to weight-bearing in the standing position, *pronation* will indicate the position in which the foot is everted and the forefoot is abducted. *Supination* will indicate the position in which the foot is inverted and the forefoot is adducted. It should be noted that the terms *pronation* and *supination,* from a purely anatomic standpoint, apply only to the action that takes place at the radio-ulnar joints of the forearm. However, these terms have a functional application when dealing with postural position and movements of the feet. Foot positions are structurally related to rotation of the thighs when the knees are extended. Therefore, when the thigh is rotated inward and the foot is free to move, that is, held above the floor, the whole foot is adducted. If the foot is not free to move, as in the weight-bearing position, torsion from inward rotation of the thigh is then referred to the foot and ankle. The resultant force brings about pronation. Under similar conditions, but as a result of outward rotation, the positions of adduction and supination of the whole foot are achieved.

While the foot is bearing weight, any foot position that shifts the weight to the medial border of the longitudinal arch will also abduct the forefoot. This is a passive rather than voluntary movement that is caused by the upper portion of the calcaneus rolling downward and inward. In addition, the position of the talus changes in relation to the other tarsal bones. The tarsal, metatarsal, and metatarsophalangeal articulations also make adaptations, which result in slight turning outward of the forefoot. This position is referred to as *pronation. Supination* is a foot position with the weight on the outer border and adduction of the forefoot.

The effect of gravity applying stress to the weight of the body is the major cause of most foot problems. Special attention must be paid to the interrelationships between foot positions and gravitational pull. The individual's weight-bearing characteristics must be determined in order to make referrals to the physician for diagnosis and further recommendation. Correction of severe postural deviations must be based upon the medical diagnosis and the recommendation from the physician.

Weight-Bearing Screening Devices

The Pedo-graph (fig. 4.4) and the podiascope (fig. 4.5) are two devices often used by physical educators for determining foot divergencies. The Pedo-graph is a foot-impression device that provides an inked footprint. A rubber sheet inked on its underside is pulled from a

Figure 4.4.   Pedo-graph. (The Scholl Mfg. Co., Inc., Chicago, Ill.)

roller within the device and is placed above a special paper. Although these impressions are commonly used, they are of questionable value because they place undue emphasis on the height of the arch as an indicator of foot strength. There is little or no direct relationship between the height of the arch and the strength of the foot. Two of the difficulties concerning the use of the inked foot impressions are (1) it is difficult to determine correctly the amount of ink to use in order to achieve the best impression and (2) the impression is actually a composite of non-weight-bearing and weight-bearing because of the way the subject must step up on the equipment. Nevertheless, the device does provide an aid to student motivation.

The podiascope is of great value in determining the weight-bearing areas of the sole of the foot. This device consists of a three-sided box, approximately 16 x 16 x 12 inches. The front of the box is open, and an adjustable mirror is inserted into the box. The optimum angle is

Figure 4.5. Podiascope

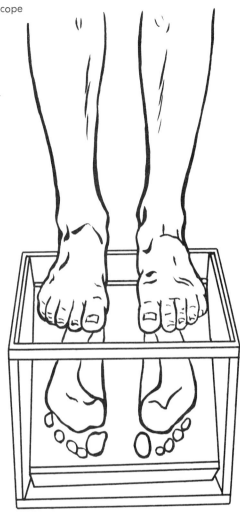

forty-five degrees to the bottom of the box. The top of the box is a
plate glass, not less than one-half inch in thickness. The individual
to be evaluated stands on the glass top. The reflection of the feet in
the mirror indicates the weight-bearing areas. The non-weight-bearing
areas are a different color from the weight-bearing areas. An additional advantage of the podiascope is that the examiner can accurately
determine the effect of any weight-bearing changes the subject makes
at his suggestion. Photographs of the image on the mirror may be
taken for a permanent record to be used for later comparisons.

Foot-Leg Alignment

From a functional approach, it is recommended that the foot position be one in which the feet are parallel from two to four inches apart. This foot position is the natural or anatomic position. Correct foot-leg alignment implies that certain bony landmarks will fall in a vertical line. The checkpoints for such alignment, when viewed from the front, are the anterior superior iliac spine, the center of the patella, the midpoint of the ankle, and the second toe. When viewed from the rear, a straight line should run through the midpoint of the popliteal space, the midline of the Achilles tendon, and the midline of the calcaneus. A plumb line or posture grid screen may be used to check foot-leg alignment. Any marked deviations from the previously described vertical alignment should be evaluated for possible referral to the student's physician for his diagnosis and further recommendation.

Adaptations Resulting from
Faulty Weight-Bearing

The body weight should be equally distributed between the calcaneus and the metatarsal heads. Because of the difference in the height of the medial and lateral borders of the longitudinal arch, the lateral border of the foot is designed to absorb the imposed weight. It is not unusual, therefore, for a foot impression to show some degree of contact with the supporting surfaces as a result of the flexibility of the longitudinal arch in weight-bearing. If the weight-bearing distribution is not normal as shown by the podiascope, it indicates that certain adaptations have occurred.

Pronation has resulted if there is weight-bearing on the inner border of the foot. The bony arch must rely on ligaments and muscles to maintain its integrity. Continuous weight-bearing with the foot in a pronated position tends to cause the arch to become lower or flattened. It has been pointed out that flattening of the arch is due largely to continual stress rather than to the intensity of the stress, and these are the individuals who develop arch problems (Grant and Basmajian, 1965). Therefore, although pronation may result from the lowering of the arch, *it must not be assumed that a pronated foot is also a flat foot.*

The determination of whether or not an individual's arch has fallen and whether he has a flat foot or not may be indicated by either the use of the podiascope or a functional arch-height test.

The *functional arch-height test* consists of the examiner sliding his extended second and third fingers (with hand supinated) under the medial aspect of the longitudinal arch at the articulation of the first cuneiform and first metatarsal bones. The subject should be in his habitual standing position. If the fingers cannot slide under the arch or if the arch is contacting the bony surface, the foot is classified as a flat foot or *pes planus* (fig. 4.6). If the fingers will slide only under the base of the first metatarsal, the foot may be classified as having

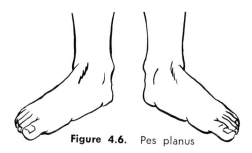

Figure 4.6. Pes planus

an unusually low arch. If the fingers can slide under the base of the second metatarsal, the foot may be classified as having a normal arch. If the fingers can slide under the base of the third or fourth metatarsal, then the foot is classified as having a high arch. If the fingers can slide under the base of the fifth metatarsal or completely under the lateral border, the foot is classified as having a high arch or *pes cavus* (fig. 4.7).

Figure 4.7. Pes cavus

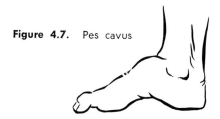

Although this discussion concerning the identification of the foot adaptations resulting from improper weight-bearing has dealt with the use of the Pedo-graph, podiascope, and the functional foot test, there are also other signs and procedures that may be used to determine the presence of foot adaptations. The plumb line may be used to check the vertical alignment of the foot and leg. If undesirable foot positions have resulted from poor standing postures, certain signs will be obvious. The normal foot is slightly concave on the medial side due to the increased height of the medial aspect of the arch. The lateral border is slightly convex due to the lowness of the lateral aspect of the arch and the widening of the foot as a result of weight-bearing. Therefore, the appearance of a convexity on the medial border of the foot is an important sign. This is an indication that the individual has assumed a position of pronation with excess weight being borne on the medial aspect of the foot. This change may indicate that the individual has a low arch or flat foot. Additional screening with the use of the podiascope or the functional arch-height test is necessary for classifying the foot as flat.

When the upper portion of the calcaneus rolls inward and downward in a position of pronation, there is a "jamming" of the heel toward the lateral malleolus in which the malleolus seems to disappear (fig. 4.8). The medial malleolus appears to be farther from

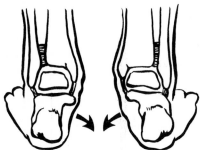

Figure 4.8. Inward tilting of calcaneus

the heel; consequently it is more prominent. There is a reverse of this appearance when the foot is in a position of supination. In observing foot-leg alignment from the rear of the subject, attention should be paid to the Achilles tendon and the malleoli of the ankle. Normally, the Achilles tendon should be straight from its distal attachment on the calcaneus to the broadening of its junction with the belly of the gastrocnemius and soleus muscles. A bowing inward of the tendon toward the medial aspect of the leg indicates an adaptation in which the calcaneus has rolled inward and downward. The lateral edge of the tendon is prominent and sharp while the medial edge is rounded and tends to disappear. Bowing inward of this tendon is called *Achilles flare* or *Helbing's sign* (fig. 4.9). This is associated with pronation of the foot.

Outward bowing of the Achilles tendon is an indication that an adaptation of a supinated position of the foot has occurred. Care should be taken to avoid identifying the natural flaring of the triceps surae muscle at its tendinous junction as being an indication of flaring

Figure 4.9. Helbing's sign

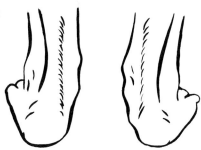

of the tendon. Comparison of the prominence of the malleoli is possible from a rear view of the ankle.

The literature indicates a difference of opinion about the divergencies of pronation, flat feet, and weak feet. Definitions and relationships of pronation and flat feet have been presented previously. The concept of weak feet should be discussed in some detail.

Some authorities have treated weak feet as being synonymous with the position of pronation in which the arch may or may not be depressed. They regard a pronated foot as a weak foot. Flat feet are also classified as weak feet. However, the same authorities maintain that the presence of pain should serve as an indicator of weak feet. Morrison and Chenoweth have developed a *functional foot test.* They indicate that if the exercises recommended in the test cause pain, then the individual may have weak feet (Morrison and Chenoweth, 1955).

The functional foot test is useful in determining whether or not the foot is to be classified as a weak foot. This test consists of four foot exercises. If the individual experiences pain during or immediately after the exercises, he should be classified as having weak feet. The test is designed to place increasing stress on the feet. When pain is experienced, the individual should not complete further exercises in the test. The exercises are as follows (when the exercise includes the phrase "on the toes" it means on the balls of the feet and toes; the phrase "feet abducted" implies the whole foot is pointing diagonally outward): (1) rise on toes (feet abducted); (2) walk on toes (with sole nearly vertical to the floor); (3) hop on toes; and (4) jump into the air and land on the toes with the feet abducted (knees relaxed).

Other Common Foot Divergencies

The most frequent cause of malalignment of the bones in the anterior portion of the foot is improper weight-bearing. A shift of the weight from the medial to the lateral aspect of the forefoot is often due to (1) a short first metatarsal bone and/or (2) a hypermobile first metatarsal segment which includes the first metatarsal and the first cuneiform bone (Morton, 1935). Because of these two factors, the other metatarsal heads must assume a disproportionate share of the load. This in turn produces pain in the area of the metatarsal heads. The condition is known as *metatarsalgia*. This simply means that there is pain in the area of the metatarsal heads. A frequent site of pain is the articulation of the fourth metatarsal with the first phalanx of the first toe. This pain is referred to as *true metatarsalgia* or as *Morton's metatarsalgia*. Associated with this condition is the formation of a neuroma on the digital nerve near the head of the metatarsal. In some cases, surgical excision of this neuroma may be necessary.

In normal weight-bearing, the weight is borne anteriorly on the heads of the metatarsals except for the first metatarsal where the weight is taken by the two sesamoid bones under the head of that bone. If there is excess pressure on the metatarsophalangeal joint for any reason, the toe involved is unable to maintain its normal position. As a consequence, the first phalanx is hyperextended, the second phalanx is flexed, and the third phalanx may be either flexed or extended. As a result, the toe assumes the appearance of a hammer. This divergency is called *hammer toe* (fig. 4.10). In addition to the hammer shape, there will be a prominence of the extensor tendon of the first phalanx. This prominence is due mostly to hyperextension at that joint. Also, there will usually be a *callus* (thickening of the skin) under the head of the metatarsal of the affected toe. Another divergency usually involving the third toe is known as *mallet toe* (fig. 4.11). This

Figure 4.10. Hammer toe
(second toe).

Figure 4.11. Mallet toe
(third toe).

condition is characterized by extreme flexion of the distal phalanx with extension of the proximal phalanx. There will usually be a callus on the dorsal surface of the involved toe.

Poorly fitting shoes often tend to increase pressure which results in friction of the skin of malformed toes. As a defense to this force, the skin thickens. When located on the superior aspect or between the toes, this thickening of the skin is referred to as a *corn*. Pressure or friction continuously applied by poorly fitting shoes causes crowding of the toes. Frequently, the fourth and fifth toes overlap. The fifth toe is usually forced over the fourth toe (fig. 4.12). This divergency is called *overlapping toe*.

Figure 4.12. Overlapping toe (fifth toe).

Improperly fitting shoes may cause the great toe to change its alignment in relation to the first metatarsal. The great toe is deflected or turned toward the four lesser toes. This divergency is called *hallux valgus* (fig. 4.13) and tends to be fifteen to twenty times more prev-

Figure 4.13. Hallux valgus

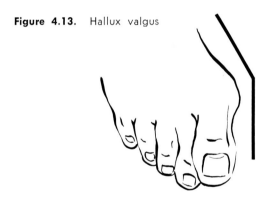

alent in women than in men. Often associated with this condition is the development of a *bunion* and *exostosis* of the bone. With the increased angulation of the great toe toward the other toes, the pressure of poorly fitting shoes is exerted against the side of the head of the first metatarsal. The articulation of the first metatarsal and the proximal phalanx of the great toe is unique in that a *bursa* is present. The pressure results in irritation of the bursa, which becomes inflamed and is known as *bursitis*. Enlargement of the bursa is called a bunion. Increased irritation in the area of the head of the first metatarsal often results in calcium deposits in that area. These deposits of calcium increase the size and alter the shape of the metatarsal. The growth of bone in the area is called an *exostosis*. Surgical intervention is required in most cases to correct the condition.

ANTEROPOSTERIOR POSTURAL ADAPTATIONS

The postural grid screen (fig. 4.14) or plumb line (fig. 4.15) may be used as guides for the screening of anteroposterior postural adaptations. The standing position is viewed from the *side* which demonstrates

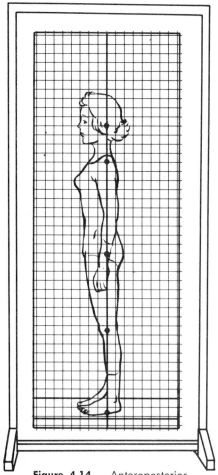

Figure 4.14. Anteroposterior postural alignment with grid screen.

Figure 4.15. Anteroposterior postural alignment with plumb line.

anteroposterior postural alignment (fig. 4.14). In checking for a marked deviation in vertical alignment, the following anatomic landmarks may serve as a guide: base of the fifth metatarsal (approximately one to one and one-half inches in front of the lateral malleolus), midpoint of the knee joint, midpoint of the hip area, midpoint of the shoulder area, and the lobe of the ear.

Foot-Leg Alignment

From an anteroposterior standpoint, the normal position of the foot is at a *right angle* to the leg. The line of gravity falls at the anterior edge of the tibia and in front of the malleolus in the area of the navicular-cuboid articulation. The checkpoint for normal foot-leg alignment, therefore, is just behind the patella and from one to one and one-half inches in front of the fibular malleolus.

Any deviation from this line will indicate an increase or decrease in foot-leg angle. If the checkpoint of the knee—middle of the knee joint—is noticeably forward of the reference line, the individual has assumed a position of partial dorsiflexion or forward inclination of the leg at the ankle. If the checkpoint is considerably behind the vertical, the individual has assumed a position of partial plantar flexion or backward inclination of the leg at the ankle joint.

Leg-Thigh Alignment

The normal position of both the knee and the hip joint is extension. The femur and tibia should form a straight line. The line of gravity passes through the greater trochanter, and the checkpoint for vertical alignment of the thigh is the midpoint of the hip area.

Any deviation of the foot-leg angle will affect leg-thigh alignment because of the relationship of the foot-leg alignment to the knee. Dorsiflexion will place the tibia anterior to the vertical. This will cause flexion of the thigh at the hip in order for the femur to articulate with the tibia. This action results in partial flexion of the knees. An increase in foot-leg angle (plantar flexion) causes the thigh to be hyperextended. This position is referred to as "back knee" or *genu recurvatum.*

Pelvic Girdle Alignment

The pelvic girdle is considered the keystone of standing posture because of its function of supporting the upper body weight and transferring it to the feet. Normal anteroposterior alignment of the pelvis consists of a slight forward and downward inclination. This is when the anterior superior iliac spine and the anterior aspect of the pubic crest are vertically aligned (fig. 4.16). If the anterior superior iliac spine is forward of the pubic crest, the position is called *increased pelvic inclination* (fig. 4.17). Conversely, if the pubic crest is anterior to the anterior superior iliac spine, the position is called *decreased pelvic inclination* (fig. 4.18).

Figure 4.16. Normal pelvic alignment.

Figure 4.17. Increased pelvic inclination.

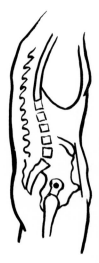

Figure 4.18. Decreased pelvic inclination.

Thigh-Pelvic Relationships

Pelvic inclination is controlled by the hip flexors and extensors, the extensors of the lumbar spine, and the abdominal muscles. In the balanced position, there is equal muscle tension exerted on the pelvis by these muscle groups. If, however, there is greater muscular tension exerted by the hip flexors or the extensors of the lumbar spine, the inclination of the pelvis will be increased; whereas, if there is greater muscular tension exerted by the hip extensors and/or the abdominal muscles, the inclination of the pelvis is decreased.

The rectus femoris and the hamstrings are biarticular or two-joint muscles. They have functions at both the knee and hip joints. Flexion of the knees in the standing position results in lengthening the rectus femoris. This, in turn, creates a downward pull on the anterior aspect of the pelvis. This downward pull increases pelvic inclination. Hyperextension of the knees, on the other hand, results in placing the hamstrings on stretch, and this creates a downward pull of the posterior of the pelvis, thereby decreasing pelvic inclination. There is, therefore, a relationship between flexion or hyperextension of the knees and inclination of the pelvis.

Pelvic-Lumbar Relationships

Because of the immovable nature of the joints between the sacrum and the pelvic bones, any movement of the pelvic girdle will have a direct relationship to the positions of the lumbar spine. Thus, it is impossible to separate the anteroposterior curve of the lumbar spine from inclination of the pelvis. Consequently, if pelvic inclination is increased, the sacrum rotates forward and downward, causing the lumbar vertebrae also to assume a position of forward inclination. The body, in an attempt to maintain a balanced upright position, will compensate by assuming a posterior inclination of the upper portion of the lumbar spine and lower portion of the thoracic spine. This position results in an exaggeration of the lumbar curve (fig. 4.17). If pelvic inclination is decreased, compensating adaptations for this position result in a decrease in the lumbar curve (fig. 4.18).

The abdominal muscles, through their attachment to the pubis, influence pelvic inclination. When pelvic inclination is increased, the abdominals are elongated and the pressure of the viscera adds further stress to these muscles. The protrusion or sagging of the abdominal viscera is known as *visceral ptosis*. When pelvic inclination is decreased and the pubis is moved forward and upward, the lower portion of the abdominal area becomes prominent (fig. 4.17). This prominence is most noticeable in the female because of the development of a layer of adipose tissue in the area between the pubis and the umbilicus. However, it must be remembered that ptosis is an actual sagging of the abdominal viscera and is not necessarily synonymous with a prominent abdomen.

Lumbar Spine

There is no absolute standard for the determination of the degree or extent of an anterior convexity of the normal lumbar curve. A marked increase in a lumbar curve is called a *hollow back*, or *lumbar lordosis* (fig. 4.17). Lordosis indicates an increase of the anterior curve. A decrease in the lumbar curve is called a *flat back*, or *lumbar kyphosis* (fig. 4.18). Kyphosis indicates a decrease or reversal of an anterior curve or an increase or exaggeration of a posterior curve.

Thoracic Spine and Shoulder Girdle

A marked increase in the thoracic or dorsal curve is called a "round upper back" or *thoracic* or *dorsal kyphosis*. The checkpoint for alignment of the shoulders in relation to the plumb line is the midpoint of the conformation of the shoulder.

Manipulative activities of the hands and arms require that the shoulder girdle habitually assume a position of protraction. Continuous use of the upper limbs in this position may result in adaptive shortening of the anterior muscles which pull the shoulders forward and abduct the scapulae. Because of the forward position of the shoulders, the chest may appear sunken or shallow. If the forward position or protraction is a marked divergency, the midpoint of the shoulder will be anterior to the plumb line reference. This condition is called "round shoulders" or "forward shoulders."

An apparent increase in the thoracic curve may be just protraction of the shoulders and abduction of the scapulae. This confusion frequently results in the faulty assumption that forward shoulders and round upper back are synonymous. Erroneous identification of a thoracic divergency is fairly complicated since forward shoulders frequently accompany thoracic kyphosis. Therefore, one must be especially careful to differentiate between these two divergencies.

Another divergency associated with protraction of the shoulder girdle with accompanying abduction of the scapulae is the protrusion of the vertebral border of the scapulae from the rib cage. This condition is influenced by muscular imbalance between the middle trapezius and rhomboid muscles (scapular adductors) and the serratus anterior (scapular abductor). Excessive posterior projection of the vertebral border of the scapula is known as "winged scapulae."

Lumbar-Thoracic Relationships

Although an adaptation may occur exclusively in one spinal segment, a change in alignment generally involves more than one segment due to the process of compensation. The most common combined lumbarthoracic adaptation is one in which there is an increase in the lumbar and thoracic curve. This is referred to as "round hollow back," or *kypholordosis.*

An adaptation which includes both the lumbar and thoracic curves is one in which the thoracic curve tends to obliterate the lumbar curve. This deviation terminates in sharp hyperextension of the lumbosacral junction and is called "round swayback." At first glance, there appears to be an increase in the thoracic curve. Closer examination will reveal that neither the lumbar nor the thoracic curve is increased. The thoracic curve is not increased, but it does extend through the thoracic as well as the lumber segments of the spine. Consequently, the lumbar curve is decreased or reversed as characterized by the "flat back," or lumbar kyphosis. Because of the resultant posterior overhang of the trunk, however, there is a sharp hyperextension of the lumbosacral junction. Because of the prominence of the gluteal area, one is frequently led to assume falsely that the lumbar curve is increased.

Cervical Spine and Head Relationships

A marked increase in the cervical curve is called a "poke neck," or *cervical lordosis.* A decrease in the cervical curve is called "flat neck," or *cervical kyphosis.*

A balanced position of the head is one in which the vertical alignment passes through the midpoint of the shoulder and the lobe of the ear. If the vertical reference checkpoint of the head and ear lobe is anterior to the line, and if the chin is down and back, the position is referred to as "forward head." Conversely, if the lobe of the ear is posterior to the reference line and the chin is forward and up, the position is referred to as "back head." A "forward-head" position is commonly associated with a decreased cervical curve. The "back-head" position is usually associated with an increased cervical curve.

One may speculate about the validity of the commonly held vertical head positioning. The study of Braune and Fischer, previously cited, utilized frozen cadavers. It is assumed that the cadavers were frozen in the anatomic position. If this assumption is correct, the head, because of its relationship to the supporting surfaces, may have assumed an extreme posterior position. Ironically, this may account for the unusually high incidence of students who are assigned to adapted physical education and posture classes because of a "forward-head" divergency.

Thoracic-Cervical Relationships

Although adaptations may be confined to only one segment, any change in the thoracic curve is generally compensated by, or affects, the cervical segment of the spine. When the body attempts to compensate for the posterior stress of the increased thoracic curve, the shoulders tend to be brought forward so that the arms may assist in the maintenance of balance. A similar relationship exists between the position of the head and the adaptations of the thoracic area. The head is thrust partly forward as a compensatory reaction. In addition, the head is frequently held in a forward position as a result of concentrating on such activities as reading or in the performance of the daily manipulative skills. Consequently, "forward head" and a decreased cervical curve are generally associated with "round upper back" and "forward shoulders."

Compound Anteroposterior Postural Adaptations

Segmental anteroposterior adaptations in the standing position have been previously discussed. However, no attempt has been made to demonstrate total body adaptations which are usually assumed in the standing position. Postural reflexes operating involuntarily are consequently involved in the maintenance of a balanced posture in which the head is centered over the trunk. The weight is born equally by the thighs and distributed to the legs and finally to the feet (fig. 4.19). Thus, any change in normal alignment will affect other body segments.

Because the feet provide a base of support, the analysis of standing posture should begin with the feet. Any deviation of the feet will cause adaptations in other segments of the body at a higher level.

The commonly assumed standing postural adaptation is called the "fatigue slump" posture (fig. 4.20). This position is characterized by the weight being borne on the medial-posterior aspect of the feet. There is an increase in the foot-leg angle, hyperextension of the knees, increased pelvic inclination, increased lumbar curve, sagging abdominal

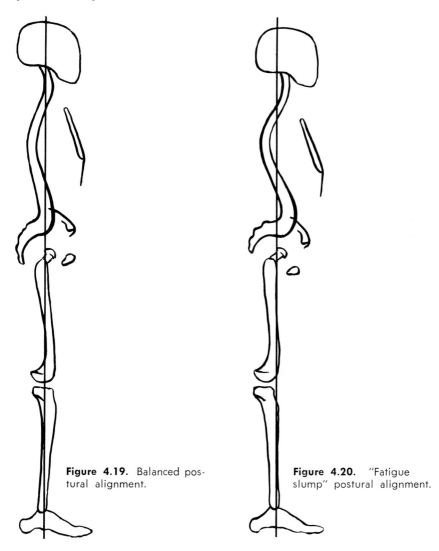

Figure 4.19. Balanced postural alignment.

Figure 4.20. "Fatigue slump" postural alignment.

viscera, increased thoracic curve, protracted shoulders, apparent sunken chest, abducted and protruding scapulae, decreased cervical curve, and a forward head. This position has been described as one in which the individual is "hanging" on his ligaments. In such areas as the knee and the hip joint, the ligaments are at their extremes, and any habitual maintenance of these positions tends to place undue stress on these structures.

Another rather common anteroposterior postural adaptation is known as the "fashion model slouch" posture (fig. 4.21). This position is frequently associated with the wearing of high-heeled shoes. This posture is assumed constantly by teen-age girls and by women. Often an attempt is made to decrease the posterior projection of the gluteal area. This emphasis is promoted by the clothing industry, particularly through the professional fashion model. The major differences between the "fatigue slump" posture and the "fashion model slouch" posture is in relation to hip and leg, knee, pelvic inclination, and lumbar curve. The "fashion model slouch" posture is characterized by the weight being borne on the medial-anterior aspect of the feet, decreased foot-leg angle, partial flexion of the knees, decreased pelvic inclination, prominent abdomen, decreased lumbar curve, increased thoracic curve, protracted shoulders, apparent sunken chest, abducted and protruding scapulae, decreased cervical curve, and forward head.

LATERAL POSTURAL ADAPTATIONS

Both the *anterior* and *posterior* views of the body are required for the determination of marked *lateral* deviations of body segments in a standing position. Screening for lateral postural adaptations should include the use of a posture grid screen. This helps the examiner determine both vertical and horizontal alignment.

Viewing the normal vertical alignment from the rear (fig. 4.22), the reference line falls equidistant between the ankles and the knees, passes through the cleft of the buttocks, and bisects the midline of the spinous processes of the vertebrae and the midline of the head. When viewed from the front (fig. 4.23), the reference line is equidistant between the ankles and knees; passes through the point of the symphysis pubis; bisects the umbilicus and the midline of the sternum, chin and nose; and passes between the eyes. A check of horizontal alignment is required to determine adequately whether

Figure 4.21. "Fashion model" postural alignment.

Figure 4.22. Lateral postural alignment (posterior view).

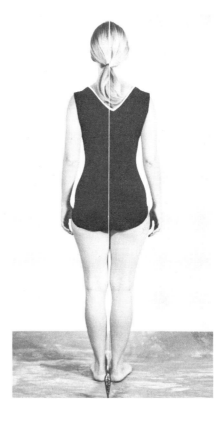

Figure 4.23. Lateral postural alignment (anterior view).

there is lateral asymmetry of the body segments in the standing position. When viewed from the front, the following body structures should be in horizontal alignment: the patellae, the anterior superior iliac spines, and the shoulders. The scapulae and the shoulders should be horizontally aligned when viewed from the rear (fig. 4.24).

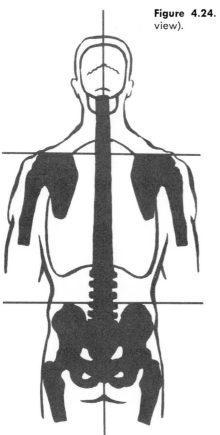

Figure 4.24. Lateral postural alignment (posterior view).

Foot-Ankle Postural Adaptations

Although an extensive discussion of the feet has previously been presented, this section concerning the feet is a brief review because of the relationship of faulty weight-bearing to lateral deviations. Pronation of the foot, in addition to weight-bearing on the medial border of the foot, is characterized by a prominent medial malleolus. This sign may be viewed from either a front or rear view. The posterior view will also show a medial bowing of the Achilles tendon. The feet may, however, have assumed a position of supination as a result of faulty weight-bearing. Signs of such a position of the foot are a prominent lateral malleolus and an outward bowing of the Achilles tendon.

Leg-Thigh Alignment

The normal standing position is with the feet parallel and the knee joints extended. There should be no rotation of the thighs. The presence of rotation of the thighs can be viewed from a front view; the position of the patellae serves as a sign of rotation. If the patellae are turned inward, giving the appearance of looking at each other, they indicate *medial rotation* of the thighs; whereas, if the patellae are rotated outward, they indicate *lateral rotation* of the thighs.

The normal position of the knees when viewed from the front is one of vertical alignment. A simple check in which the reference line intersects the midpoint of the ankle, the midline of the knee, and the anterior superior iliac spine may be used. A further check for lateral adaptation of the knee position is one in which the subject stands with the feet together and parallel and with the patellae pointing straight ahead (fig. 4.25A). In this position the medial malleoli and

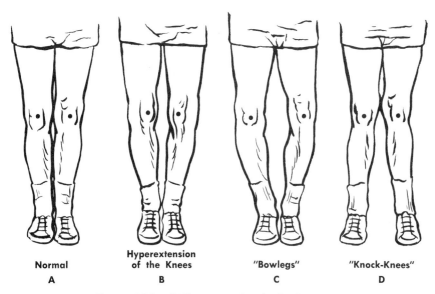

| Normal | Hyperextension of the Knees | "Bowlegs" | "Knock-Knees" |
| A | B | C | D |

Figure 4.25. Difference in leg-thigh alignment

the medial aspect of the knees should be in contact. If the knees are not in vertical alignment, it is indicative that some adaptation has taken place in relation to knee position. Frequently, the common functional adaptation is mistakenly identified as "bowlegs" (fig. 4.25B). This apparent bowing of the legs at the knee is due to the individual's assuming a position of hyperextension of the knees. This position is associated with medial rotation of the thighs as indicated by the apparent medial rotation of the patellae. This condition is appropriately called "functional bowlegs" since its characteristics readily disappear when the subject rotates the thighs laterally while assuming the normal extended position of the knees. If the knees do not touch when standing with the feet together, the individual then has "bowlegs," or *genu varum* (fig. 4.25C). If the knees are in contact and the subject is unable to place the feet together and parallel so that the medial malleoli are in contact, the individual has "knock-knees," or *genu valgum* (fig. 4.25D).

Continuous weight-bearing in a pronated foot position tends to cause the legs and thighs to rotate medially. This places unusual stress on the medial aspect of the knee and tends to cause slight flexion and a knock-knee adaptation to occur. An assumed knock-knee position tends to shift the weight toward the medial border of the foot and brings about a foot position of pronation. A similar relationship exists between pronation of the foot and bowlegs. It is important to determine the relationship between weight-bearing of the foot and lateral adaptations at the knee. Rasch and Burke point out that before good posture can be attained, such divergencies must be corrected or compensated for (Rasch and Burke, 1967).

Pelvic Girdle Alignment

Viewed from the front, normal pelvic girdle alignment is characterized by horizontal alignment of the anterior superior iliac spine. This alignment may be checked by use of the horizontal lines on a posture grid screen. If the points are not aligned, it is indicative of a lateral tilt of the pelvic girdle. This deviation may result from a difference in leg length that may be due to improper foot position, knee deviation, or a structural disorder. If the pelvic girdle has a lateral tilt due to a difference in leg length, the curve of the waistline on the side of the longer leg is projected inward and is accompanied by a soft tissue fold at the waistline. The hip area on the side of the longer leg is prominent and projected slightly forward. These characteristics are due to a shifting of the trunk from a vertical alignment so that it is no longer equally balanced over the base of support. Displacement of a body segment can be determined by the use of a plumb line (figs. 4.26 and 4.27).

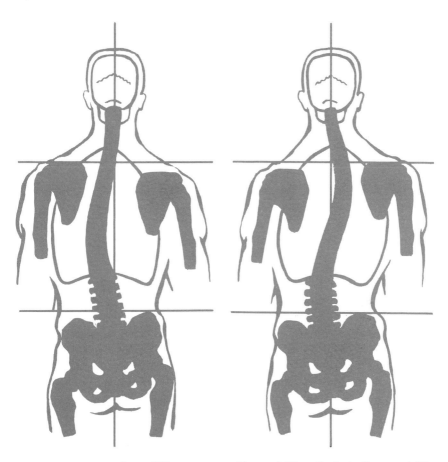

Figure 4.26. Scoliotic "C" curve   **Figure 4.27.** Scoliotic "reversed 'S' curve."

Lateral Spinal Postural Adaptations

A lateral postural adaptation in the spine is called *scoliosis*. Scoliosis means bending, twisting, or rotating. Two of the characteristics of scoliosis are primarily concerned with vertebral adaptations. They are identified as deviations and rotations. The term *deviation* is used to indicate lateral movement of the vertebrae from the normal vertical alignment. The term *rotation* is used to indicate the turning or twisting of the spinous process of the vertebrae about the normal vertical alignment. An additional characteristic of scoliosis which is primarily concerned with the segments of the trunk is *displacement*. This term refers to the shifting of the body segment from the normal balanced position over the base of support, the feet. Deviation and displacement may be evaluated by the use of a plumb line. Rotation may be checked by having a subject bend forward from the waist with the arms hanging down. This position is called the *Adam's position* (fig. 4.28).

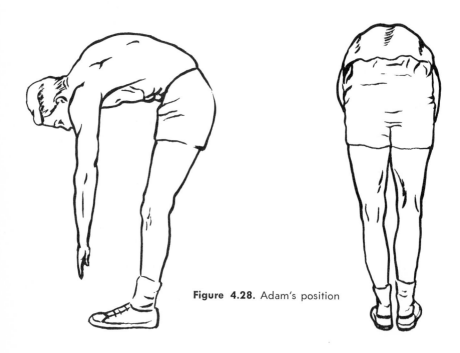

Figure 4.28. Adam's position

Muscular adaptation is an additional characteristic of scoliosis. If a position in which the spine is laterally flexed is habitually assumed, the muscles on the right side will undergo an adaptive shortening. The atrophied muscles on the left side will elongate. In addition, muscular imbalance of the deeper muscles must be considered, since they may be a major factor in producing scoliosis. Lateral flexibility of the spine is limited because of the resultant muscular imbalance.

Functional postural adaptations involve changes in the muscular or ligamentous tissue. The signs of this divergency tend to disappear when the individual is hanging suspended by the hands, lying in a prone or supine position, or assuming the Adam's position.

Structural adaptations involve a change in the shape of the bone. The atypical characteristics do not disappear when the vertical compression effect of gravity is eliminated. An additional characteristic that may be used to classify lateral divergency as either functional or structural is the appearance of a bulge on either side of the spine while standing. This prominence may also be seen in the Adam's position. In a functional scoliosis, there is a muscular bulge in the area of the *concavity* of the curve that results from adaptive shortening of the muscles. Although the lateral curve may disappear, this bulge is evident in the Adam's position. A bony bulge on the side of the *convexity* of the curve is characteristic of a structural scoliosis. This bulge is due to protrusion of the ribs as a result of rotation by the thoracic vertebrae.

In the previous discussion of anteroposterior postural adaptations, it was impossible to separate pelvic inclination and the changes in the lumbar curve because of the fixed position of the sacrum; the same types of relationship exist—lateral pelvic girdle tilt and lateral deviation of the lumbar spine. When viewed from the rear, therefore, a lateral pelvic girdle tilt from right to left (high to low) causes the lumbar spine to deviate or curve so that the convexity is to the left (fig. 4.26).

A similar relationship exists between the balanced horizontal alignment of the shoulders and the vertebrae of the upper thoracic spine. In the balanced position, the shoulders form a ninety-degree angle with the thoracic spine (fig. 4.24). A lateral deviation of the thoracic spine results in an imbalance or a displacement of the shoulders. An equality of the axillary angles (angle formed by the medial border of the upper arm and the lateral border of the chest) results. The converse is also true in that the exaggerated difference in shoulder heights with the associated difference of the axillary angle indicates a deviation of the thoracic vertebrae. For example, if the thoracic spine deviates so that the convexity is to the left, the left shoulder will be higher than the right; the left axillary angle is smaller than the right (fig. 4.26).

Scoliotic curves are defined in terms of their convexities. They are identified, for example, as either *convexity right* or *right convexity*. A single or simple curve to the left, or *convexity left*, is commonly called *C* curve (fig. 4.26). A lateral curve to the right, or convexity right, is called a "reversed *C*" curve. Although a lateral deviation of the spine may involve only one spinal segment, it frequently involves more than one segment. In either instance, as long as the deviation is in only one direction, the curve may be appropriately called a *C* or "reversed *C*" curve.

Scoliotic curves are often compound. They can consist of two different curves in which convexities of the curves are in opposite directions (fig. 4.27). Such compound curves are defined two ways: (1) by the uppermost segment of the spine that deviates and (2) in terms of the direction of the convexity of the curves. For example, the compound curve in which the thoracic curve is to the left and the lumbar curve is to the right is defined as a *thoracic left-lumbar right*. It can also be called an *S* curve. A compound curve in which the thoracic curve is to the right and the lumbar curve is to the left is defined as *thoracic right-lumbar left*. It can also be called a "reversed *S*" curve (fig. 4.27).

Some of the characteristics of scoliosis may be generalized. If there is a lateral pelvic girdle tilt, the convexity of the lumbar spine will be in the direction of the lower hip. If there is a lateral thoracic curve, the highest shoulder will be on the side of the convexity. In simple or single curves, the low hip and high shoulder are on the same side. If there is a compound curve, the low hip and shoulder are on the same side. One should differentiate between scoliotic curves by either defining them in terms of the convexity of the curves or describing them in terms of their characteristics of deviations, displacement, and rotation. So far, this discussion has been in terms of asymmetry of body segments—displacement—and a spinal deviation. Scoliosis possesses a third characteristic, rotation of the vertebrae.

The rotation of the vertebrae in scoliosis is most noticeable in the thoracic area when the ribs are affected by the rotation of the vertebrae. Thoracic rotation is indicated by the prominence of one side of the chest when viewed from the front. The rear view will also show a prominence of one side of the rib cage when rotation is present. For example, in a "reversed *C*" curve of the thoracic area, the thorax is more prominent in the front on the left side. A further check for vertebral rotation utilizes the forward-bend or Adam's position. In this position a prominence of the thorax on the side of the convexity is noticeable if rotation is present.

The interrelations between the characteristics of deviation and rotation of the thoracic vertebrae in scoliosis are often a source of misunderstanding. The lateral adaptation is primarily one of lateral flexion. Part of the confusion arises from the fact that although the spine is laterally flexed, the direction of the scoliotic curve is described in terms of the convexity. For example, if the thoracic spine is laterally flexed to the right, the resultant curve is described as a *dorsal* or a *thoracic left scoliosis*. In order to perform marked lateral flexion, the vertebrae must rotate. Thus, in order to laterally flex the thoracic spine to the right to its anatomic limits of motion, the thoracic vertebrae must rotate to the left. This means that the bodies of the vertebrae move to the left and the spinous processes move to the right around a longitudinal axis which runs through the intervertebral joints that are posterior to the bodies of the vertebrae. The ribs, in turn, move along with the vertebrae. In this case, the bony bulge formed by the ribs projects posteriorly on the left side, the side of the convexity. In terms of the direction of vertical deviation or lateral curve, using the spinous processes as an indication of the direction of rotation, the spinous processes move toward the side of the convexity. Rotation of the vertebrae is a result of superimposing one curvature upon another. Normally an anteroposterior curve exists in the thoracic area. Upon lateral flexion in that area, a lateral curve is produced. The combination of these two curves results in rotation of the vertebrae.

Unilateral exercises may be prescribed for the correction or amelioration of the scoliotic curve. This will involve the "derotation" principle in which the exercises are intended to rotate the thoracic spine in the direction opposite to its assumed position. For example, in the case of a dorsal left scoliosis, derotation exercises will involve rotation of the vertebrae to the left. In terms of the characteristics of the curve, rotation will be in the direction of the curve's convexity. The derotation will also involve lateral flexion of the thoracic spine. Lateral flexion in the above case will be to the left, the direction of the convexity of the curve.

Generally, bilateral exercises are prescribed for scoliosis. The exercises are performed through the anteroposterior plane of motion. The objective, while the individual is moving through the anteroposterior plane, is to assure balanced, symmetrical motion in the spinal column.

SELECTED REFERENCES

1. ABRAMSON, ARTHUR S., and DELAGI, EDWARD F. "The Contributions of Physical Activity to Rehabilitation." *Research Quarterly* 31 (May 1960): 365-375.
2. CLARKE, H. HARRISON, and CLARKE, DAVID H. *Developmental and Adapted Physical Education.* Englewood Cliffs, N. J.: Prentice-Hall, Inc., 1963.
3. *Corrective Physical Education: Teaching Guide for Junior and Senior High Schools.* Pub. No. SC-566. Los Angeles City Schools, Division of Instructional Services.
4. DANIELS, ARTHUR S., and DAVIES, EVELYN A. *Adapted Physical Education.* 2nd ed. New York: Harper & Row, Publishers, 1965.

5. DAVIS, ELWOOD C.; LOGAN, GENE A.; and McKINNEY, WAYNE C. *Biophysical Values of Muscular Activity.* 2nd ed. Dubuque, Ia.: Wm. C. Brown Company Publishers, 1965.

6. DREW, LILLIAN CURTIS, and KINZLY, HAZEL L. *Individual Gymnastics.* 5th ed. Philadelphia: Lea & Febiger, 1949.

7. FAIT, HOLLIS F. *Special Physical Education.* 2nd ed. Philadelphia: W. B. Saunders Company, 1966.

8. GOFF, CHARLES WEER. "Orthograms of Posture." *The Journal of Bone and Joint Surgery* 34-A (January):115-122.

9. GRANT, J. C. BOILEAU, and BASMAJIAN, J. V., eds. *Grant's Method of Anatomy.* 7th ed. Baltimore: The Williams & Wilkins Co., 1965.

10. HIRT, SUSANNE E.; FRIES, CORRINE; and HELLEBRANDT, FRANCES A. "Center of Gravity of the Human Body." *Archives of Physical Therapy* 29 (1944):280-287.

11. KELLY, ELLEN DAVIS. *Adapted and Corrective Physical Education.* 4th ed. New York: Ronald Press Co., 1965.

12. ———. *Teaching Posture and Body Mechanics.* New York: A. S. Barnes & Co., 1949.

13. KENDALL, HENRY O.; KENDALL, FLORENCE P.; and BOYTON, DOROTHY A. *Posture and Pain.* Baltimore: The Williams & Wilkins Co., 1952.

14. KLEINBERG, SAMUEL. *Scoliosis.* Baltimore: The Williams & Wilkin Co., 1951.

15. LOGAN, GENE A. *Adaptations of Muscular Activity.* Belmont, Calif.: Wadsworth Publishing Co., Inc., 1964.

16. LOWMAN, CHARLES LeROY, and YOUNG, CARL HAVEN. *Postural Fitness.* Philadelphia: Lea & Febiger, 1960.

17. LOWMAN, CHARLES LeROY; COLESTOCK, CLAIRE; and COOPER, HAZEL. *Corrective Physical Education for Groups.* New York: A. S. Barnes & Co., 1928.

18. MATHEWS, DONALD K.; KRUSE, ROBERT; and SHAW, VIRGINIA. *The Science of Physical Education for Handicapped Children.* New York: Harper & Row, Publishers, 1962.

19. METHENY, ELEANOR. *Body Dynamics.* New York: McGraw-Hill Book Co., Inc., 1952.

20. MORRISON, WHITELAW REID, and CHENOWETH, LAURENCE B. *Normal and Elementary Physical Diagnosis.* 5th ed. Philadelphia: Lea & Febiger, 1955.

21. MORTON, DUDLEY J. *The Human Foot.* New York: Columbia University Press, 1935.

22. MORTON, DUDLEY J., and FULLER, DUDLEY DEAN. *Human Locomotion and Body Form.* Baltimore: Williams & Wilkins Co., 1952.

23. RASCH, PHILIP J., and BURKE, ROGER K. *Kinesiology and Applied Anatomy.* 3rd ed. Philadelphia: Lea & Febiger, 1967.

24. RATHBONE, JOSEPHINE L., and HUNT, VALERIE V. *Corrective Physical Education.* 7th ed. Philadelphia: W. B. Saunders Company, 1965.

25. WILES, PHILIP, and SWEETNAM, RODNEY. *Essentials of Orthopaedics.* Boston: Little, Brown and Company, 1965.

congenital
and pathological
conditions

Environmental stresses that affect human motion were previously defined as gravity, congenital and pathological conditions, and trauma or injury. In an effort of the body to counteract these forces, certain adaptations occur in the musculoskeletal system. One can readily observe the relationship between the force of gravity and the adaptations that the individual makes to resist its downward pull. The relationship between the magnitude, direction, and point of application of force to a body segment and the resultant injury to the musculoskeletal system may be determined logically. However, musculoskeletal deformities whose origin is either congenital or pathological are not easily comprehended.

The assumption that adaptations of human motion involve only the musculoskeletal system is without basis. Although most of the factors that elicit movement adaptations do involve these systems, there are numerous pathological conditions capable of modifying or remedying one's movement patterns. Since the effects of movement are organismic rather than systemic, it is logical to assume that any marked abnormalities in the structure or in the function of one anatomic system will bring about an adaptation in the function of the others, since the function is based on the physiologic interrelationship that exists between the anatomic system.

Individuals whose physical condition prohibits their participation in the regular physical education program are considered to be physically handicapped. The physically handicapped individual is generally assigned to the adapted physical education program. Consequently, the physical educator is primarily concerned with the nature of the student's physical condition and its implications for his physical education. This chapter deals with the specific congenital and acquired divergencies and disorders that are most likely to impair one's locomotion or health to the extent that he is unable to receive maximum benefits from participation in the regular physical education program. In addition to being unable to participate in the regular physical education program, many physically handicapped children require other specialized educational services. These services may include the utilization of modified methods of instruction, specially designed materials and equipment, and other services deemed necessary to meet the educational needs of the children (Dunkelberg, 1958).

An educational program for those physically handicapped children who are unable to benefit from participation in the regular instructional program is often referred to as *special education*. Special education programs are commonly organized to provide (1) itinerant teachers; (2) remedial classes such as speech therapy, adapted physical education, sight-saving classes, and lip-reading; (3) special day classes—special classes for the handicapped in the same building or on the same campus as the regular school; (4) special schools; (5) hospital classes; and (6) home teaching for those unable to attend school.

Individuals with a wide range of handicaps will be assigned to the adapted physical education classes. They may also require and may be receiving other special education services as well. It is imperative, therefore, that all teachers of adapted physical education be familiar with the practices in the field of special education so that they may be able to provide a physical education program which will better meet the requirements of these individuals.

It should be emphasized that adapted physical education programs for the physically handicapped must be based on and guided by the physician's diagnosis and recommendations. The implications concerning the various physically handicapping conditions, therefore, must be understood to be general, and as such provide a guide within which the specifics of the physician's recommendations can be implemented.

The two major classifications of physically handicapping conditions are *congenital* and *acquired*. The word *congenital* means "born with." Thus, the anomalies are generally genetic or hereditary in origin. Congenital conditions are those anomalies or malformations which are present at birth. These may or may not be evident at birth. Acquired malformations are not present at birth. They are not traceable to a genetic or hereditary origin. Acquired abnormalities are primarily the result of injury and disease.

ORTHOPEDIC HANDICAPS

Orthopedic handicaps are commonly classified as follows:

1. Crippling due to infection. This category includes joint tuberculosis, poliomyelitis, and osteomyelitis.
2. Crippling resulting from birth injury: Erb's palsy, fractures, and similar disorders.
3. Congenital anomalies such as congenital amputation, congenital dislocation, talipes equinovarus, torticollis, and spina bifida.
4. Traumatic crippling: amputation, fractures, and dislocations.
5. Tumors: bone tumors, bone cysts, and similar conditions.
6. Developmental conditions, including coxa plana, spinal osteochondritis, and Osgood-Schlatter disease.
7. Other conditions, such as multiple sclerosis and muscular dystrophy.

The following estimates of frequency of the various kinds of orthopedic handicaps in children who require special education services were derived from a survey by James G. Dunkelberg, California State College, Los Angeles.

Cerebral palsy 33%
Infection (musculoskeletal) 25%
Cardiovascular conditions 20%
Congenital anomalies 6%
Developmental conditions 6%
Trauma (musculoskeletal) 2%
Tumors (skeletal) 1%
Birth injury 1%
Other 6%

The majority of handicapping conditions are not correctable through the use of exercise. Consequently, a large proportion of individuals assigned to the adapted physical education program will benefit most from a program of sports that have carry-over value. This does not imply that exercise has no place in a program for physically handicapped children with permanent disabilities. However, it does mean that the emphasis is changed from that of correcting the condition to that of providing the student with the opportunity to achieve maximum physical conditioning that his physical disability will permit. It is possible that some of the secondary changes affecting these children may respond favorably to exercise. It is imperative, therefore, that both the sports and exercise phases of adapted physical education be made available to all physically handicapped children.

TALIPES: A congenital malformation in which the foot is fixed in any of the normal positions such as plantar flexion, dorsiflexion, inversion, eversion, adduction, and abduction of the forefoot. Talipes implies that the fixed position involves both the ankle and foot. The usual classification of the fixed position is as follows:

Figure 5.1. Talipes equinus

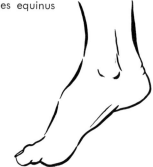

1. Talipes *equinus:* A position of plantar flexion (fig. 5.1). In the standing position, the body weight is borne on the metatarsal heads and on the toes.

Figure 5.2. Talipes calcaneus

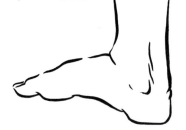

2. Talipes *calcaneus:* A position of dorsiflexion (fig. 5.2). In the standing position, the weight is borne on the heel.

Figure 5.3. Talipes valgus

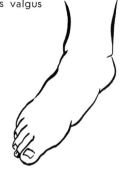

3. Talipes *valgus:* A position of eversion and abduction of the forefoot (fig. 5.3). In the standing position, the weight is borne on the medial border of the foot (pronation).

Figure 5.4. Talipes varus

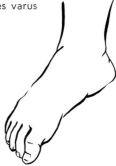

4. Talipes *varus:* A position of inversion and adduction of the forefoot (fig. 5.4). In the standing position, the weight is borne on the lateral border of the foot (supination).

A talipes malformation is usually a condition involving a combination of a fixed ankle and foot position. The most common combination is one in which the ankle is fixed in plantar flexion and the foot is inverted and adducted. This condition, *talipes equinovarus* (fig. 5.5), is commonly known as clubfoot. This constitutes about 75 percent

Figure 5.5. Talipes equinovarus

of all talipes divergencies. Other combined fixed ankle-foot conditions are identified as (1) talipes *equinovalgus,* (2) talipes *calcaneovarus,* and (3) talipes *calcaneovalgus.*

Although therapeutic exercise is of little value in the correction of a talipes divergency, it may be useful in increasing the strength of the involved muscles and improving the range of motion of the ankle and foot. A general conditioning program and selected sports may benefit the student. Because of the severe adaptations of the individual's weight-bearing, sports that require extensive running, jumping, and kicking are contraindicated.

ERB'S PALSY: A birth injury to the brachial plexus that results in paralysis of the upper limb. The injury is limited to the roots and trunk of the fifth and sixth cervical nerves. The individual loses the ability to abduct or laterally rotate the upper limb at the shoulder joint, to supinate the forearm, and sometimes to extend the wrists and fingers. Because of the visual characteristics of this birth injury, it is commonly referred to as a "waiter's tip" deformity.

Therapeutic exercise is generally of little value in the correction of Erb's palsy. Exercise may, however, prevent the formation of additional connective tissue adaptations by assisting in the maintenance of range of motion. Participation in sports that are within the limitations of this disability should be encouraged.

CONGENITAL DISLOCATIONS: The prenatal displacement of one or more bones of a joint from a normal position. Generally, this condition affects the shoulder and hip joints. Congenital dislocation and *dysplasia* (abnormality of development) of the hip is usually characterized by upward and backward displacement of the head of the femur as well as by a thickening at the base of the acetabulum. The left hip is more frequently affected than is the right. The condition may be sex-linked because it affects more females than males. If the condition is unilateral, the individual has a lurching walk in which he appears to sink down on the affected side as weight is borne on that limb. All weight-bearing activities are contraindicated. Exercises for general conditioning may be used if they do not require standing. Games which do not require standing and use of the lower limbs should be encouraged.

COXA VARA AND COXA VALGA: The normal angle between the neck of the femur and its shaft is approximately 135 degrees. A marked increase or decrease from this angle is abnormal.

Coxa vara is characterized by a decrease in the angle of the femoral neck as it relates to the shaft. The affected limb is usually shorter, and its lateral rotation is limited. Coxa vara may occur as a congenital or as an acquired defect, the latter more commonly.

Coxa valga is characterized by an increase in the angle of the femoral neck as it relates to the shaft of the femur. The affected leg is usually longer. Rotation is limited. This condition is congenital.

General conditioning exercises are recommended. Prolonged weight-bearing is contraindicated unless prescribed by the physician. Participation in sports which do not require extensive use of the lower limbs is also recommended.

OSTEOCHONDROSIS OR OSTEOCHONDRITIS: A disease of children that affects the growth of the epiphyseal centers in such a manner that inflammation of bone and cartilage occurs. It successively results in fragmentation and degeneration of the cartilage, which is followed by regeneration of the bone. Subsequently, there is a return to the normal hardness and strength of the involved surface. Various epiphyses may be involved, but certain ones seem to be more commonly affected. These are known by various names, and these names are dependent upon the site of involvement. Osteochondritis usually begins in children between four and twelve years of age and has a tendency to affect more boys than girls. The outstanding symptom is pain in the affected part which causes a voluntary limitation of movement and a protective limp.

Coxa Plana: A condition most commonly known as Perthes' disease (fig. 5.6). It is also known as *osteochondritis deformans juvenilis, Calve-Perthes' disease, Legg's disease* and *Legg-Calve-Perthes' disease.* It is characterized by atrophy and rarefaction of the head of the femur. As a result, a shortened and thickened femoral neck, a broad, flat femoral head, and a flattening of the capital femoral epiphysis appear. Onset is insidious between the ages of five and twelve years. Since the disease is not primarily inflammatory, no fever or evidence of inflammation is present. The presence of pain in the affected hip is the outstanding symptom; however, pain is frequently referred to the medial aspect of the knee since the obturator nerve may be involved.

Part of the treatment for this condition is to have the individual avoid weight-bearing. This is usually accomplished by the use of crutches in addition to a supporting shoulder harness attached to the ankle of the affected limb. These children may participate in selected sports during this period provided weight-bearing is avoided.

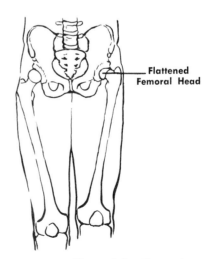

Flattened
Femoral Head

Figure 5.6. Coxa plana

OSGOOD-SCHLATTER DISEASE: An inflammation or partial separation of the tibial tuberosity. It is characterized by pain and tenderness on deep pressure, and swelling in the area of the tibial tuberosity. Pain becomes especially marked after physical activity such as kicking or kneeling, or when the knee is forcibly extended against resistance. In the acute stage of the condition, therapeutic exercise is usually contraindicated.

SCHEUERMANN'S DISEASE: Also known as *osteochondritis deformans juvenilis dorsi,* a condition confined to the vertebral epiphysis. It frequently results in producing kyphosis of the affected vertebrae. Individuals with osteochondritis should avoid weight-bearing activities. General conditioning exercises are indicated. Special unilateral exercises may be employed, because the contralateral effects of exercise may help to maintain tone and strength of the affected limb. Sports appropriate to the individual's limitations are recommended.

SLIPPED FEMORAL EPIPHYSIS: This condition closely resembles osteochondrosis. It results in a nontraumatic separation of the femoral head from the epiphysis and is often associated with children who are excessively obese, tall and thin, or who have recently experienced a period of rapid growth. The individual walks with the foot in a toes-out position as a result of lateral rotation of the thigh. Medial rotation, an early characteristic of the condition, is limited.

Sports requiring excessive use of the lower limbs and prolonged weight-bearing are contraindicated. General conditioning is recommended. Exercises may also be used that will maintain the range of motion of the affected limb.

SPONDYLOLISTHESIS: An anterior displacement of the 5th lumbar vertebrae on the sacrum (fig. 5.7). This vertebrae overhangs the brim of the pelvis and may cause pressure on the spinal nerves. About one in five persons has some congenital structural variation of the lumbosacral joint. This disability generally manifests itself as the child approaches puberty. The onset of the condition may be the result of trauma. Consequently, all children with acute or exaggerated lordosis or sharp hyperextension of the lumbosacral junction should be closely scrutinized.

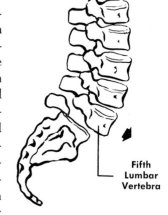

Fifth
Lumbar
Vertebra

Figure 5.7. Spondylolisthesis

Due to the possibility of traumas eliciting this divergency, the individual with an extreme lordotic curve of the lumbar spine should not engage in contact sports and gymnastics without medical approval. Heavy resistance exercises may be contraindicated for this individual. However, in many cases where spondylolisthesis is chronic in nature, the use of progressive resistance exercises to develop the abdominal and back muscles to a high level of strength is often recommended by the physician.

BRITTLE BONES: Also known as *osteogenesis imperfecta,* or *osteopsathyrosis.* This is a familial disease of the long bones characterized by abnormal brittleness leading to a history of numerous fractures, marked atrophy of the extremities, and the presence of a marked change in the anatomical characteristics of the limbs and joints. Vigorous physical activities, resistance exercises, and sports are contraindicated.

SPINA BIFIDA: A congenital defect in which there is incomplete closure of the vertebral lamina and, occasionally, protrusion or herniation of the meninges of the spinal cord. This defect is most common in the lumbosacral area of the spine. Its characteristics include loss of tactile sensitivity of the legs, and incontinence. Physical activity, other than sedentary games, is contraindicated if a meningocele is present.

SKELETAL TUBERCULOSIS: A tubercular infection of the bones and joints. Usually, it develops insidiously during the first ten years of life. About one-half of all cases occur in the spine. The hip area is also very vulnerable to tubercular infection. Vigorous physical activities are contraindicated.

POTT'S DISEASE: Also called *tuberculous spondylitis* or tuberculosis of the spine. This disease is characterized by the development of an abnormal prominence at some level of the spine. This localized kyphosis usually occurs in the thoracic spine, but it can also occur in the cervical and lumbar regions of the spine. Vigorous physical activities are contraindicated.

OSTEOMYELITIS: An inflammation of the bone caused by pyogenic (pus-producing) bacteria, especially staphylococci and streptococci. It is frequently characterized by destruction of the bone. It is recurrent and usually involves several bones unless the infected bone is completely removed. It is seen mostly in young children who are between the ages of three and ten years. Vigorous physical activities are contraindicated.

POLIOMYELITIS: This disease is a virus infection that attacks the central nervous system. Damage or destruction occurs to the motor cells of the gray matter in the anterior horn of the spinal cord. The voluntary muscles innervated by these motor cells become paralyzed, atrophic, and flaccid. Poliomyelitis, also known as infantile paralysis, accounted for the largest single enrollment of children in special education classes in 1939-1942. With the discovery of vaccines, however, the incidence of paralytic polio has markedly decreased in recent years.

Individuals with poliomyelitis may receive benefits from an appropriate exercise program. The program should be designed to increase strength, muscular endurance, and range of motion. Participation in selected sports should also be of value to the individual during his leisure time.

MUSCULAR DYSTROPHY: A crippling disease which mysteriously attacks the muscles. The disease usually affects the proximal muscles first, and a progressive wasting and weakness occurs. Eventually, the condition extends to practically all voluntary muscles of the body. The disease itself is not considered fatal, but the debility it causes makes slight illnesses extremely dangerous. The disease is characterized by four types: (1) *Pseudohypertrophic,* the most prevalent form, commences in childhood between the ages of three and ten. Its course is more rapid than that of any other type. It is considered to be hereditary in 35 percent of the cases, and it affects three times as many boys as girls; (2) *Juvenile form*—onset in childhood or adolescence—has a progression that is slower. Individuals may reach middle age, and boys and girls are affected equally; (3) *Facioscapulohumeral* affects young adults; attacks the facial muscles, the shoulders, and the upper arms; (4) *Mixed types* is a combination of the aforementioned conditions. The onset of the disease may be between the ages of thirty and fifty. This type is not inherited, and it can strike anyone. The course of the disease is rapid and is often terminal in five to ten years.

Exercise will not arrest the dystrophic process nor restore wasted muscles. However, general conditioning exercises may delay the stage of complete helplessness. Recreational games and sports are indicated when they are within the limitations of the physician's recommendations.

AMPUTATION: The removal, wholly or in part, of a limb or of a projecting process. Amputation may be indicated in the course of pathological processes such as gangrene or constriction. *Traumatic* amputation may result from an accident. *Surgical* amputation may be undertaken in order to remove a malignant tumor. *Congenital* amputation is the result of prenatal processes that may be either developmental or pathologic in nature. It may also be due to genetic or hereditary factors.

The loss of a limb or a part thereof involves an irrevocable anatomical and physiologic impairment of major proportions. The individual who has had an amputation may participate in any physical activity, exercise, game, or sport of which he is capable.

WRY NECK: Generally a congenital defect but may be induced by psychic stresses as a result of excessive emotional tensions. Because of muscular imbalance of the sternocleidomastoid muscles, the head is laterally flexed and rotated to one side. This condition is also referred to as *torticollis*.

The individual may participate in most sports. Exercise may be used to increase the strength of the lengthened muscle and thereby increase the range of motion of the neck.

VISUAL HANDICAPS

It has been estimated that one in four children has some type of visual anomaly. The differentiation between "normal vision" and the various degrees of deviation is made on the basis of *visual acuity*.

The Partially Seeing

Partially-seeing children are defined as those with visual acuity of less than 20/70 or more than 20/200. This acuity is of the best eye after all necessary medical and surgical treatment has been given and compensating lenses have been provided. Hathaway feels, also, that the individual must have a sufficient residue of sight to make it possible to use sight as the chief avenue of approach to the brain (Hathaway, 1959). She also includes those children whose visual deviations are such that they may benefit from the special educational services provided for the partially seeing.

The following kinds of visual defects may be found among partially-seeing children and are listed here in order of their frequency: (1) *refractive errors* (myopia, hyperopia); (2) *developmental anomalies* of structure (cataracts, albinism); (3) *defects of muscle function* (strabismus, nystagmus); and (4) *disease* or *defects* of the eye (caused by infection, injuries).

Children with these conditions require slight modifications of physical activity, games, and sports. Care should be taken when the student must wear glasses. It is recommended that glass-guards be worn.

Due to the possibility of retinal detachments, students with high myopia should not be permitted to engage in contact sports.

The Blind

Individuals whose vision affords them no practical value for the purposes of education and activities of daily living are considered to be blind. However, any definition depends upon the purpose for which it is made. For educational purposes, the person is blind if his vision is so defective that he cannot be educated through visual methods. Or he is blind if he must be taught through his auditory and tactile senses. There is a lack of evidence to substantiate the belief that because of blindness the individual gains in other senses. In terms of visual acuity, the educationally blind are those whose acuity is 20/200 or less in the best eye after all the necessary medical and surgical treatment and compensating measures have been provided. According to Kerby, there were 7,000 blind children attending schools or classes for the blind in 1954-55 (Kerby, 1958). This number increased to 13,491 by 1959. Kirk indicated that this marked increase in blind children attending school was mainly attributed to the coming of school age of those children who have been made blind by *retrolental fibroplasia* (Kirk, 1962). The major causes in terms of the frequency are (1) unspecified prenatal causes; (2) poisoning, including those of excessive oxygen; (3) heredity; (4) infectious disease, tumors, and injuries. Excessive amounts of oxygen administered to premature children has been found to be the major cause of retrolental fibroplasia. This form of oxygen poisoning causes a complete detachment of the retina. This condition was nonexistent prior to 1938, and it had virtually disappeared in 1955. This is an example of how a medical advance in one area can produce a handicapping condition that is otherwise unrelated.

The blind may benefit from participation in a wide variety of physical education activities. However, the instructor must utilize the auditory and tactile senses in his instruction almost exclusively.

AURAL HANDICAPS

There are different degrees of hearing loss, which vary from a very slight loss for certain sounds to complete loss of hearing for all sounds. In addition to the degree of loss, the severity of the disability is influenced by the age for the onset of the impairment. The educational programs for children with aural handicaps differ according to the nature and extent of their hearing acuity. At the Conference of Executives of American Schools for the Deaf, the classification of the deaf was made. The two classes of the deaf are (1) congenitally deaf and (2) the adventitiously deaf (born normal but became deaf through illness or injury). The hard-of-hearing are those with defective but functional hearing (Committee on Nomenclature, Conference of Executives of American Schools for the Deaf, 1938).

Streng and others have further classified the auditorily handicapped in accordance with the degree of hearing loss. For example, those students whose hearing loss is greater than 75 decibels even with amplification are unable to use hearing to understand language. They require specialized instruction in all areas. These authors classified such children, for educational purposes, as deaf (Streng and others, 1958).

Auditory handicaps are also classified on the basis of cause as either *endogenous* or *exogenous*. Endogenous refers to hereditary causes; exogenous refers to accidents and disease as causative factors. The most common exogenous causes are meningitis, scarlet fever, pneumonia, whooping cough, ear infections, and accidents that injure the ear. Estimates concerning the prevalence of impaired hearing range from 1.5 to 5 percent of the school-age population.

Individuals with moderate hearing losses are able to participate in the regular physical education program with little or no modification of the activities. For those students who are educationally deaf, the physical education instructor must utilize the sense of vision in his instruction. The deaf child also requires physical education to develop and improve his balance.

CEREBRAL PALSY

Cerebral palsy is a condition resulting from damage or from a dysfunction of those portions of the brain that govern or control muscular function. The term is derived from *cerebral* meaning "brain" and *palsy* meaning "a motor disability."

Motor dysfunction may involve different groups of muscles of one or more of the limbs. If only one limb is involved, the condition is called *monoplegia*. If both limbs on the same side are affected, it is called *hemiplegia*. If both of the lower limbs are involved, it is called *paraplegia*. If three of the limbs are affected, it is called *triplegia*. Triplegia usually involves both lower limbs and one upper limb. If all four limbs are involved, it is called *quadriplegia*. Often the head and trunk are also involved. Cerebral palsy takes different forms with different neuromotor involvements and characteristics. These are differentiated as *spasticity, athetosis, ataxia, tremor,* and *rigidity.* Furthermore, there are combinations of these called *mixed types.*

Spasticity is characterized by muscle stiffness in which the muscles remain in a state of tension. The normal muscular balance between the muscles most involved (agonists) and the contralateral muscles (antagonists) is absent. Volitional movements tend to be jerky and uncontrolled as a result of spasmodic contraction of the muscles. They also evidence the "overflow" phenomenon which may manifest itself by participation of muscles not primarily concerned with the performance of the movement or skill. This syndrome may involve facial contortions, increased respiratory rate, and the production of guttural sounds. The stretch reflex is also a distinctive characteristic of this kind of cerebral palsy.

Athetosis is characterized by bizarre twisting, writhing muscular movements. Walking is characterized by a lurching and a stumbling nonrhythmical pattern. Voluntary movements do not seem to follow any established sequence, and they are characterized by various uncontrolled movements.

Ataxia is characterized by impaired or lost kinesthetic sense and equilibrium. A person suffering from ataxia is very unsteady in his movements, walks with a high step, and frequently falls. The eyes are often uncoordinated, and *nystagmus*—jerky tracking movement of the eyes—is common.

Tremor is characterized by slow, involuntary, rhythmic shaking or vibrating movements of an irregular nature. This condition may be present at rest, but usually is most marked when voluntary muscle action is attempted.

Rigidity is characterized by interference with postural tone as a result of simultaneous contraction of the muscles most involved in the movement (agonistic) and the contralateral (antagonistic) muscles. There is more of a diminished or limited amount of movement rather than abnormal movement.

It has been estimated that there is one child born with cerebral palsy for approximately every two hundred live births, or that a cerebral-palsied or brain-injured child is born every 53 minutes (Deaver, 1955; Rusk, 1964).

Special adaptation of most of the sports which comprise the physical education program are required for these children. Attention should be centered on the development of neuromuscular coordination and tension release. Fine and rapid muscular movements are extremely difficult. These children will exaggerate their muscular dysfunction as a result of increased tension. When introducing any new activity or new equipment, the child should be allowed enough time to become acquainted with the situation. This procedure will avoid the development of increased tension that tends to limit the child's ability to perform new skills.

SPECIAL HEALTH PROBLEMS

Students with special health problems are those whose weakened physical condition renders them relatively inactive or who require special precautions within the school program. They may be described as children with low vitality.

CARDIAC ANOMALIES: The two main kinds of cardiac disturbances may be classified as *functional* and *organic*. Functional disturbances are those that do not involve any structural changes in the heart. Organic disturbances refer to a permanent malformation of the cardiac structure. Some children are born with congenital organic problems. The most common cause of acquired heart disabilities is rheumatic fever. This disease often strikes school-age children, and it may or may not result in organic involvement. Regardless of the nature or cause of the disturbance, the physical educator should be primarily interested in the effect of the disability upon the individual student's physical activity. The physician is primarily concerned with the classification of the cardiac disturbance or heart damage as it relates to functional capacities.

The energy output should be kept minimal for individuals with heart conditions. These students should avoid dyspnea (labored, difficult breathing) and fatigue. However, they may participate in all activities within their limitations.

ASTHMA: The cause of asthma is not known, but there is some evidence that it may be psychologically induced. It is generally thought to be the result of some allergic phenomenon. It is characterized by recurrent attacks of labored breathing due to an obstruction of the bronchial tubes. As a result of reflex spasms of the bronchial musculature, accompanied by edema of the mucous membranes, the student with asthma may have an obstruction of the airflow to the lungs. As an asthma attack continues, thick mucus fills the bronchial tubes. The individual produces a characteristic wheezing as he exhales.

Most individuals benefit from a general conditioning program, but care should be taken to avoid labored breathing and fatigue. If the individual reports an asthmatic attack prior to attending the adapted physical education class, these activities may have to be further limited during that particular day of attendance. Breathing exercises may help by restoring the individual's confidence, and this may lessen his fear during the asthmatic attack.

DIABETES MELLITUS: A complex hereditary metabolic disease in which the ability to oxidize carbohydrates is faulty. This is due to the diminished production of insulin secreted by the islands of Langerhans in the pancreas. The disease is characterized by an increase of sugar in the blood (hyperglycemia) and an excretion of sugar in the urine (glycosuria). Through the injection of insulin, the carbohydrate tolerance of the diabetic is increased. Consequently, the individual may overindulge in exercise. This may bring about hypoglycemia—a sudden reduction of the blood-sugar level below normal. If this condition occurs, the diabetic needs to ingest carbohydrates.

The individual with diabetes should engage only in sports that do not require physical contact because of the possibility of receiving an abrasion or laceration and because of the diabetic's susceptibility to infection. This susceptibility to infection and inability of abrasions or lacerations to heal adequately in many cases leads to the necessity of amputation. The diabetic should be encouraged to engage in standardized amounts of physical activity, and he should participate daily to establish a uniform metabolic base. Exercises for general conditioning requiring increased cardiovascular output, which, in turn, result in increased caloric consumption, are often used by the diabetic to regulate intake and output.

DYSMENORRHEA: This condition of painful or difficult menstruation may have a number of physiological and psychological causes. Dysmenorrhea may be caused by congestion of the blood in the abdominal cavity, lack of exercise, fatigue, poor posture, or by structural and organic abnormalities. However, there is a close relationship between emotional states and the events associated with menstruation. Adolescent girls who have not succeeded in establishing mature attitudes toward menstruation may experience "premenstrual tension" or incapacitating dysmenorrhea. Their reactions to menses may include such symptoms as anxiety, unhappiness, depression, and moderate discomfort to severe pain. Dysmenorrhea may occur at the beginning of the menstrual cycle or before the flow is fully established. It is characterized by uterine cramps, backache, leg aches, and nausea.

A survey of the literature indicates the general agreement that regular intervals of physical activity tend to decrease the pain and difficulty associated with dysmenorrhea. Specific exercises have proven to be of value in preventing or lessening the severity of dysmenorrhea.

Exercises that increase the mobility of the fascial ligamentous bands located in the lumbar spine, anterior pelvis, and in the general area of the hip flexors are useful. It is believed that stretching of these fascial ligamentous bands decreases pressure on the nerves in this area which reduces pain associated with the menstrual cycle (Billig and Lowendahl, 1949). One of the exercises (Billig) often used to help relieve dysmenorrhea is illustrated in figures 8.89 and 8.90. Fascial stretching is recommended for those cases in which the student complains of leg and back aches.

HERNIA: A protrusion of a loop of an organ or tissue through an abdominal opening. Hernias may occur at many different places within the body. *Abdominal* hernias, the protrusion of some internal structure through an abnormal opening in the abdominal wall, are the most frequent types. The names of the various abdominal hernias are taken from their anatomic locations. For example, an *umbilical* hernia indicates that it involves the umbilicus; and the *inguinal* hernia occurs at the inguinal canal. Inguinal hernia, the most common type, results from the . protrusion of the intestine into the inguinal canal. If the intestine protrudes completely through the canal, it may become estrangulated, closing off the supply of blood, and may result in the development of gangrene.

Undue weaknesses of the abdominal wall, as the result of under-developed abdominal muscles, general muscular debility, injury, or any unusual or sudden increase or rise in the intra-abdominal pressure, will predispose or may cause a hernia. Activities—such as weight lifting, wrestling, or similar sports—in which the individual exerts maximum pressure or force with the epiglottis closed can cause a significant increase in the intra-abdominal pressure. It is important, therefore, to instruct students not to hold their breath with the mouth closed or to close the glottis while lifting heavy weights. It is suggested that the individual breathe during the most difficult part of a given performance.

Physical activities that significantly increase the intra-abdominal pressure are contraindicated for those individuals with unrepaired hernias. In severe cases, running may cause herniation of the viscera through a weakened abdominal wall. Once the hernia has been repaired, a rehabilitation program involving strengthening of the muscles of the abdominal wall may be recommended by the physician.

EPILEPSY: This condition is a series of symptoms—a syndrome which is characterized by seizures or convulsions. The seizures differ in type and form, and in intensity of the loss of consciousness. A seizure may involve a convulsive jerking of parts of the body, emotional outbursts, and periods of mental confusion or amnesia. There are three major types of epilepsy that are of particular concern to the physical education teacher. These are (1) major motor seizure including *grand mal,* (2) minor motor seizure including *petit mal,* and (3) psychomotor seizure. The grand mal is a true convulsion in which the individual falls and loses consciousness. Generally, the attack lasts from about two to five minutes. It is followed by a period of mental confusion, fatigue, and headache. The individual who has this type of seizure often experiences an aura or sensation which may be motor, sensory, or visceral. The sensation tends to remain constant for that individual. Petit mal is characterized by transient periods of unconsciousness that last approximately five to twenty seconds. During this time, the person has a blank, staring expression. He may become immobile, or he may demonstrate rhythmic movements such as blinking, nodding the head, and twitching of the limbs and trunk. There is no general convulsion of the body. The individual does not fall, but he may drop objects that he is holding in his hands. In the period of a day, he may experience from one to one hundred or more seizures.

Psychomotor epilepsy is characterized by a period of amnesia. The symptoms are extremely varied. The manifestations may be chiefly motor, in the form of automatisms such as rubbing and masticatory movements, or they may be chiefly psychic in the form of confused, dreamlike states, hallucination, and temper outbursts. Duration of the seizure may vary from a few minutes to several hours.

Because of the successful medical control of epilepsy, a high percentage of school-age individuals with epilepsy are attending regular schools. In terms of physical activity, the major problem confronting the epileptic is the losing of consciousness. Therefore, he should not be permitted to work with gymnastic equipment or to engage in activities in which he is not in contact with the floor. Participation in physical activity may be of potential value for the epileptic student, however, because the incidence of seizures is often lessened for the epileptic while he is engaging in vigorous activity (McKinney, 1959). Generally, the epileptic should not be permitted alone in swimming pools because of the possible loss of consciousness. But, under close supervision and the use of the buddy system, he may benefit from swimming instruction.

SELECTED REFERENCES

1. ANDERSON, THERESA W. "Swimming and Exercise During Menstruation." *Journal of the Association for Health, Physical Education and Recreation* 36 (October 1965):66-68.

2. BASMAJIAN, J. V. *Muscles Alive. Their Functions as Revealed by Electromyography.* 2nd ed. Baltimore: The Williams & Wilkins Co., 1967.
3. BILLIG, HARVEY E. JR., and LOWENDAHL, EVELYN. *Mobilization of the Human Body.* Stanford, Calif.: Stanford University Press, 1949.
4. COMMITTEE ON NOMENCLATURE, CONFERENCE OF EXECUTIVES OF AMERICAN SCHOOLS FOR THE DEAF. *American Annals of the Deaf* 85 (January, 1938):1-7.
5. COZEN, LEWIS. *Office Orthopedics.* 3rd ed. New York: Hafner Publishing Co., Inc., 1969.
6. DEAVER, G. G. *Cerebral Palsy: Methods of Evaluation and Treatment.* Rehabilitation Monograph IX (Institute of Physical Medicine and Rehabilitation, New York University Medical Center, 1955).
7. DUNKELBERG, JAMES G. "Criteria for Evaluating Special Education Programs for Physically Handicapped Children." Unpublished Ed.D. dissertation. Los Angeles: University of California, 1958.
8. GALLAGHER, J. ROSWELL. *Medical Care of the Adolescent.* New York: Appleton-Century-Crofts, Inc., 1960.
9. GRANT, J. C. BOILEAU, and BASMAJIAN, J. V., eds. *Grant's Method of Anatomy.* Baltimore: The Williams & Wilkins Co., 1965.
10. GREEN, MORRIS, and RICHMOND, JULIUS B. *Pediatric Diagnosis.* Philadelphia: The W. B. Saunders Company, 1955.
11. HATHAWAY, WINIFRED. *Education and Health of the Partially Seeing.* 4th ed. New York: Columbia University Press, 1959.
12. KASCH, FRED W. "The Exercise Tolerance of Normal Children and Those with Congenital Heart Disease." Paper presented to Research Section, Convention of the California Association for Health, Physical Education and Recreation, San Diego, California.
13. KERBY, EDITH. "Causes of Blindness in Children of School Age." *Sight Saving Review* 28 (Spring 1958):18-21.
14. KIRK, SAMUEL A. *Educating Exceptional Children.* Boston: Houghton Mifflin Co., 1962.
15. LOGAN, GENE A. *Adaptations of Muscular Activity.* Belmont, Calif.: Wadsworth Publishing Co., Inc., 1964.
16. MCKINNEY, WAYNE C. "*A Study of the Problem of the Epileptic Student in Physical Education.*" Unpublished Research, Department of Physical Education, Long Beach State College, 1959.
17. MAYER, D. MCCULLAGH, and SWANKER, WILSON A. *Anomalies of Infants and Children.* New York: McGraw-Hill Book Co., Inc., 1958.
18. NOLEN, JEWEL. "Problems of Menstruation." *Journal of the Association for Health, Physical Education and Recreation* 36 (October 1965): 65-66.
19. RUSK, HOWARD A. *Rehabilitation Medicine.* 2nd ed. St. Louis: The C. V. Mosby Co., 1964.
20. STRENG, ALICE, and OTHERS. *Hearing Therapy for Children.* 2nd ed. New York: Grune & Stratton, Inc., 1958.

musculoskeletal injuries

A large percentage of students in adapted physical education have some form of musculoskeletal disability or deviation that has resulted from *trauma.* Trauma is an injury caused by some form of external force. Traumatic injuries seen in the adapted physical education class are typical of the injuries received in contact sports. These injuries are often received while the individual is in an awkward or unprotected position. The students with traumatic disabilities usually have damaged the musculoskeletal system. Generally, the mechanism involved in the injury consists of the part being either *compressed* or *elongated.* Compression injuries are often either soft-tissue contusions or fractures. Elongation injuries usually involve stretching or tearing of connective tissue or muscle fibers. Musculoskeletal injuries usually include sprains, strains, dislocations, and fractures.

Students with acute or chronic traumatic musculoskeletal injuries are frequently assigned to the adapted physical education class. The benefits of therapeutic exercise or sports have applications to both of these injury states. Usually, however, the acute phase of the injury has subsided before the individual is referred to the adapted physical education class. The task of the adapted physical education teacher becomes one of following the medical recommendation by administering therapeutic exercises and other forms of physical activity to aid in the rehabilitation of the individual.

Musculoskeletal injuries may be classified as *sprains, strains, dislocations,* and *fractures.* Sprains are by far the most frequent injury seen in the adapted physical education class. Therefore, much attention should be directed toward proper rehabilitative procedures for this condition. Strains, dislocations, and fractures, although less frequent, constitute another large proportion of injuries requiring therapeutic exercises for functional recovery. The adapted physical education teacher must have an understanding of the mechanisms or causative factors of each injury, the effect of the injury upon the individual, and the specific implications for programming.

A sprain is an injury to *ligamentous* tissue. Ligaments function to hold bones together to form joints. Ligaments are also structures that limit the extremes of joint motion. A movement of the body is performed by the muscles, which act upon the joints by way of their tendinous attachments. Injury to ligaments occurs when the joint is forced beyond a position normally held by the ligaments. Ligaments are generally nonelastic and, therefore, either stretch or tear when violent force causes the joint to be separated beyond its normal limits.

A strain is an injury that results in damage to *muscle*. This trauma is usually manifested by a tearing of the tendon or the muscle fiber. From a functional standpoint, the muscle fibers *and* the tendon that attaches the muscle fibers to other structures actually form a unit. The term *strain,* therefore, indicates an injury to one or more of the structures. A common site of the injury is at the junction of the muscle fibers and the tendon. Severe strains in the belly of a muscle are usually called "pulled muscles."

A dislocation occurs when the *articular surfaces* of a joint are completely separated. Many severe sprains are, in reality, dislocations in which the joint surfaces have realigned themselves to their original positions. If the bones remain separated, the injury is a dislocation. A partial separation of the joint surfaces is known as a *subluxation.* The tissues injured in a dislocation often include muscles, ligaments, and the joint capsule-lining—the synovial membrane, nerves, and blood vessels that supply the joint structures.

Restabilization of joints that have been dislocated is an important aspect of adapted physical education. Properly applied therapeutic exercise aids in the prevention of recurrent dislocations. Also, strength-developing exercises are useful for bringing the involved musculature up to an optimum state before surgery is performed on the injured joint.

A fracture is a *break* in a bone in which the continuity of the bone's surfaces is disrupted. Fractures in the area of joints often involve connective tissues that surround the joint. Associated injuries may involve sprains, strains, and dislocations. For example, the *Pott's fracture* (fig. 6.3) of the ankle involves a chip fracture of the medial malleolus and a fracture of the lower end of the fibula, usually with an associated dislocation of the ankle joint. This type of fracture is seen most frequently in contact sports such as football.

A selected number of often-encountered traumatic musculoskeletal injuries are presented in the following pages. The students with the injuries discussed are usually referred to the adapted physical education class by the orthopedic physician. The high incidence of traumatic musculoskeletal injuries seen in the adapted physical education class requires the teacher to have a thorough knowledge and understanding of the mechanisms of the injury and the implications for programming. Obviously, not all of the musculoskeletal disabilities that may occur can be presented here. Further reference should be made to standard texts on the subject. Most of the important anatomic structures that are related to the injuries illustrated and discussed in this chapter are described in chapter 3.

THE ANKLE

Sprain

MECHANISM OF THE INJURY: Sprains of the ankle usually involve extremes of either *inversion* or *eversion*. The *inversion sprain* is the most common of the two. Excessive pressure on the foot from above, when the sole of the foot is turned inward, is the most frequent cause of this injury. The typical position of an inversion sprain is illustrated in figure 6.1. When the weight of the body falls directly over the area just anterior to the lateral malleolus, a number of ligaments and other structures may be injured. In figure 6.1, the three most often involved ligaments in such injuries are indicated: anterior tibiofibular, anterior talofibular, and calcaneofibular. Although authorities disagree as to which of these ligaments is injured most frequently, it can be safely stated that one or more of them will be involved in inversion sprains.

Eversion sprains are seen much less frequently than inversion sprains. The eversion sprain primarily involves the deltoid ligament—the medial collateral ligament of the ankle. The deltoid ligament, however, has such great tensile strength that it may resist the injuring force and pull off part of the end of the medial malleolus, causing a chip fracture of the tibia. Chip fractures are not uncommonly associated with severe sprains to either the medial or the lateral aspects of the ankle. If a fracture does occur, the implications for adapted physical education are the same as for other types of fractures. But, in the case of a ligament injury, it should be remembered that *once ligaments are elongated by stretching or tearing, they will not return to their original length except through surgical intervention.* Fortunately, the trend in medical treatment is toward immediate immobilization of severely torn ligaments and their associated structures. This prac-

Figure 6.1. Most frequently injured ankle ligaments.

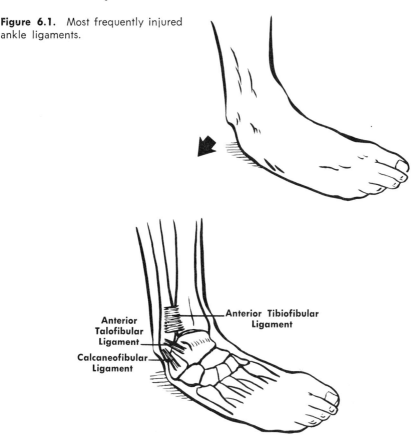

Anterior Talofibular Ligament

Anterior Tibiofibular Ligament

Calcaneofibular Ligament

tice tends to lessen the high incidence of joint instability due to elongated ligaments.

IMPLICATIONS FOR PROGRAMMING: Students with traumatic musculoskeletal injuries who are referred to the adapted physical education class are usually sent there after the acute stage of the injury has subsided. The joint may require flexibility exercises. The recommendation generally given for chronic or recurrent ankle sprains calls for therapeutic exercises which develop strength and muscular endurance to help restabilize the joint.

Dislocation

MECHANISM OF THE INJURY: Dislocations of the ankle are not common. However, many authorities believe that severe sprains result when a joint dislocates but returns to its original position of alignment without requiring manipulative reduction. The most frequent dislocation is characterized by a *posterior projection* of the foot on the lower leg. This position is shown in figure 6.2. Indicated are the fibula and talus bones. Since two peroneal tendons on the lateral side and two long flexor tendons of the foot on the medial side pass behind the malleoli on both sides of the ankle, there is a tendency for the bones of the leg, the tibia and the fibula, to be forced forward when the individual is standing on the ball of the foot. If extreme downward force is exerted while in this position, there is a tendency for these tendons to dislocate, in effect, the ankle. There is little muscular support from the front to prevent this action. Numerous ligaments are attached in such a way that they resist this force; but if the action is violent, there is a tendency for the ankle to dislocate. In any case, severe

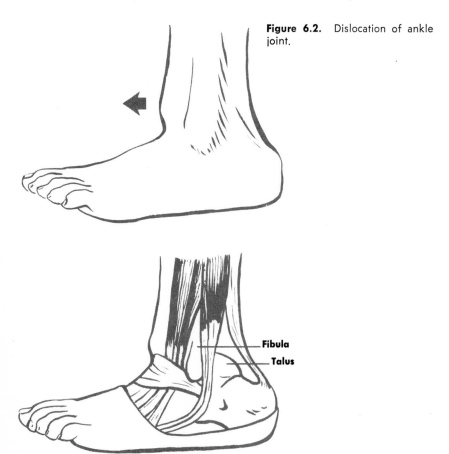

Figure 6.2.   Dislocation of ankle joint.

Fibula

Talus

damage is sustained that could result in a dislocation. This injury is seen most often in such activities as gymnastics where the individual lands forcibly on the edge of a mat while the total body is turning in an anteroposterior plane.

PROGRAMMING: Since dislocation of the ankle results in damage to the ligaments, which maintain normal joint relationships, the rehabilitation exercise program in adapted physical education would be similar to that recommended for severe ankle sprains. Again, the purpose is to help restabilize the joint through strength-developing exercises.

Fracture

MECHANISM OF THE INJURY: A Pott's fracture is illustrated in figure 6.3. This injury is characterized by an indentation on the medial side

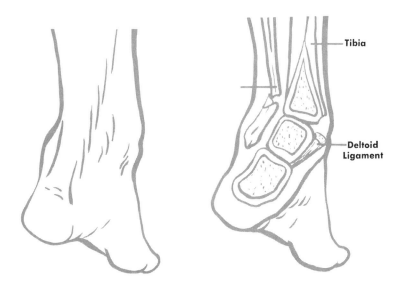

Figure 6.3. Pott's fracture

of the ankle that has been caused by a chip fracture in that area. A Pott's fracture involves a fracture of the lower end of the fibula while the deltoid ligament pulls away part of the medial malleolus from the tibia.

PROGRAMMING: Recommended therapeutic exercises are similar to those for fractures that are placed in immobilizing casts. Since inactivity usually results in atrophy and adaptive shortening of muscles and tendons, strengthening and stretching are necessary.

THE KNEE

MECHANISM OF THE INJURY: The arrows in figure 6.4 indicate the direction of force that usually causes stretching or tearing of the *medial collateral ligament*—the most frequently injured knee ligament. The medial collateral ligament is attached to the meniscus (interarticular or semilunar cartilage) by fibrous connective tissue. There is not a corresponding attachment between the lateral meniscus and the lateral collateral ligament. The medial meniscus is attached to the superior surface of the head of the tibia and also to the medial collateral ligament. A blow to the lateral side of the knee stretches or tears the medial collateral ligament, which in turn may dislodge the medial meniscus from the head of the tibia. Therefore, if a severe medial

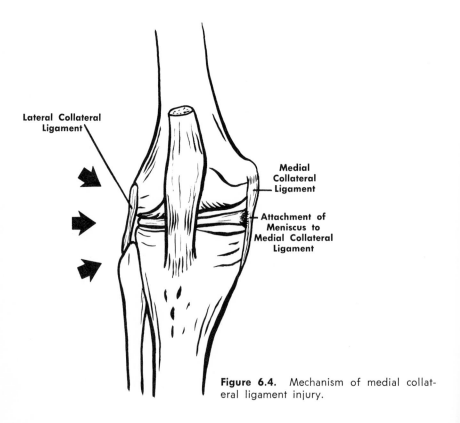

Figure 6.4. Mechanism of medial collateral ligament injury.

collateral ligament injury occurs, an associated injury to the medial meniscus may be anticipated.

If the knee is hit from the medial side, a tearing of the lateral collateral ligament may be expected. However, fewer lateral meniscus injuries result than medial meniscus injuries. This is because the lateral meniscus does not attach to the lateral collateral ligament.

The *cruciates* are the second most frequently injured ligaments of the knee joint. Of the two cruciates, *anterior* and *posterior*, the anterior cruciate is damaged more often than the posterior cruciate. The mechanism whereby these ligaments are torn is shown in figure 6.5. If the

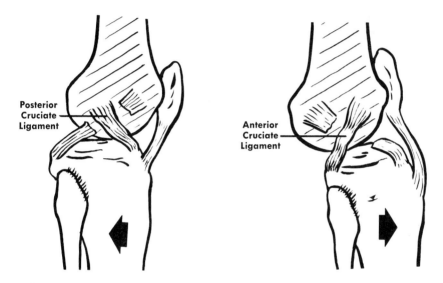

Figure 6.5. Mechanism of cruciate ligament injury

head of the tibia is forcefully driven backward in the direction of the arrow when the femur is fixed or stationary, the posterior cruciate ligament may be injured. On the other hand, if the tibia is driven forward when the femur is fixed or stationary, the anterior cruciate ligament may be torn. Anterior cruciate injuries in sports occur most often when the knee is partially flexed during running and another individual falls across the back of the leg below the knee. This action drives the head of the tibia toward the ground, while the femur tends to move forward by its own inertia. In football, this mechanism is called "clipping" and frequently results in an injury to the anterior cruciate ligament.

PROGRAMMING: A knowledge of specific exercises for restabilizing the knee joint is extremely important. Muscles or muscle groups involved at this joint are described in chapter 3. All three muscle groups involved in maintaining knee stability should be strengthened for optimum results.

THE HIP

MECHANISM OF THE INJURY: The hip is structured primarily for weight-bearing and is relatively stable. Hip stability comes from the deep articulation of the head of the femur with the acetabulum of the innominate bone, strong ligaments, and heavy musculature surrounding the joint. Due to the nature of the joint, dislocations are much less frequent than fractures. Most fractures occur to the neck of the femur and are, in many cases, the result of automobile accidents. Fractures of the hip are common in individuals over sixty years of age, since there is a tendency for the bone to become abnormally porous in the aging process.

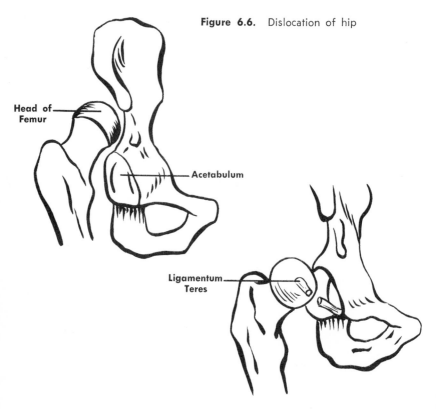

Figure 6.6. Dislocation of hip

Head of Femur

Acetabulum

Ligamentum Teres

A dislocation of the hip is shown in figure 6.6. The head of the femur is completely separated from the acetabulum. Occasionally in a dislocation of this type, the *ligamentum teres* may be torn or completely severed. The blood supply to the head of the femur runs through this ligament. Injury to the ligamentum teres, therefore, may result in disintegration of the head of the femur.

PROGRAMMING: Students with hip injuries are not too common in adapted physical education programs. Increasing the strength and flexibility of the hip is a major purpose of therapeutic exercise for these students.

THE BACK

MECHANISM OF THE INJURY: Traumatic musculoskeletal injuries of the spine usually present a complex picture. A majority of the structures that compose the back may be traumatized. In addition, referred pain may exist in the areas that were not actually involved in the specific injury. Therefore, considerable difficulty arises in accurately determining the nature of the injury. Traumatic disabilities may be either sprains, strains, or fractures. Along with these injuries, *compression herniations* of the *intervertebral discs* may occur. Some medical authorities believe that most back pain is related to some form of damage to the discs. Others are of the opinion that only a small proportion of back problems result from disc injury (Williams, 1962). Although traumatic injury is a cause of back disability, Kraus and Raab indicate that over 80 percent of lower-back pains are a result of physical inactivity. They stress the use of preventive and therapeutic exercise for disabilities of the back (Kraus and Raab, 1961).

A sagittal section of the lumbar spine is shown in figure 6.7. The spinous process, the pedicle, and the vertebral body are indicated. A normal intervertebral disc with its anulus fibrosus and its nucleus pulposus is indicated. The nucleus pulposus is a semifluid material and the anulus fibrosus is a fibrocartilaginous capsule. Trauma which forces the bodies of the vertebrae together, especially when the lumbar curvature is reversed, may force the nucleus pulposus through the anulus fibrosus and cause pressure on the posterior longitudinal ligament of the spine. Posterior herniation is often called a "slipped disc." This condition is illustrated (fig. 6.7). Protrusion of the disc in this area places pressure on the nerve roots, which may in turn result in pain in the lower back and legs. The nucleus pulposus protruding into the spongy part of the vertebral body is pointed out in the illustration.

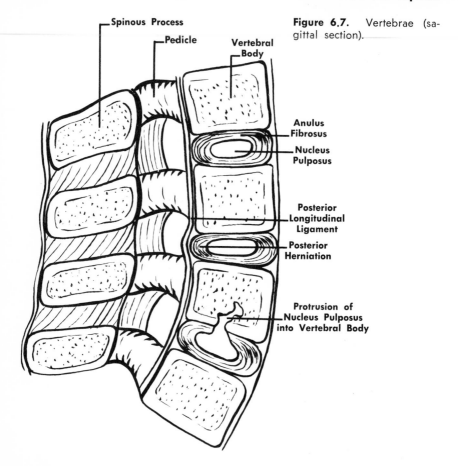

Spinous Process

Pedicle

Vertebral Body

Figure 6.7. Vertebrae (sagittal section).

Anulus Fibrosus

Nucleus Pulposus

Posterior Longitudinal Ligament

Posterior Herniation

Protrusion of Nucleus Pulposus into Vertebral Body

The mechanism involved in many back injuries caused by lifting is related to an increase in the hydraulic pressure of the nucleus pulposus (Keegan, 1953). If an individual attempts to lift a weight with the lumbar spine in a position that places undue pressure on the anterior portion of the disc (decreased lumbar curvature), the disc may herniate posteriorly. When a rapid, jerking motion is exerted at the start of lifting an object, the hydraulic pressure within the intervertebral disc increases manyfold. With greatly increased pressure, severe injury can occur even though the weight lifted is relatively light. The position just described is sometimes called the "7" position, because flexing at the hip joint with the knees in extension resembles the number seven. In order to avoid extreme reversal of the lumbar curve and to place less strain on the long straplike extensor muscles which run from the base of the skull to the sacrum, the knees should be flexed before lifting. This precaution releases the pull from the hamstring muscles since the hamstrings have a two-joint action crossing both the hip and knee joints posteriorly. In this position, the tension is removed from the hamstrings, and the lumbar spine is allowed to assume a more normal curvature. The weight should be lifted with the knee extensors rather than with the back extensors. The starting position for lifting a weight, with the knee extensors rather than the back extensors, has been called the "4" position, because it resembles the number four. Many potential injuries may be avoided through proper lifting mechanics.

Along with compression injuries in which the intervertebral discs may be damaged, the body of a vertebrae will fracture occasionally. Fortunately, these injuries are uncommon. A compression fracture of a vertebral body is indicated in figure 6.8. Also noted is a chip fracture of a vertebral body. Injuries of this type are found more frequently in the cervical area than in other areas in the spinal column. Fractures in which the spinous and transverse processes become detached from the vertebrae are the most common types of athletic injuries to the spinal column. A fracture of the spinous and transverse

Figure 6.8. Spinal fractures

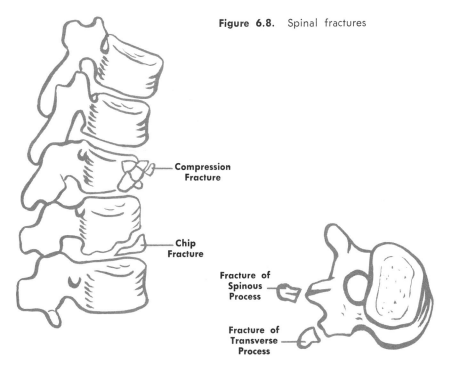

Compression Fracture

Chip Fracture

Fracture of Spinous Process

Fracture of Transverse Process

processes is also noted. Muscles pulling on the bony attachments may actually exert enough force to cause the fracture.

PROGRAMMING: Students with traumatic back injuries often comprise a large portion of those individuals who require therapeutic exercise in the adapted physical education program. Although there is a wide variety of differences in the injuries received, the exercise recommendations for back disabilities will be quite similar. The general purpose of exercise for these injuries is to provide increased stability through the provision of stronger muscles.

THE SHOULDER

MECHANISM OF THE INJURY: The shoulder involves three joints: the glenohumeral, the acromioclavicular, and the sternoclavicular. Injury to the acromioclavicular joint ranks first in order of frequency, followed by the glenohumeral and the sternoclavicular joints. Injuries in this area may involve spraining of ligaments, straining of muscle and connective tissue, and dislocation of any of these three joints. Since a dislocation is defined as the complete separation of the surfaces of a joint, the injury illustrated in figure 6.9 is in reality a dislocation.

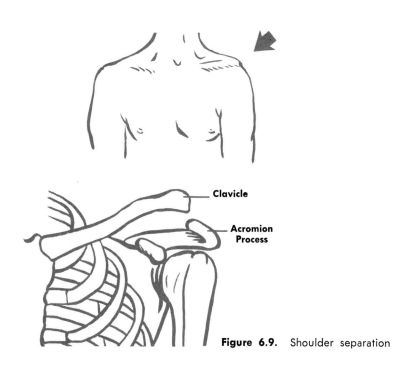

Figure 6.9. Shoulder separation

However, subluxations or partial dislocations of the acromioclavicular joint are called *separations*. This terminology is used in order to differentiate between injuries to these two joints and to the glenohumeral joint. When it is said that an individual has a dislocation of the shoulder, reference is made to a dislocation only at the glenohumeral joint. A shoulder separation at the acromioclavicular joint is commonly referred to as a *shoulder point*. This injury may be caused by the individual's falling directly on the point of the shoulder or by his breaking a fall with the arm extended. The injury shown in figure 6.9 is considered a separation of the acromioclavicular joint. The clavicle and acromion process are indicated.

Shown in figure 6.10 is a dislocation of the glenohumeral joint. Viewing the shoulder from an anterior view, the protrusion of the

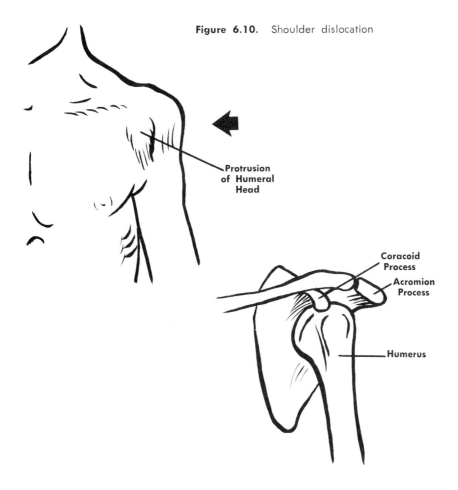

Figure 6.10. Shoulder dislocation

Protrusion
of Humeral
Head

Coracoid
Process

Acromion
Process

Humerus

humeral head is indicated. The corocoid process, the acromion process, and the humerus are pointed out. This is called a subcoracoid dislocation of the humerus. Dislocations may also occur with the humeral head posterior to the scapula or inferior to the glenoid fossa of the scapula. The dislocation is brought about when the humerus is at least at shoulder level while being laterally rotated.

With the exception of clavicular fractures, fractures in the shoulder area are infrequent. Falling on the tip of the shoulder or with the arm outstretched may result in such a fracture. Once the fracture has healed, rehabilitative therapeutic exercises are usually indicated to overcome atrophy caused by inactivity.

PROGRAMMING: The glenohumeral joint of the shoulder depends largely upon muscular function to maintain its integrity. Since dislocations of this joint are frequent, developing the musculature around the joint becomes a major task in the adapted physical education program. Once a dislocation of the shoulder joint has occurred, recurrences of the injury may progressively increase. In order to prevent these recurrences, a judiciously applied therapeutic exercise routine is extremely important.

A major precaution must be taken in relation to exercise for recurrent shoulder dislocations. *The individual must never be allowed to exercise with the humerus at shoulder level or above, and with the arm in a laterally rotated position.* For example, if the individual should attempt to press a barbell over his head and allow the weight to move slightly posterior to his line of gravity, the chances of a recurrent dislocation would be greatly increased. Experience indicates that this mechanism does happen. Every attempt should be made to inform the student of this possibility. Furthermore, close supervision is required to see that such an exercise is not attempted.

Surgical procedures are required in most recurrent dislocations of the shoulder. These surgical techniques involve some form of "tightening" or shortening of the joint structures, particularly the subscapularis muscle. Operations for the prevention of recurrence of shoulder dislocations are quite effective. Excellent results are seen in most cases. Prior to and following surgery, the physician may recommend therapeutic exercises for the muscles involved in the area. Exercise is almost always recommended following surgery for shoulder dislocation.

Strength-developing exercises, unfortunately, have little effect on restabilizing the acromioclavicular and sternoclavicular joints, because the muscles in these areas do not actually cross these joints. Strengthening exercises, therefore, do little for increasing acromioclavicular joint stability.

THE ELBOW

MECHANISM OF THE INJURY: Because of the deep socket formed by the articulation of the humerus with the ulna, the elbow joint is normally quite stable. It allows a hinge action between these two bones. Furthermore, there is a rotation action between the humerus and the ulna. Much force is required to dislocate this joint. Up to the point of dislocation, the injury is called a sprain. Sprains of the elbow joint are frequent. Although the elbow joint is stable, any slight amount of injury tends to result in discomfort, and the individual is unable to make effective use of the limb.

The elbow sometimes becomes injured when the individual attempts to break a fall with an outstretched, hyperextended elbow joint. This hyperextension may result in a sprain to the limiting ligaments, or if enough pressure is applied, the joint may dislocate. An upper limb that is struck from the rear while the elbow is hyperextended is susceptible to being dislocated because the retaining ligaments are at their limits of motion. The force tends to drive the joint forward. The ulna, in a hyperextended position, provides a type of "door-stop" action which, when driven hard enough, will aid in the dislocation of the joint. Chip fractures may be associated with this type of injury. These chips may become loose bodies within the joint and subsequently roughen the articular surfaces on the ends of the bones. Surgery is often required in such instances.

An elbow dislocation is illustrated in figure 6.11. The ulna is displaced posteriorly, resulting in an indentation in the posterior aspect

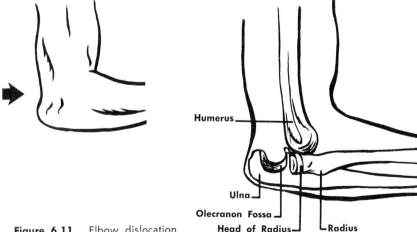

Figure 6.11.   Elbow dislocation

of the elbow. The humerus, ulna, olecranon fossa, and head of the radius are noted.

PROGRAMMING: Exercises for improving the stability of the elbow joint involve the application of resistance against the motions of flexion and extension of the elbow.

THE WRIST

MECHANISM OF THE INJURY: Wrist injuries are most often a result of hyperextension of the joint. Other than sprains, the most common injury to the wrist is a fracture of the navicular bone which is indi-

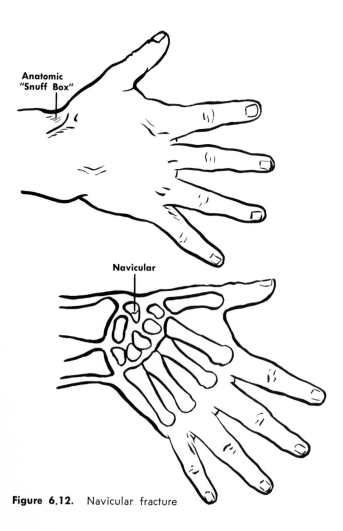

Figure 6.12. Navicular fracture

cated in figure 6.12. Long after a diagnosis of a "wrist sprain" in which there is persistent pain, it is often discovered that a fracture was the original problem. The damage resulting to the bone may necessitate surgical removal of the bone. The site of pain related to the navicular fracture is located at what is often called the anatomic "snuff-box." This is an indentation formed between the extensor tendons of the thumb on the radial side of the wrist when these tendons are placed under tension. Some medical services have a standing order that all X rays of the wrist should be repeated two weeks after the original examination. This is done to ascertain whether or not fractures of the bone have actually occurred. Many times the fracture is not seen on the first X ray. The subsequent X ray may show a more delineated fracture site because the healing process may have begun by that time.

PROGRAMMING: Therapeutic exercises for the wrist involve flexion and extension motions of the wrist joint against resistance. Exercises for these joints and the other musculoskeletal injuries included in this chapter are dealt with in detail in chapter 8.

SELECTED REFERENCES

1. HELFRICH, H. *Fractures and Dislocations.* London: New Sydenham Society, 1899.
2. KEEGAN, JAY J. "Alterations of the Lumbar Curve Related to Posture and Seating." *Journal of Bone and Joint Surgery* 35-A (July 1953): 589-603.
3. KRAUS, HANS, and RAAB, WILHELM. *Hypokinetic Disease.* Springfield, Ill. Charles C Thomas, 1961.
4. LOGAN, GENE A. *Adaptations of Muscular Activity.* Belmont, Calif.: Wadsworth Publishing Co., Inc., 1964.
5. ————, and LOGAN, ROLAND F. *Techniques of Athletic Training.* 3rd ed. Los Angeles: Franklin-Adams Press, 1967.
6. MOREHOUSE, LAURENCE E., and RASCH, PHILIP J. *Sports Medicine for Trainers.* 2nd ed. Philadelphia: The W. B. Saunders Company, 1963.
7. MOSELEY, H. F. "Disorders of the Hip." *Ciba Clinical Symposia* 5, no. 2 (March-April 1953):35-60.
8. ————. "Disorders of the Knee." *Ciba Clinical Symposia* 5, no. 6 (November-December 1963):171-201.
9. ————. "Disorders of the Shoulder." *Ciba Clinical Symposia* 11, no. 3 (May-June-July 1959):75-102.
10. ————. "Traumatic Disorders of the Ankle and Foot." *Ciba Clinical Symposia* 7, no. 6 (November-December 1955):167-194.
11. THORNDIKE, AUGUSTUS. *Athletic Injuries.* 5th ed. Philadelphia: Lea & Febiger, 1962.
12. WILES, PHILIP, and SWEETNAM, RODNEY. *Essentials of Orthopaedics.* 4th ed. Boston: Little, Brown and Company, 1965.
13. WILLIAMS, J. G. P. *Sports Medicine.* London: Edward Arnold (Publishers) Ltd., 1962.

principles
of exercise

Exercise may be used for the prevention, rehabilitation, and prevention of recurrence of adaptations made to internal and external forces that have been imposed on the body. When exercise is used for the purposes of rehabilitation, it is generally referred to as *therapeutic exercise*. The only difference between therapeutic exercise and exercise in general is that the former is being used as a form of therapy for disabilities or divergencies on the recommendations of a physician. Therapeutic exercise is exercise used to improve or prevent regression of some physical disability or deviation.

A major objective of physical education programs should be to provide physical conditioning that aids the body in withstanding external forces which may be injurious to muscles, bones, and joints. Through conditioning exercise programs, the body is better able to resist situations that are potentially hazardous. A program of injury prevention involves many factors. The individual is capable of reacting faster to a potential injury situation if his neuromuscular mechanism is in a well-conditioned state. Although basic reaction time is not improved, the body is able to respond in a more skillful way to avoid hazards. The basic elements of a physical education program involve the development of strength, cardiovascular endurance, muscular endurance, flexibility, and neuromuscular skill.

Therapeutic exercise may be used for both general and specific outcomes. General outcomes of exercise include raising the threshold of physiological responses—better oxygen delivery, lowered pulse rate, increased cardiac output, more rapid recovery from exertion, and other similar changes. These benefits accrue provided that sufficient stress is applied to increase the tolerance level of the individual. The specific outcomes of therapeutic exercise are primarily concerned with strength, cardiovascular endurance, muscular endurance, flexibility or range of motion, tension release, and neuromuscular skills.

There are basically four kinds of therapeutic exercise: (1) passive, (2) active-assistive, (3) active, and (4) resistive. These classifications indicate a progression from very mild to intense, vigorous exercise. Application of exercise progression may include one or more of these categories.

Passive exercise is exercise in which a body segment or limb is moved through a specific range of motion by another person. The involved individual may or may not be volitionally making an effort to perform the movement while the exercise is being administered to him. In most cases, however, he is attempting to move the part but is unable to initiate or demonstrate overt movement. This type of exercise is rarely used in the adapted physical education program.

Active-assistive exercise involves the movement of a body part or limb through a range of motion as far as possible by a volitional effort with assistance being given by another person to complete the motion. This type of exercise is usually performed against gravity, with the body segment or limb acting as resistance against which the muscles are required to work.

Active exercise consists of moving a body part through a range of motion against gravity, unassisted by another person. Technically, this type of exercise is a form of resistive exercise.

Resistive exercise is that type of exercise in which external forces are used to provide additional loads to increase the resistance to the motion. Various kinds of external forces may be used to provide the resistance. These include weights (in the form of metal plates), springs, rubber bands, resisted ropes, pulleys, and other equipment of this nature. Also, resistance to one body segment or part may be resisted by another body part.

Because therapeutic exercise is administered for specific disabilities or divergencies, certain factors must be taken into consideration. These concerns are not ordinarily of importance in an exercise program for normal students. Such problems include pain, limited flexibility, and uncoordinated neuromuscular relationships. Many times, the intensity of the exercise being performed by the individual is modified by his ability to withstand pain while the segment or limb is moved through a range of motion. Since pain is often heightened by the fear of pain, a twofold problem exists for the adapted physical education teacher.

Joint swelling or fluid within a joint may result in the limitation of flexibility. This is not necessarily related to shortened tendons or adaptation of other structures. A careful consideration of the causes of decreased flexibility will provide a better foundation on which to base the exercise program. The term *uncoordinated* is used here to relate to the inability of muscles to function in a normal relationship with one another. A coordinated movement is one in which the muscles work together to provide a desired motion. If an uncoordinated movement results, it may be due to pain. On the other hand, certain congenital or pathological conditions are characterized primarily by uncoordinated movements. An example of this is cerebral palsy.

As previously emphasized, the body is waging a constant battle against such external forces as gravity and other kinds of stresses. These may or may not result in adaptations that are disadvantageous to the individual. If the results are disadvantageous, a reversal of these changes may be made through judiciously applied therapeutic exercise. Because the body has many mechanisms that provide it with the ability to adapt favorably in the direction desired by the individual, it can be said that exercise facilitates the performance of subsequent exercise. The obverse holds also, because inactivity results in lessening the ability to do exercise, and many of the undesirable adaptations which are seen in inactive people result. The use of exercise for ameliorating adaptive changes that stem from the force of gravity, congenital and pathological anomalies, and traumatic injuries is the major concern of adapted physical education.

Performance of exercise for either normal or therapeutic purposes causes the body to respond in specific ways. Demands which are sufficient to increase the tolerance for more exercise must be placed on the organism in order for favorable adaptations to occur. Since the body has this ability for specific adaptation to the demands placed upon it, a unifying principle has been suggested to serve as a general guide for the deveolpment or design of an exercise program. This concept has been called the SAID principle (Logan and Wallis, 1960). The name, an acronym, is composed of the first letters of the following words: "Specific Adaptation to Imposed Demands." The SAID principle offers a guide to gain maximum effect in the least amount of time with a minimum amount of effort. Strength, cardiovascular endurance, muscular endurance, flexibility, and neuromuscular skill may be developed by using this principle in the application of exercise.

In designing specific exercises based upon general principles of exercise, the three-I principle suggested by Metheny is helpful (Metheny, 1956). The three *I*'s represent these three words: "Identify, Isolate, and Intensify." Application of these three procedures is essential when designing exercises or routines of exercises for students in the adapted physical education class.

The following is an example of how the three-I principle may be applied with an exercise such as the sit-up. One must *identify* the area to be exercised. The general area involved with this exercise is the abdominal muscle group. In order to *isolate* as much as possible the muscles to be exercised, the body should be in a position which allows the most effective and efficient application of resistance in the desired area. When isolating the area for exercise, attention must be given to the stabilization of other parts of the body. Stabilization for adequate exertion of the muscles in the abdominal area requires that the individual lie on his back with his knees and hips flexed. The feet should be placed under some permanent structure in order that they be firmly anchored. This prevents the feet from coming up from the floor during the exercise. The flexed knees and hips tend to place the hip flexor muscles in a slackened state, thereby reducing their function during the sit-up. This tends to place more emphasis on the contraction required by the abdominal muscles. Generally, in order for progression to occur as strength increases, the individual must *intensify* the exercise within his tolerance to perform the exercise. This is done by changing the position of the arms, for example, from a position along the side of the trunk to a position with the hands clasped behind the head. A further progression is to apply resistance to this movement through the use of weights held in the hands. As strength increases, the amount of weight held behind the head should be increased.

STRENGTH

Strength undergirds all factors when one considers the total functioning of the body in movement. The ability of the muscles to exert force has been studied more than any other single element of human performance. The importance of adequate levels of strength is universally recognized. Without sufficient strength, factors such as cardiovascular endurance, muscular endurance, flexibility, and neuromuscular skill cannot be developed effectively. Continued physical activity is required to prevent the deterioration of these factors. When activity which is necessary for normal functioning of the body is decreased, strength, along with other performance factors, also decreases. Wasting away of muscle and surrounding tissues as the result of inactivity is known as *atrophy*.

Principles of Strength Development

The development of strength is perhaps the most beneficial aspect of therapeutic exercise. Strength development exercises result in increased ability to exert force, increased muscle bulk (hypertrophy), and increased tone or firmness of the muscular tissues.

Regardless of the method utilized for strength development, the SAID principle serves as a guide. This is the application of *overload.* Increased demands must be applied beyond those levels of activity previously attained. In order to raise the tolerance level of the individual, there must be intensification of imposed demands. When the ability to exert force at a given level is reached, increased demands must be applied for additional increases in performance.

Two forms of strength conditioning are in general use. These involve working against resistance in such a way that the muscles either create muscular tension without changing their length, or do so while changing their length. Exercise in which exertion is made without changing the length of the muscle or moving the part or body segment through a range of motion is known as *isometric* exercise. Exercise which employs a change in length of the muscle while a limb or body part is being moved through a range of motion is known as *isotonic* exercise. In terms of strength development, there are advantages and disadvantages in the use of these two kinds of exercise.

Research investigations comparing the outcomes of isometric and isotonic strength-development exercises have indicated very little difference in the development of strength, i.e., the ability to exert force. In terms of time spent, isometric exercise is more efficient than isotonic exercise. Although isometric exercise is more efficient in terms of time expenditure, it has limitations. Isometric exercise has little effect on the development of cardiovascular endurance because it places little stress on the circulatory and respiratory systems (Wells, 1966). Also, hypertrophy, or increase in muscle bulk, does not accrue at as rapid a rate as in isotonic exercise. Isometric exercise has a specific advantage in its application for strength development where little or no joint motion is to be performed. This type of exercise is particularly useful, for example, for individuals in the rehabilitation phase after spinal fusions. Strength can be developed in the supporting musculature without motion in the involved area.

Isotonic strength-development exercise is of value where reduction of pain and an increase in the range of motion are desired. With isotonic exercise, the individual is able to observe increases in his ability to overcome applied resistances. When resistances of known increments are overcome with this type of exercise, it is obvious to the person exactly how much improvement he has made from one exercise period to the next. The factor of motivation may cause the individual to respond more rapidly through the use of isotonic exercises. For individuals requiring therapeutic exercises, isotonic programs are believed to be superior to isometric programs. Authorities on this subject have indicated that isotonic exercise is the preferred exercise for strength development (Hellebrandt, 1962; Morehouse and Rasch, 1963).

Procedures for the Development of Strength

The two basic methods in use for the development of strength involve isometric muscle contraction and isotonic muscle contraction. The most widely accepted and recommended technique is based upon the work of DeLorme (DeLorme and Watkins, 1951). The method is called progressive resistance exercise (P.R.E.). This procedure involves determining the resistance which can be lifted or overcome ten times, or ten *repetitions*. The performance of ten repetitions through a range of motion is called a *bout*. Recommended are the use of either two or three bouts per day per exercise. The first step in this method is the determination of the ten-repetition maximum (10 R.M.). The R.M. is the most resistance with which the individual may complete no more than ten repetitions through the range of motion. The resistance is determined through a process of trial and error. When three bouts are used, the first bout consists of one-half maximum resistance, the second bout involves three-fourths maximum resistance, and the third bout consists of the maximum resistance (10 R.M.). The first two bouts in the series serve as a warm-up for the final maximum effort.

The procedure recommended by DeLorme may be modified for use in adapted physical education classes. When the two-bout-per-day-per-exercise procedure is used, the first bout should consist of one-half maximum resistance performed for ten repetitions. The second bout consists of maximum resistance performed for ten repetitions. The two-bout program is desirable for those individuals who are apprehensive about performing a maximum level due to their specific disability. From empirical observation, the two-bout program is more applicable in adapted physical education class than three bouts.

The two-bout procedure is illustrated in the following example. If the individual found that he could lift twenty pounds of resistance no more than ten repetitions during a trial-and-error initial session, then in the succeeding exercise period he would begin by performing with ten pounds of resistance. He would complete the session by executing ten repetitions with twenty pounds (the 10 R.M.). As the ability to perform more than ten repetitions with twenty pounds of weight is developed, more repetitions should be attempted by the individual. When twelve to thirteen repetitions can be performed, the resistance or weight should be increased to cause him to return to approximately ten repetitions. In practical application, it is suggested that the repetitions remain between eight and twelve, because it is difficult to reach an exact number of ten repetitions at all times. The point to remember here is that repetitions should remain fairly constant while the resistance is progressively increased in subsequent exercise periods.

If the individual is recommended for a general conditioning program for the development of strength through isotonic procedures, and he has no problem concerning apprehensiveness, pain, or range of motion difficulties, the use of only one bout per exercise period may be sufficient. A consensus of the studies, which involved determination of optimum resistance and number of repetitions for the development of strength at a maximum rate, indicates that to use one bout of between five to fifteen repetitions with maximum resistance is sufficient for each exercise. More repetitions fail to increase strength significantly. It is recommended, therefore, when only one bout is performed, that the number of repetitions should fall somewhere between eight and twelve. If eight repetitions cannot be performed, too much resistance is being used. On the other hand, if the student can execute more than twelve repetitions, the resistance should be increased so that the performer works within the eight-to-twelve range.

The second method of strength-development exercise involves the use of isometric muscular contractions. There is no movement of the body segment or limb during the exercise. This form of exercise received impetus shortly after the original publications of Hettinger and Müller of Germany (Müller, 1957). Although this form of exercise was promoted as "dynamic tension" prior to that time, its use was not widespread. The original recommendations made by Hettinger and Müller were to apply *two-thirds maximal* effort to a muscle group. This contraction was to be held for *six seconds per day*. Subsequent studies have indicated that the application of *maximal* resistance up to ten seconds per day will yield greater results (Ball, Rich, and Wallis, 1964; Rasch and Pierson, 1963; Rich, Ball, and Wallis, 1964). It is recommended here that a maximal effort lasting for approximately ten seconds applied once per day is sufficient.

ENDURANCE

Endurance is the ability to sustain prolonged physical activity. It is gained by regularly increasing effort and gradually progressing in repetitions and/or rate of activity. Consequently, the individual's tolerance for more of the same type of activity will be increased. This is another example of the SAID principle in which demands must be imposed, that in turn cause the body to make specific adaptations in the desired direction.

Factors of strength and endurance are closely related. When one of these factors is developed, the other demonstrates an increase (Yessis, 1963). The development of strength must precede endurance training. Endurance development is at least a twofold phenomenon. The two types of endurance which have been identified are general and local. Examples of overall elevation of the basic adaptations in general endurance development are (1) increased oxygen-carrying capacity of the blood, (2) increased capillarization, and (3) greater output of the heart. When local endurance is developed, specific endurances result in areas of the body when they are called upon to exert continued and prolonged effort. As a result, various parts of the body may develop greater endurance than other parts, provided that sufficient training is done. There is a close relationship between general and specific endurance because they both depend upon strength in the involved muscles and an adequate supply of oxygen. It can be said, however, that specific endurance that results from specific training in a muscle or group of muscles is *muscular endurance*. General endurance basically involves the circulatory and respiratory systems. This type of endurance is referred to as *cardiovascular endurance*.

Endurance is usually considered a part of strength-development exercises when applied to specialized areas or specific parts of the body in the adapted physical education program. In general conditioning programs, cardiovascular endurance helps to reduce physical fatigue and allay the discomforts associated with low physical fitness.

When the development of both strength and endurance are desired at the same time, a program of circuit training is recommended (Morgan and Adamson, 1958). This is an invaluable procedure in an adapted physical education class where several students have common disabilities for which a general conditioning program is medically recommended. It is particularly useful where little equipment is available. It should be emphasized, however, that when utilizing this type of program in adapted physical education classes, very careful attention must be given to the tolerance level of the individual students.

Circuit training should be limited to those individuals requiring a general type of activity. The diagnosis and medical recommendation received from the physician must guide the application of such a program. Since circuit training involves the "station" approach with groups of students moving from one exercise or exercise area to another, class administrative problems can be reduced. This procedure may utilize active and/or resistive exercises established on the basis of the abilities and tolerances of the students. Generally, a series of six to ten exercises usually comprise a circuit. Examples of the exercises of stations are (1) flexed-knee sit-up, (2) biceps curl, (3) bench press, (4) half squat, (5) pull-up, (6) back-raise, or any similar kinds of activities. The resistance may be the body itself, barbells, metal plates and dumbbells, an exerciser such as the Exer-Genie Exerciser, or an exercise machine such as the Universal Gym which is composed of nine different exercise stations. Any combination of the exercises illustrated in the general conditioning section of chapter 8 may be used for the circuit. The amount of resistance for each of these activities depends on the abilities and tolerance of the individuals involved. Thus, the resistance or load for each activity is established in relation to the student with the lowest exercise tolerance. He must be able to perform at least ten repetitions of the exercise. For example, for the biceps curl exercise in a class, the weight to be lifted may be determined by trial and error to be thirty pounds. This weight is used by all individuals in the class.

After the resistance is established at each station, each individual on the first day performs as many repetitions as he can at each exercise station. The number of repetitions for each individual for each station is recorded. Prior to the next exercise period, the number of repetitions is arbitrarily reduced by one-third (or one-half, if desired). For example, if a student performs fifteen repetitions, his repetitions would be reduced to ten. On succeeding days, the exercise would be performed for ten repetitions with thirty pounds of resistance during one trip around the circuit. Three trips around the circuit would be completed during a class period of approximately thirty minutes.

Seven exercises might be established as a circuit for a class of twenty-one students to be completed within thirty minutes. The class might be divided into seven groups of three each. These groups would continue as units in order to assist each other in maintaining proper exercise positioning. They would also stand ready to receive the weight or resistance as a safety precaution. Furthermore, this procedure would facilitate a continuous movement around the circuit. As the performance of each exercise becomes easier, the number of repetitions at each station can be increased, for example, by two. Thus, a student who was originally performing ten repetitions would perform two more repetitions of the exercise on each of the three trips around the circuit. Where weights are used at stations, the weight might be increased five to ten pounds depending upon the group's tolerance. These increases may be made at different intervals during the semester.

The development of endurance usually involves a specific part of the body when applying therapeutic exercise. Therefore, if more endurance is desired than that which is obtained through strength-development exercises previously discussed, the rate and number of repetitions should be increased while using low resistance. As the individual is able to increase the rate and number of repetitions of the exercise over previous levels, the amount of resistance should be gradually increased. The exercise must be such that it involves the cardiovascular mechanism to a greater degree than does strength development exercise. For example, an exercise used for strength development may involve ten pounds of resistance for ten repetitions. The same exercise, when used for the development of endurance, might be performed with five pounds of resistance for twenty or more repetitions and at a more rapid rate. The desired outcomes will determine the resistance and number of repetitions to be used.

There are a number of ways in which endurance may be developed in the adapted physical education program. The development of cardiovascular endurance is one of the major outcomes of the sports phase of the program. In addition to these sports, such supplementary activities as jogging and cycling might be recommended. Running is perhaps the best cardiovascular activity in which the individual can participate. It is less time-consuming than most activities, and no special equipment is needed. The state of one's endurance or cardiovascular fitness can be measured through the use of a simple test. The test is known as Cooper's 12-minute field test for fitness (Cooper, 1968). It consists of determining how far one can go by running and walking within a period of twelve minutes. Standards of performance for individuals at different age levels are available in Cooper's recent publication (Cooper, 1970).

FLEXIBILITY

Flexibility is the range of motion of joints or body parts. The term *flexibility* has connotations applying only flexion. As widely employed in physical education, the term indicates the total range of movement possible at a joint. This may involve flexion *or* extension or any other type of joint motion.

It is possible that a person may have too much as well as not enough flexibility. The latter is usually the case. Adequate flexibility is usually the result of adaptive shortening of the connective tissues that cross and surround joints. Undesired extremes of flexibility due to injury or congenital and pathologic involvement of these same structures may result in their being elongated. Many of these hyper-flexible areas may not return to a desired state of flexibility without surgical intervention. However, therapeutic exercise is extremely bene-ficial in strengthening the muscles whose major function is to sta-bilize these joints. Strengthening the muscles in areas where the con-nective tissues, ligaments, and other joint structures allow more range of motion than is desired will tend to provide better functioning.

Individuals differ in the amount of flexibility which they possess. Differences in bodily proportions may cause people to appear less flexible than they really are. Also, there are differences in degree of flexibility within the individual. Flexibility tends to be specific for body parts (Holland, 1968). An indication of the flexibility in one joint or body segment does not necessarily indicate flexibility of other joints (Rasch and Burke, 1967). This is another application of the SAID principle. If the activity involves a continual application of stretching-type activities in one particular body part, this part will become more flexible. This is a change in flexibility as a result of adaptations made to demands that are specifically imposed.

The problem of limited flexibility is of great concern to many people. The constant pull of gravity on the erect human organism is largely responsible for decreased range of motion. This is particularly true in individuals who are inactive and have a low level of physical fitness. Where inactivity, no matter what the cause, prevents optimum strength, flexibility often becomes a problem. For example, if the abdominal muscles are in a weakened state, there is a tendency for the pelvis to have increased inclination with a resultant increased lum-bar curve. If this increased lumbar curve is maintained for a long period, the fascial structures and other connective tissues in that area will adapt to this habitual position by shortening. Once this adap-tation has occurred the range of motion in the area is limited to such an extent that no matter how strongly the abdominal muscles are developed, their ability to shorten to their potential is seriously curtailed. It follows that in order to bring about proper alignment of the pelvis, the shortened connective tissue in the lumbar area must be increased in length. This relationship of adaptively shortened struc-tures on one side of the body or joint and weakened muscles on the other side calls for a reversal of these conditions for optimum func-tion. The reversal involves increasing the flexibility in the lumbar area by stretching (lengthening) the posterior structures and strengthening the abdominal muscles.

Having shortened connective tissue on one side of the joint or body part and weakened muscles on the other side may be likened to the bow of an archer. The bowstring in this analogy would represent the adaptively shortened structures. This concept which shall be referred to as the *lengthening-strengthening principle* should be applied where such a relationship exists: one should *stretch* the shortened structures and *strengthen* the opposite weakened muscles.

Flexibility exercises in a general exercise program should follow endurance exercises and precede strength-development exercises. Endurance exercises tend to stimulate the cardiovascular system and, in turn, aid the flexibility procedures. This probably is a result of an increase in temperature within the connective tissue. The effect of temperature increase is not fully understood. The whole concept of "warm-up," whether for normal or therapeutic purposes, requires additional research.

Muscles on opposite sides of a joint function reciprocally with each other. Therefore, one muscle or muscle group might lengthen while the contralateral (antagonistic) muscle or muscle group shortens. In order to stretch adaptively shortened connective tissue in an area, the contralateral muscles must relax to allow elongation of these structures. A resistance to the stretching procedures exists if relaxation of the opposite muscles does not take place. When the muscles opposite those being stretched are contracted, the muscles of the involved area are reflexly inhibited (Loofburrow, 1960). This reflex inhibition allows for a more favorable setting in which increased range of motion may occur. The myotatic stretch reflex in the muscle being stretched is one of the limiting factors in the development of flexibility (Holland, 1968). This reflex is probably a protective mechanism where there is fast, uncontrolled movement. Walker has shown that the tension within the muscle is more than doubled when there is a rapid muscle stretch than when the stretch is slow (Walker, 1961). In order to minimize this reflex contraction, it is recommended that stretching be controlled and done slowly without momentum.

Observation and investigation appear to substantiate the slow stretching procedures advocated by Shelton (Shelton, 1949). Empirical observation led him to propose that fast, uncontrolled stretching prior to an athletic event may be a predisposing cause of subsequent soft-tissue damage. This damage is often in the form of pulled muscles, particularly when maximum exertions are made. The evidence seems to justify the preference for slow versus fast stretching (de Vries, 1962; Logan and Egstrom, 1961; Ryan, 1961). Both the studies of de

Vries and Logan and Egstrom showed no significant differences between the slow and fast stretching procedures. In addition, muscle
soreness was observed in the fast groups. These results have led de
Vries to conclude that (1) slow or static stretching offers less danger
of going beyond the limits of extensibility in soft tissues, (2) less
energy is required, and (3) static stretching not only does not cause
muscle soreness, but it may, in fact, relieve muscle soreness (de Vries,
1966).

Individuals requiring flexibility exercises in the adapted physical
education class are often placed there immediately after the removal
of plaster casts. Immobilized joints soon lose flexibility. Pain and swelling usually accompany these cases. There is often apprehension on
the part of the individual. There is a tendency for the person to
resist movement of the part because of anticipation of pain during
movement. Caution must always be taken when these exercises are
performed.

In order to increase range of motion, the part must be carried to
the point of pain and slightly beyond. In the adapted physical education class, flexibility exercises are usually performed actively by
the individual himself. He should be instructed in what to expect and
how the part should be carried through a given range of motion.

RELAXATION

Relaxation or the ability to release tension in muscles is a skill which
can be learned. The objective is to decrease the amount of electrical
activity in the muscle. An ability to release "tension" or reduce electrical activity within the muscle is becoming increasingly important.
With increased "stresses" of contemporary living, it is obvious that
the ability to relax under stress is of value.

Relaxation can be approached from at least two viewpoints: (1)
natural relaxation and (2) conscious relaxation. In either case, the
major purpose is for the provision of emotional release from tensions.
The ability to relax at will appears to be an important tool for the
release of tension.

The first approach to relaxation is natural relaxation. This form
of relaxation comes as a result of an individual having participated
in physical activity in the form of sports and other physical activities.
There is an awareness of an exhilarating feeling, which provides for
an emotional release from stresses. If the activity in which the individual participates is pleasant and satisfying, the subsequent result
is general relaxation. De Vries reports that a vigorous five-minute bout
of exercise can make a significant contribution to neuromuscular ten-

sion release in normal adult subjects as measured by electromyography (de Vries, 1966). It would appear that tension release through vigorous physical activity would be preferred to other forms of neuromuscular relaxation.

The second approach to relaxation is concerned with teaching the individual techniques through which he may become consciously aware of muscular tension. Several methods have been advocated, but the most widely used and accepted is that developed by Jacobson (Jacobson, 1938). This technique is called *progressive relaxation.* The method involves a person's learning to recognize the "feeling" of muscular tension in a muscle or group of muscles. The subject then learns to decrease the level of muscular tension to the smallest degree possible. After this is learned in one muscle group or body part, he then concentrates on other body parts until almost total electrical silence is attained.

The ability to relax volitionally is acquired in about the same manner as any other neouromuscular skill is learned. "Feeling" of relaxation must be perceived in order for it to become a learned skill which can be reproduced when desired. This form of relaxation involves the conscious awareness of the individual and requires the continued practice and application for optimum outcomes. A program of motor learning for the development of the neuromuscular skill of relaxation is beyond the scope of this text. The reader should consult the list of selected references on the subject.

NEUROMUSCULAR SKILL

Neuromuscular skill is a factor for consideration in the therapeutic exercise program. As discussed previously, it was indicated that the body responds rather specifically to demands placed upon it (SAID Principle). This concept also applies to the development of neuromuscular skill. When a skill is being developed, it must be repeated until there is a "connection" between the input and the desired response. Repetitive practice tends to cause the impulses to flow more freely. Neurologists term this *neurofacilitation.* Conditioned reflexes must be established in learning a skill (Falls, Wallis, and Logan, 1970).

The development of a neuromuscular skill requires a *specific* approach. As a result, many patterns of movement develop within the body. If these patterns are developed to a high degree, the end result could be called *general* coordination.

The development of strength, cardiovascular endurance, muscular endurance, and flexibility provide a base upon which specific coordinations may be developed. The development of these factors does not necessarily bring about better coordination. They do, however, contribute a foundation upon which skill can be developed. If a person desires to develop a particular pattern of movement, he must practice that movement pattern in the way in which the subsequent performance is to be demonstrated.

The administration of therapeutic exercise sometimes involves the use of "coordination exercises" to improve the working interrelationships between and among muscles and muscle groups. Specific patterns of movement must be practiced in order to accomplish these relationships. Coordination in this sense means an ability of parts to work together in a smooth-functioning unity. For example, if one part of a muscle is weakened through disease, the pattern of movement of the lever upon which this muscle acts may not be that which is desired. This is because only a part of the muscle was doing its share of the movement. The individual must either strengthen this part of the muscle to where it was before the disability, or he must learn to use it in such a way as to demonstrate a smooth, efficient movement pattern.

Exercises for coordination development are often required in the early stage of rehabilitation of injuries and debilitating diseases. The exercises recommended in chapter 8 for the development of strength of different areas of the body may serve as coordination exercises. In instances where exercise is to be administered for certain neurological conditions, cerebral palsy for example, specific recommendations would be made by the physician.

Selected References

1. BALL, JERRY R.; RICH, GEORGE, Q.; and WALLIS, EARL L. "Effects of Isometric Training on Vertical Jumping." *Research Quarterly* 35 (1964): 231-235.
2. CLARKE, H. HARRISON, and CLARKE, DAVID H. *Developmental and Adapted Physical Education*. Englewood Cliffs, N. J.: Prentice-Hall, Inc., 1963.
3. COOPER, KENNETH H. "A Means of Assessing Maximal Oxygen Intake." *Journal of the American Medical Association* 203 (1968):201-204.
4. ————. *The New Aerobics*. New York: M. Evans and Company, Inc., 1970.
5. DAVIS, ELWOOD C.; LOGAN, GENE A.; and McKINNEY, WAYNE C. *Biophysical Values of Muscular Activity*. 2nd ed. Dubuque, Ia.: Wm. C. Brown Company Publishers, 1965.
6. DeLORME, THOMAS L. "Restoration of Muscle Power by Heavy-Resistance Exercises." *Journal of Bone and Joint Surgery* 27-A (October 1945):645-667.
7. ————, and WATKINS, ARTHUR L. *Progressive Resistance Exercise*. New York: Appleton-Century-Crofts, Inc., 1951.

8. DE VRIES, HERBERT A. "Evaluation of Static Stretching Procedures for Improvement of Flexibility." *Research Quarterly* 33 (1962):222-229.

9. ————. *Physiology of Exercise for Physical Education and Athletics.* Dubuque, Ia.: Wm. C. Brown Company Publishers, 1966.

10. FALLS, HAROLD B.; WALLIS, EARL L.; and LOGAN, GENE A. *Foundations of Conditioning.* New York: Academic Press, Inc., 1970.

11. FREDERICK, A. BRUCE. "Tension Control in the Physical Education Classroom." *Journal of the Association for Health, Physical Education and Recreation* 38 (September 1967):42-44, 78-80.

12. HELLEBRANDT, FRANCES A. "The Scientific Basis of Weight Training." In *Weight Training in Sports and Physical Education.* Washington: American Association for Health, Physical Education and Recreation, 1962.

13. HOLLAND, GEORGE. "Specificity of Flexibility." In *Kinesiology Review—* 1968. Washington: American Association for Health, Physical Education and Recreation, 1968.

14. JACOBSON, EDMUND. *Progressive Relaxation.* Chicago: University of Chicago Press, 1938.

15. ————. *Self Operation Control.* Philadelphia: J. B. Lippincott Co., 1964.

16. KRAUS, HANS. *Therapeutic Exercise.* Springfield, Ill.: Charles C Thomas, 1949.

17. ————, and RAAB, WILHELM. *Hypokinetic Disease.* Springfield: Charles C Thomas, 1961.

18. LIGHT, SIDNEY, ed. *Therapeutic Exercise.* 2nd ed. New Haven: Elizabeth Licht, 1965.

19. LOGAN, GENE A. *Adaptations of Muscular Activity.* Belmont, Calif.: Wadsworth Publishing Co., Inc., 1964.

20. ————. "Weight Training in the Prevention and Rehabilitation of Athletic Injuries." In *Weight Training in Sports and Physical Education.* Washington: American Association for Health, Physical Education and Recreation, 1962.

21. ————, and EGSTROM, GLEN H. "The Effects of Slow and Fast Stretching on the Sacro-femoral Angle." *Journal of the Association for Physical and Mental Rehabilitation* 15 (May-June 1961):85-89.

22. LOGAN, GENE A., and WALLIS, EARL L. "Recent Findings in Learning and Performance." Paper presented at the Southern Section Meeting, California Association for Health, Physical Education and Recreation, Pasadena, California, 1960.

23. LOOFBURROW, G. N. "Neuromuscular Integration." In *Science and Medicine of Exercise and Sports.* Edited by W. R. Johnson. New York: Harper & Row, 1960.

24. MATHEWS, DONALD K.; KRUSE, ROBERT; and SHAW, VIRGINIA. *The Science of Physical Education for Handicapped Children.* New York: Harper & Row, Publishers, 1962.

25. METHENY, ELEANOR. *Body Dynamics.* New York: McGraw-Hill Book Co., Inc., 1952.

26. ————. Personal communication. University of Southern California, 1956.

27. MORGAN, R. E., and ADAMSON, G. T. *Circuit Training.* New Rochelle, N. Y.: Sportshelf & Soccer Associates, 1958.

28. MOREHOUSE, LAURENCE E., and RASCH, PHILIP J. *Sports Medicine for Trainers*. Philadelphia: W. B. Saunders Company, 1963.

29. MÜLLER, ERICH A. "The Regulation of Muscular Strength." *Journal of the Association for Physical and Mental Rehabilitation* 11 (March-April 1957):41-47.

30. RASCH, PHILIP J., and BURKE, ROGER K. *Kinesiology and Applied Anatomy*. Philadelphia: Lea & Febiger, 1967.

31. RASCH, PHILIP J., and PIERSON, WILLIAM R. "Isometric Exercise, Isometric Strength, and Anthropometric Measurements." *Internationale Zeitschrift Fuer Angewandte Physiologie* 20 (1963):1-4.

32. RATHBONE, JOSEPHINE L., and HUNT, VALERIE V. *Corrective Physical Education*. 7th ed. Philadelphia: W. B. Saunders Company, 1965.

33. RATHBONE, JOSEPHINE L. *Teach Yourself to Relax*. Englewood Cliffs, N. J.: Prentice-Hall, Inc., 1957.

34. RICE, GEORGE Q.; BALL, JERRY R.; and WALLIS, EARL L. "Effects of Isometric Training on Strength and Transfer of Effect to Untrained Antagonists." *Journal of Sports Medicine and Physical Fitness* 4 (1964): 217-220.

35. RYAN, A. J. "The Role of Training and Conditioning in the Prevention of Athletic Injuries." In *Health and Fitness in the Modern World*. Chicago: Athletic Institute, 1961.

36. SHELTON, ROBERT E. Personal communication. University of Illinois, 1949.

37. SILLS, FRANK D., ed. *Weight Training in Sports and Physical Education*. Washington: American Association for Health, Physical Education and Recreation, 1962.

38. WALKER, S. M. "Delay of Twitch Relaxation Induced by Stress and Stress Relaxation." *Journal of Applied Physiology* 16 (1961): 801-806.

39. WALLIS, EARL L., and LOGAN, GENE A. *Exercise for Children*. Englewood Cliffs, N. J.: Prentice-Hall, Inc., 1966.

40. ————. *Figure Improvement and Body Conditioning through Exercise*. Englewood Cliffs, N. J.: Prentice-Hall, Inc., 1964.

41. ————. *Figure Improvement Exercises for Women*. Englewood Cliffs, N. J.: Prentice-Hall, Inc. 1965.

42. WELLS, KATHARINE F. *Kinesiology*. Philadelphia: The W. B. Saunders Company, 1966.

43. YESSIS, MICHAEL. "Relationship Between Varying Combinations of Resistances and Repetitions in the Strength-Endurance Continuum." Unpublished Ph.D. dissertation, University of Southern California, Los Angeles, 1963.

exercise programs

Students are assigned to the adapted physical education class on the basis of a medical diagnosis and the recommendation of the physician. Therefore, the class is composed of students with a variety of physical disabilities. Because of the special nature of the students in this type of class, the teacher-student relationship is on a one-to-one basis. Consequently, these classes must be smaller than those offered in the regular physical education program. For optimum benefits to accrue from adapted physical education, a class of approximately twenty students is considered ideal.

Even though a great variety of physical disabilities are seen in adapted physical education classes, the individuals will generally fall into subgroups on the basis of similar disabilities. For example, in a class of twenty there might be five students rehabilitating knee disabilities; three might be taking exercises for common disabilities of the back; five might be recommended for postural exercises; the remainder might be recommended for a general conditioning program. It should be noted that the individuals in this class have disabilities requiring therapeutic exercise. Another class might consist of five students who were recommended for rehabilitation of joint disabilities. These students would be participating in therapeutic exercise, and the remaining fifteen students might be recommended for the sports phase of the program. Still another class could be composed exclusively of students requiring postural exercises. The composition of the class will depend upon the physical disabilities of the students who are unable to participate in the regular physical education program. Therefore, cooperation between the school health service and the physical education department is essential.

Individualization in adapted physical education classes presents a greater administrative problem than in regular physical education classes. It is not possible to anticipate the kinds of medical classifications and recommendations that will be presented by the students attending the class for the first time. Because activity should begin in the class as soon as possible, it becomes the task of the instructor to minimize class administrative procedures. One way to do this is to develop a student handbook or guidebook which presents to the student pertinent information concerning the adapted physical education program. Such a guide can serve at least three purposes: (1) it can facilitate the administration of a class; (2) it can provide useful guidance to the student while he is in the class; (3) it can be of value for those individuals requiring a continued exercise program throughout their lifetime. The guidebook might contain an introduction to the aims and objectives of adapted physical education, indications for specific requirements for a given class, expected outcomes of therapeutic exercise, anatomical and physiological bases of exercise for specific conditions, and a series of exercises for disabilities seen in the adapted physical education class. It might also contain information about the sports phase of the program and suggest recreational activities for students with certain physical limitations. Additional space may be provided for the student to record his progress in the program.

The frequency and similarity of certain disabilities allow the adapted physical education teacher to develop routines of therapeutic exercise which may be applied to a number of students with common disabilities. The routines should include all of the exercises usually recommended for a common disability, thereby serving to provide a more efficient and comprehensive approach to the program. Furthermore, when the student appears for the first time in the adapted physical education class, it will be possible to schedule his routine of exercises at that time on the basis of his classification and medical recommendation. It should be stressed, however, that individual modifications of the exercise routine are necessary in many cases. Nonetheless, there is enough similarity of disabilities and exercise recommendations to allow for the establishment of routines for most common conditions.

The *exercise-routine method* of administering therapeutic exercise in the adapted physical education program has been developed to a high degree of utility by Shelton (Shelton and Logan, 1952; Shelton and Logan, 1954). The routine of exercises for common back disabilities which is presented later in this chapter was adapted from a series of exercises known as the "Shelton Back Routine."

EXERCISE FOR POSTURAL ADAPTATIONS

The key to providing a basis for "good" posture lies in the development and maintenance of optimum levels of strength, muscular endurance, flexibility, and skill. Skill in this context is the ability to exhibit desired patterns of movement of the extensor mechanisms of the body which must withstand the pull of gravity. Therefore, postural exercises should serve to—

1. increase strength in specific areas,
2. increase muscular endurance to reduce the effect of fatigue,
3. increase flexibility of connective tissue which has become adaptively shortened due to immobility, and
4. improve skill in segmental body alignment.

"Good" posture is often considered synonymous with how well an individual is able to align himself with a plumb line. As related previously, this rigid standard has a questionable origin. Teaching a person to assume this static position has some merit in making him aware of body alignment. But the use of such a position as an indication of the *functional* capacity of one's body is seriously limited. An individual never assumes this stiff, rigid standing position *unless it is precisely to demonstrate his ability to align himself with the plumb line.* Rather, observing the individual from anteroposterior or lateral views while the person is standing at ease *does* have merit, particularly when the concern is with the balance of segments. Alignment of the body so that it can be held in balance with a minimum of ligamentous, fascial, and muscular strain seems more desirable than a demonstration of the ability to assume a rigid position. To counteract postural divergencies due to the pull of gravity, the exercises should be designed for the improvement of those physical fitness factors which serve to maintain the balanced alignment in many different postures.

Without proper instruction in how desired balance of segments should be maintained, little change can be expected in that direction. Some evidence is available to indicate that a positive relationship exists between trunk strength and what is generally considered "good" posture (Flint and Diehl, 1961). This evidence suggests that strengthening muscles of the trunk might result in better posture without psychological awareness. When proper emphasis is placed upon both the psychological aspect and an effective exercise program, it should follow that better results could be obtained from postural training in the adapted physical education program.

Examples of exercises are presented here to illustrate underlying principles which can serve as guidelines for the improvement of posture. In some cases, the series of exercises can be complete for a specific area of the body.

The lengthening-strengthening principle is one of the basic concepts of exercise useful in postural education. This principle suggests that areas requiring increased flexibility should be stretched and the muscles in the area contralateral (antagonistic) to these structures should be strengthened through the use of exercises involving the application of resistance.

Flexibility Development Exercises
for Postural Alignment

Insufficient muscle strength and endurance often produce increased curvatures of the spine and a forward position of the shoulders. If these positions are maintained, adaptive shortening of the connective tissues in these areas may result. The shortened connective tissues must be stretched. Stretching of these areas must precede an attempt to realign body segments. Without adequate flexibility, increased strength solves only a portion of the postural problem. Connective tissue adaptations are usually found in the posterior cervical and lumbar regions, in the anterior shoulder area, in the anterior aspect of the hip joint, and in the feet. The exercises which follow are designed to improve flexibility in these areas. The exercises included here are specific to the areas indicated. Later in this chapter, in the section on flexibility exercises for general conditioning, additional exercises to improve flexibility are presented.

When a functional flat foot (eversion and abduction of the foot—pronation) is maintained for a long period, fibers on the lateral border of the Achilles tendon tend to shorten. The fibers on the medial border become lengthened. It is necessary to reverse this relationship for normal functioning. An exercise for stretching the Achilles tendon is shown in figure 8.1. The medial border of the tendon is placed in a shortened position. The heels should be placed approximately eight to ten inches apart with the great toes on each foot held closely together. The intrinsic muscles of the sole of the foot should be strongly contracted to prevent stretching of connective tissues in the sole of the foot. The sole of the feet should face each other in a position of supination to prevent rotation of the calcaneus in a way that stretches the longitudinal arch. The individual should stand approximately three feet from a wall in a "toe-in" position with the toes flexed strongly and the hands on the wall. The trunk should be allowed to move forward very slowly while the anterior muscles of the lower limbs are strongly contracted. At the same time, the knees and hips should be held in

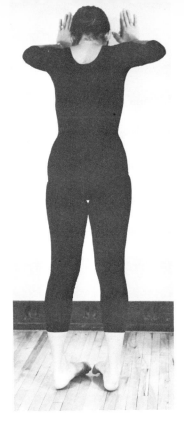

Figure 8.2. Hamstring stretch, standing—Start.

Figure 8.1. Achilles tendon stretch.

Figure 8.3. Hamstring stretch, standing—Finish.

a position of extension. The heels should remain in contact with the floor throughout the exercise. The movement should go to the point of pain and slightly beyond. This exercise should be repeated slowly five to ten times. Care should be taken to avoid jerking or movements involving momentum.

A flexibility exercise for the lumbar spine and the posterior aspect of the hip joint is shown in figures 8.2 and 8.3. The individual should

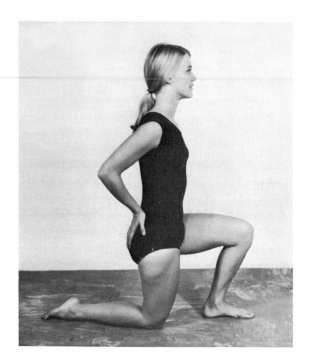

Figure 8.4. Hip flexor stretch—Start

Figure 8.5. Hip flexor stretch—Finish

attempt to straighten the knees as far as possible while the hands remain in contact with the floor. The exercise should be repeated five to ten times while contracting the muscles on the anterior aspect of the body.

A flexibility exercise for the flexors and iliofemoral ligament of the right hip is shown in figures 8.4 and 8.5. The pelvis should be pushed forward with the pressure of the right hand on the posterior hip area. The abdominals should be contracted during this exercise to help prevent excessive increase in the curvature of the lumbar spine. The exercise should be repeated on both sides from five to ten times.

A flexibility exercise for the upper back and neck regions is shown in figure 8.6. This exercise should be started from the supine position with the upper limbs away from the sides of the body at about a forty-five-degree angle. By pushing downward with the hands, assistance is given in raising the lower limbs over the head to the position shown. If difficulty is encountered in getting the lower limbs

Figure 8.6. Upper back and neck stretch

over the head when tolerance for the exercise is low, the knees may be kept flexed until sufficient strength is available to reach the proper position. The ultimate objective, however, is to assume the position with the knees as straight as possible. This exercise should be repeated five to ten times.

A flexibility exercise for the anterior shoulder girdle area is illustrated in figures 8.7 and 8.8. The individual should attempt to lower the head and trunk while holding the elbows as straight as possible. Maintaining the knees in an extended position also facilitates stretching the posterior hip and thigh muscles. The exercise should be repeated five to ten times.

Figure 8.7.   Pectoral stretch—Start

Figure 8.8.   Pectoral stretch—Finish

Isometric Strength-Development Exercises
for Postural Alignment

In addition to the development of the factors of strength, endurance, and flexibility, attention must be directed toward the improvement of skill in assuming segmental posture alignment. The individual must become kinesthetically aware of the feeling of a desired postural position in order that he may volitionally assume a given posture. The use of isometric strength-development exercises is helpful in increasing the awareness of good segmental alignment. Isometric exercises are particularly useful in helping the individual acquire postural perception.

Traditional *starting positions* for those exercises used by most advocates of static posture development can become useful isometric exercises. Early physical educators, whose posture program largely consisted of statically held positions, developed a series of rigid standardized positions. Only those basic to the erect standing position are described here. The purpose of including them is for use in helping the individual learn to assume an erect posture.

Assuming one of the traditional starting positions and holding it for approximately ten seconds with maximal contraction of one or more of the major antigravity muscle groups is an exercise in and of itself. Attention must be focused upon the desired body alignment while the exercise is being performed.

The *supine position* with the upper limbs along the sides of the body is shown in figure 8.9. An attempt should be made to flatten the lumbar and cervical regions of the spine. To perform a posture exercise from this position, the individual should tighten the abdominal and gluteal muscles. At the same time, he should press down with the back of the head, along with the forearms and the heels. Maximal contractions should be held for ten seconds. This exercise may be repeated once or twice to heighten postural awareness.

Figure 8.9. Supine position

This back-lying exercise may be varied for the purpose of improving positioning of the scapula. This can be done by changing the position of the upper limbs. In the back-lying position the upper limbs are at a ninety-degree angle to the body, the hands should be placed palms downward for the application of pressure. The exercise is performed by forcing downward with the hands. This action exerts a maximum contraction of the posterior shoulder muscles and the scapular adductors. In this position with the arms at a ninety-degree angle to the body, the elbows may be flexed to ninety degrees, with the forearms perpendicular to the floor. Pressure should be exerted downward with the back of the upper arm and elbow. It may be necessary for the knees to be slightly flexed during the attempt to align the body.

A *hook-lying position* is illustrated in figure 8.10. The knees and hips should be flexed with the feet and limbs parallel. This exercise

Figure 8.10. Hook-lying position

involves maximal contraction of the abdominal and gluteal muscles. The contraction should be held for ten seconds. The exercise may be repeated once or twice during the exercise period. Changes in the positioning of the upper limbs may be advisable as suggested for the exercise shown in figure 8.9.

The *front-lying* or *prone position* is shown in figure 8.11. The forehead may contact the floor or the face turned to one side. The upper limbs may be at the sides or in other positions depending on the comfort of the individual. This exercise consists of maximally contracting the abdominal and gluteal muscles. The contraction should be held for ten seconds. This procedure may be repeated once or twice during the exercise session.

Figure 8.11. Front-lying or prone position

The *cross-sitting* or *"tailor's sit" position* is shown in figure 8.12. The feet should be pulled in as close to the buttocks as possible. Particular attention should be paid to the erectness of the spinal regions. The hand and arm positions may be varied either by placing the arms alongside the body or the hands in contact with the shin for the maintenance of the erect position. This postural exercise consists of maximally contracting the abdominal and gluteal muscles for approximately ten seconds. In this position, it is also possible to stretch the adductor muscles of the thigh by pressing downward on the knees

Figure 8.12. Cross-sitting or "Tailor's Sit" position.

with the hands. The position of the feet should be changed frequently in order to avoid discomfort.

The *erect standing position* is illustrated in figure 8.13. The feet should be parallel to each other. The pelvic position should be in a mid-position between the extremes of anteroposterior range of motion. The abdominal and gluteal muscles should be held in a state of contraction. The chest should be lifted slightly. The head should be held erect, but not forced backward. The shoulders should be level and relaxed. Standing in this position while maximally contracting the abdominal and gluteal muscles for approximately ten seconds is an effective postural exercise. This exercise may be varied by having the individual stand with his lumbar spine against a wall with his heels approximately six inches from the wall. An attempt should be made to force the lumbar spine against the wall at the same time the abdominal and gluteal muscles are contracting. It may be necessary to have the knees flexed slightly to permit the pelvis to assume the desired position.

Figure 8.13. Erect standing position

Isotonic Strength-Development Exercises for Postural Alignment

It was seen in the previous section that isometric exercises were recommended so that an emphasis could be placed upon the assumption of an erect standing posture. Exercise in this form is especially beneficial for the development of awareness of desirable erect positioning. It is believed, however, that *function is of greater importance than the ability to assume static positions,* and, therefore, the use of *isotonic* postural exercises should be stressed. Isotonic exercises allow the individual to derive a satisfaction from seeing and knowing just how much effort he has put forth. This effort is determined by the number of times a body part has been moved through a range of motion. In addition, the individual knows how much resistance he has overcome. Overcoming a given resistance serves as a motivating factor for further improvement.

It was previously stressed that postural alignment should begin with the feet. In order for proper alignment to occur, the Achilles tendon should be stretched as indicated previously in figure 8.1. The purpose of exercise in this area is the reversal of eversion and abduction (pronation) of the foot.

An exercise is shown in figure 8.14 for strengthening the intrinsic muscles of the arch by gripping with the toes. The sitting position

Figure 8.14. Strengthening exericse for intrinsic foot muscles.

is recommended for this exercise because it places the foot in a functional position but does not require total weight-bearing during the exercise. In order to help the individual sense the feeling of toe-gripping, small wads of paper may be placed on the floor in a position that can be reached by the foot. These pieces of paper should be picked up by forcefully gripping with the toes. The student should place the papers on the hand opposite the foot being exercised. The exercise should be repeated five to ten times during each exercise session with both feet. In acute arch difficulty, the procedure may be used to advantage two or three times a day.

Shown in figure 8.15 is another foot-strengthening exercise. This exercise makes it possible to increase the resistance by placing a metal plate or other such weight on a bath towel. The towel should be stretched to its full length. The weight is placed on the towel, and the heels rest firmly on the floor. The object is to grip with the toes of each foot alternately. If done properly, the weight will be pulled toward the feet. This procedure should be repeated approximately ten to fifteen times.

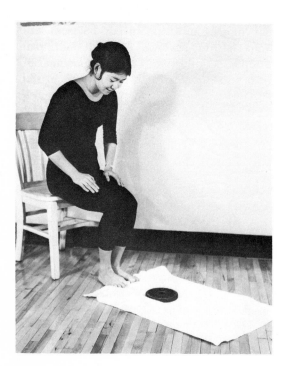

Figure 8.15.   Strengthening exercise for intrinsic foot muscles.

An exercise for the intrinsic muscles of the feet which is performed in the standing position is shown in figure 8.16. This strengthening exercise should be used only after the individual has become aware of the ability to forcefully contract the muscles in the sole of the foot. The toes should be flexed and the feet supinated so that the individual is walking on the sides of the feet. The exercise position

Figure 8.16. Strengthening exercises for intrinsic foot muscles.

should be held while the person takes short steps. When a state of mild fatigue is experienced, the walk should be terminated. As the tolerance of the individual increases, the distance of the walk should be lengthened.

Basic isotonic exercises for postural alignment should be directed toward the improvement of strength and muscular endurance in the anteroposterior antigravity muscles. Four exercises are included here for use when particular attention is focused upon aiding the individual in assuming an erect standing posture. Eight to twelve repetitions should be performed for each exercise. When the individual is able to perform more than twelve repetitions with a given resistance, the resistance should be increased to limit the participant to eight repetitions. As tolerance for the exercise increases, resistance should be progressively increased.

　　Shown in figures 8.17 and 8.18 is an exercise primarily for the abdominal muscles. The starting position is assumed with the feet an-

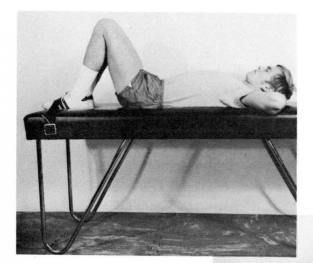

Figure 8.17. Flexed-knee sit-up—Start.

Figure 8.18. Flexed-knee sit-up—Finish.

chored as indicated. The trunk is curled up to a sitting position. Progression should be made as noted previously.

Illustrated in figures 8.19 and 8.20 is an exercise for the development of the hip and spinal extensors. This exercise should begin with the feet anchored as shown and the hands clasped behind the head. The trunk should be raised to a position parallel with the floor, held momentarily, then lowered to the starting position. The exercise should be continued according to the procedure described previously.

Figure 8.19. Back raise—Start.

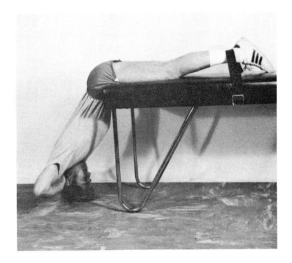

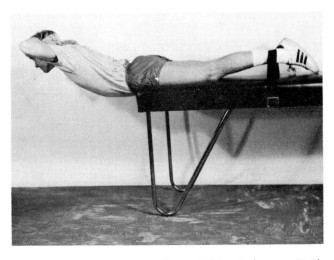

Figure 8.20. Back raise—Finish

Shown in figure 8.21 is a leg extension exercise on the Universal Gym. The individual sits in the position shown. The ankles, knees, and hips are then extended against resistance. An attempt should be made for full ankle and knee extension during this exercise. Resistance should be increased as tolerance permits.

A scapular adduction exercise utilizing the Exer-Genie Exerciser is shown in figure 8.22. The device is anchored in a door jamb. The

Figure 8.21. Leg extension.

Figure 8.22. Scapular adduction.

resistance is set in such a way that the individual may do no more than twelve repetitions and no less than eight repetitions. It is necessary to alternate from one set of handles to the other set of handles for succeeding repetitions of the exercise. It is particularly important to see that the scapulae are pulled as closely together as possible. Resistance should be increased as the ability to perform more repetitions is attained.

EXERCISE FOR CONGENITAL AND PATHOLOGICAL CONDITIONS

Disabilities, particularly musculoskeletal injuries, can be grouped in such a way that the individuals may be placed in groups in which similar routines of exercise can be administered to each individual within several subgroups. In congenital and pathological conditions, however, exact similarities of anomalies or malformations are not usually found. This is especially true in those handicapping conditions involving deformations of an orthopedic nature. Very specific classifications and recommendations are generally made for these situations. The exercise-routine method of administering exercises should not be utilized in most instances, because of the wide variation in the prescription for exercise. Exercises for these disabilities will require numerous modifications to meet the requirements of the medical recommendation.

Many congenital and pathological conditions have as their end result a debilitating effect. For example, extensive bed rest may cause atrophy or wasting away of the total musculature. In these cases, physical fitness may be improved through the use of progressive resistance exercises. For example, students with asthma may benefit from such a program. Of special application for these individuals is the general conditioning program presented in this chapter.

Many students with congenital and pathological conditions may benefit from the sports phase of the adapted physical education program. It is important that the individual participate in sports which are appropriate to his capabilities and limitations. Specific recommendations for programming may be found in chapter 5 in the discussion of the particular condition.

EXERCISES FOR MUSCULOSKELETAL INJURIES

One of the major tools of the adapted physical education teacher is the strength-developing exercise program. As noted previously, the major stabilizers of the joints are the muscles. Although the ligaments hold the joints together, they are primarily limiting structures at the extremes of range of motion. Once the ligaments have stretched or elongated beyond their normal length, it becomes necessary to substitute increased strength of the muscles spanning the joints. Injuries most common to joints are sprains and dislocations. In addition to injuries to ligaments, other limiting joint structures may also be torn. Inactivity from the injury, regardless of the structures injured, will usually result in muscle atrophy. Therefore, following almost every type of injury, some form of strength-developing exercise may be prescribed. The purpose of this strength development is to increase the stability of the joints in the involved areas.

The exercise routines suggested for the involved joint presented in this chapter are based upon DeLorme's progressive resistance exercise which was described in the previous chapter. Reference should be made to that chapter before administering the exercises which follow.

It is important to remember that if a body segment or joint is moved through all of the possible ranges of motion against progressively applied resistance, all of the muscles that act upon that segment or joint are being strengthened. Therefore, the selection of strength-development exercises must be based upon a thorough knowledge and consideration of movements that are possible at the joints.

Ankle

An exercise for the development of the lateral stabilizing musculature of the ankle is shown in figures 8.23 and 8.24. The individual moves his body weight up and down against resistance while standing on the balls of the feet. The addition of a two-inch-thick board under the forward aspect of the foot helps to increase the range of motion through which the ankle joint moves during the exercise. This exercise should be avoided by individuals with a tendency for weak longitudinal arches. Although this exercise is not specific for the lateral stabilizing muscles, they are involved in the action. As a result, they are strengthened in the process. To apply specific resistance to the movements of eversion and inversion of the foot at the subtalar and transverse tarsal joints requires some type of a device which provides lever action against which resistance can be applied. If this type of device is not available, the heel-raise exercise may serve as a substitute. A barbell across the shoulders may be used instead of the device illustrated. The resistance should be increased progressively.

Figure 8.23. Heel raise—Start   **Figure 8.24.** Heel raise—Finish

Knee

Stability of the knee joint is dependent largely upon muscle support. After an injury, the muscles will usually atrophy and the joint will become susceptible to further injury. Since pain reduces the desire to move the knee joint through the range of motion, it can be seen that a number of factors result in further disuse. Strength-development exercises are essential for proper rehabilitation of the knee joint. In addition, strong muscles are required to aid in preventing recurrence of injury.

An isometric knee-extensor exercise is shown in figure 8.25. The exercise is used when pain and swelling permit, but when the indi-

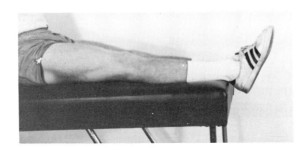

Figure 8.25. Isometric knee extensor exercise.

vidual is still unable to complete a full range of motion of the knee
through active extension. It should be performed by tensing the quadriceps muscle and holding a maximum contraction for at least ten
seconds. This action can be started by having the student attempt
to pull the patella upward. He can also attempt to push down on
the back of the knee. The knee should be held as straight as possible. Repeating this exercise once during each waking hour is recommended. Although maximum isometric strength is gained through
only a few repetitions of the exercise, additional applications of the
exercise throughout the day have other benefits such as increased
awareness of the ability to contract the muscle and lessening of pain
as a result of the contraction.

Active knee extension, that is, moving the joint through a full range
of motion without external resistance, should be started as soon as
permissible. Active knee extension is shown in figures 8.26 and 8.27.
It should be noted that a pad is placed under the knee. This pad is
for the prevention of discomfort during knee extension, particularly
when additional resistance is added. When active knee extension can
be completed at least ten times, progression of resistance should be
made by attaching a metal boot to the foot.

A metal boot strapped to the foot is shown in figures 8.28 and 8.29.
A metal bar to which metal plates may be attached to provide additional resistance is placed through the boot.

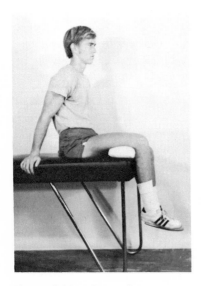 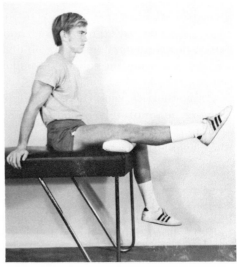

Figure 8.26. Active knee exten-   **Figure 8.27.** Active knee extension—Finish
sion—Start.

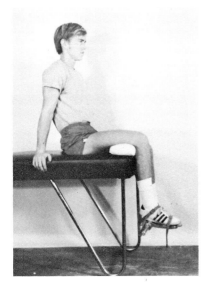 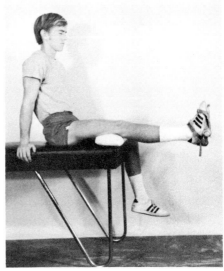

Figure 8.28. Knee extension with metal boot—Start.

Figure 8.29. Knee extension with metal boot—Finish.

Shown in figures 8.30 and 8.31 is an exercise for knee extension with metal plates attached to the boot. When the plates are thus attached, the foot should be rested on a bench or stool to prevent ex-

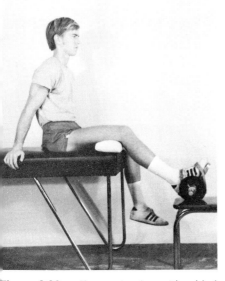 

Figure 8.30. Knee extension with added resistance—Start.

Figure 8.31. Knee extension with added resistance—Finish.

cessive strain on the knee joint before the exercise is to begin. On each repetition, the knee should be held momentarily at complete extension. Resistance should be progressively increased as tolerance permits.

In addition to the quadriceps femoris muscle group, the hamstrings muscle group and the gastrocnemius muscle also serve to stabilize the knee joint. A knee-flexion exercise is shown in figure 8.32. The exercise is started with the boot and metal plate attached to the foot with the knee extended. The weight should be moved through a range of motion to ninety degrees of flexion and returned to the starting position.

Illustrated in figure 8.33 is a heel-raise exercise which is useful in developing the strength of the gastrocnemius and soleus muscles which make up the triceps surae group. However, only the gastrocnemius muscle acts on the knee joint. The illustration shows the individual in the finish position of the exercise. From this point, he lowers himself slowly until the heels are in contact with the floor.

Increases in muscular endurance (hypertrophy) and in strength are also closely parallel in isotonic exercises. An increase in one will usually follow the other. During the application of restabilizing strength-

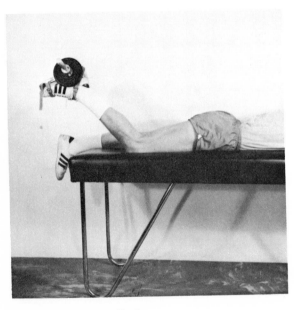

Figure 8.32. Knee flexion   **Figure 8.33.** Heel raise

developing exercises, it is advisable to measure the circumference of the thigh and calf of the injured limb for comparison to the uninjured. The measurements should be taken at approximately four inches above the upper border of the patella and approximately six inches below that point on the calf (fig. 8.34). The heel should be held approximately three to four inches above the surface on which the individual is lying in order that the muscles are in a similar state of contraction for each measurement. Continuous recording of these measurements will provide evidence of progress and also offer an opportunity for motivation of the individual.

In order to make a functional comparison of the relative strengths of the knee extensors of both limbs, the student may sit on a table with the posterior surface of his knees contacting its edge. While the knees are extended, the tester applies equal pressure just above the ankles to both limbs (fig. 8.35). The weaker of the two muscle

Figure 8.34. Girth measurement of leg and thigh.

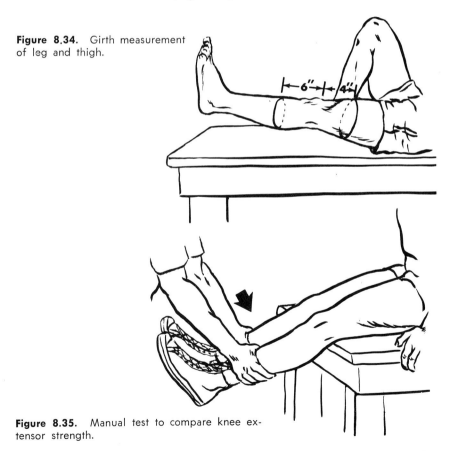

Figure 8.35. Manual test to compare knee extensor strength.

groups will "give" first. This procedure is used in making a gross determination of comparative muscle strength. When the strength is
approximately even, both limbs should be exercised against progressively increasing resistance as illustrated in figure 8.36.

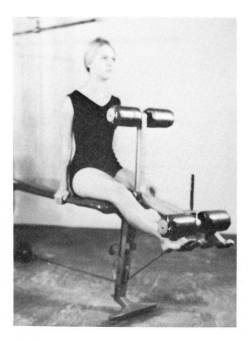

Figure 8.36. Double knee extension.

    Shown in figure 8.37 is an exercise for strengthening the ankle,
knee, and hip extensors of both limbs at the same time. When the
knees become completely extended, the feet should be pressed forward in plantar flexion in order to receive maximum strength development of the triceps surae group.

    Illustrated in figure 8.38 is a double-knee-flexion exercise. The
knees should be flexed to approximately ninety degrees on each repetition of the exercise and then returned slowly to a position of knee
extension.

Hip

Occasionally, exercises will be prescribed for common disabilities of the
hip. Resistance may be applied with weights, wall pulleys, or with
an Exer-Genie Exerciser. The device is secured in a door jamb and
is attached to the limb by way of a pulling strap. Resistance should

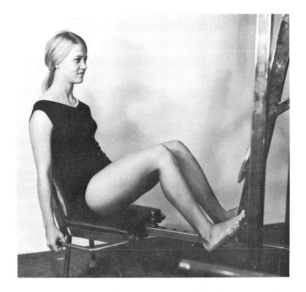

Figure 8.37. Leg extension

Figure 8.38. Double knee flexion

be increased as previously recommended. Shown in figure 8.39 is an exercise for the hip flexors. The individual should move through the range of flexion of the hip with the knee in an extended position. The body should be stabilized by placing the hand against the wall.

Illustrated in figure 8.40 is a strengthening exercise for the extensor muscles of the hip joint. The exercise should start with the hip in a position of flexion, and the part should then be moved to full extension of the hip.

Shown in figure 8.41 is an exercise for diagonal adduction of the hip joint. The starting position should be at the position of diagonal abduction and the part moved through a full range of diagonal adduction.

A resistance exercise for diagonal abduction of the hip joint is shown in figure 8.42. The exercise should be begun in a position of diagonal adduction and carried through the range of diagonal abduction.

Shown in figure 8.43 is an exercise for abduction of the joint. The limb should be moved from a position of adduction to a full range of abduction against resistance.

An exercise for hip adduction is shown in figure 8.44. The exercise should begin with the limb abducted and then moved through a full range of motion to a position of adduction.

Figure 8.39. Hip flexion

Figure 8.40. Hip extension

Figure 8.41. Hip diagonal adduction

Figure 8.42. Hip diagonal abduction

Figure 8.43. Hip abduction

Figure 8.44. Hip adduction

Resistance in the form of weights may be attached to the foot for hip exercise. However, positioning of the body to attain proper resistance against gravity is difficult with this form of resistance. As indicated previously, wall pulleys with an attachment close to the floor may serve the purpose where the application of resistance is to the foot.

Back

Two separate routines of exercises for the back are recommended and illustrated in this section. The first routine is for individuals with acute back disabilities. Obviously the tolerance of the individual for exercise at a given time during the rehabilitation of a back disability is a determining factor for the intensity of the exercise to be performed.

The first routine of back exercises is basically isometric. An abdominal and gluteal strengthening exercise is illustrated in figure 8.45. The knees should be flexed, as shown, to allow flattening of the lumbar area of the spine against the supporting surface. The upper limbs are folded across the chest. The abdominal and gluteal muscles should be contracted simultaneously to cause the pelvis to move through decreased pelvic inclination in order to force the lumbar spine downward against the surface on which the individual is lying. The number of repetitions the individual performs will depend upon his tolerance. In the early acute stages, an individual may not be able to complete one repetition held maximally for ten seconds. Approximately three ten-second repetitions should be executed as tolerance permits. The purpose of the exercise is to decrease the lumbar curvature while strengthening the muscles involved.

An abdominal isometric strengthening exercise is shown in figure 8.46. This exercise is done from a hook-lying position. In this exer-

Figure 8.45. Isometric abdominal and gluteal strengthening exercise

Figure 8.46. Isometric abdominal strengthening exercise

cise, the individual should attempt to raise his head and shoulders from the supporting surface. This position should be held momentarily and the shoulders and head then lowered slowly to the starting position. Raising the head and shoulders adds additional resistance to the abdominal muscles. It is important in the exercise that the pelvis and lumbar area remain in contact with the surface on which the individual is lying.

Figure 8.47 is an exercise for the hip flexors. The purpose of the exercise is to increase the mobility of the pelvic region. The same starting position is assumed as shown for the two previous exercises. One hip should be flexed with the thigh being brought as close to the chest as possible, held there momentarily, then returned to the starting position. This exercise should be repeated alternately with the opposite limb until the hip flexors have been exercised for ten repetitions each.

Figure 8.47. Hip flexion

An exercise for strengthening the hip extensors is shown in figure 8.48. The exercise should be begun in a position with one knee flexed to approximately ninety degrees. That limb should be raised to the position indicated and returned to the starting position. The exercise is then performed with the other limb. This exercise should be continued until ten repetitions have been performed with both lower limbs.

Figure 8.48. Flexed-knee hip extension

At the beginning of each attempt to raise the knee from the surface, the individual should simultaneously contract the abdominal muscles so that no increase in lumbar curvature will occur. The last exercise in this series is illustrated in figure 8.49. This is an isometric abdominal and gluteal strengthening exercise. It is also known as gluteal "pinching." With the individual in a prone position, an attempt should be made to strongly contract the gluteal muscles. They should be held in this state for approximately ten seconds and then allowed to relax. Tightening the abdominal muscles at the same time adds to the bene-

Figure 8.49.   Isometric abdominal and gluteal strengthening exercise

fits of this exercise. Once the previously described series of exercises can be executed without difficulty, more strenuous progressive resistance exercise should be performed. Because of the large and potentially strong muscle group such as the erector spinae, exertions of high magnitude are required to increase strength and to improve stability of the trunk. Generally, quite strenuous exercises are required for most long-term back disabilities.

The second routine of back exercises designed for strengthening the trunk musculature was adapted from the "Shelton-Back Routine" (Shelton and Logan, 1952). These exercises should be performed in the sequence indicated. The procedures for the applications of progressive resistance exercises recommended in chapter 7 should be used for these exercises. Shown in figure 8.50 is a passive hang exercise. The hanging bar should be high enough from the floor for the feet

Figure 8.50. Passive hang

to be clear from the supporting surface. The purpose of this exercise is to promote muscular relaxation and passive stretching. The individual should increase his tolerance for this exercise to a maximum of one minute of hanging.

Illustrated in figure 8.51 is an active hanging exercise. The posterior muscles of the body are contracted which results in the position illustrated. This movement should be executed without swing or momentum. A full isometric contraction should be held at the finish of the exercise before a return is made to the starting position. Time should be increased in order that the individual is able to perform three ten-second repetitions of the exercise.

A double-leg hip-extension exercise is illustrated in figures 8.52 and 8.53. The extensors of the hip and the lumbar spine are exercised.

Figure 8.52. Double-leg hip extension—Start

Figure 8.51. Active hang.

Figure 8.53. Double-leg hip extension—Finish

The lower limbs are raised simultaneously to the point where the body is in full extension as shown in figure 8.53. The knees should be kept as straight as possible. Momentum is to be avoided. The exercise should be continued according to progressive resistance exercise procedures.

An exercise primarily for the abdominal muscles is illustrated in figures 8.54 and 8.55. The exercise is started from a hook-lying position with the feet anchored by a strap as indicated. The trunk should be curled up to a sitting position. Progression should be made by the application of weight held in the hands behind the head.

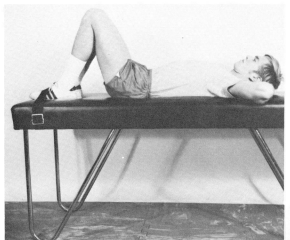

Figure 8.54. Flexed-knee sit-up—Start.

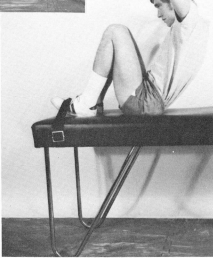

Figure 8.55. Flexed-knee sit-up—Finish.

The last of the exercises in this back routine is illustrated in figures 8.56 and 8.57. This is a back-raise exercise for the hip and back extensors. The exercise should start with the feet anchored and the hands clasped behind the head. The trunk is then raised to a horizontal position, held momentarily, and then lowered to the starting position. Resistance should be increased by the application of a weight held in the hands behind the head.

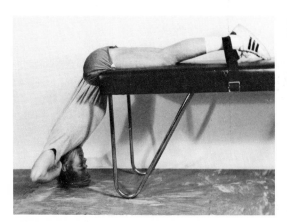

Figure 8.56. Back raise – Start.

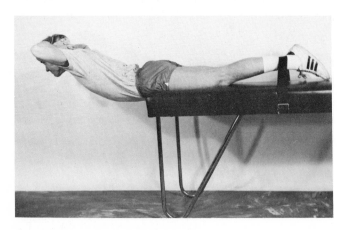

Figure 8.57. Back raise—Finish

It should be noted that these exercises are specifically *bilateral* exercises. The movements should be performed only through one plane of motion, the anteroposterior plane. For example, when the trunk raise is being performed, one shoulder may come up before the other.

This may result in undesirable rotary motion. Therefore, the individual should be instructed to move in such a way that the shoulders remain parallel to the floor throughout the exercise. Emphasis should be placed upon symmetrical development throughout the anteroposterior range of motion by executing bilateral exercises designed to strengthen the trunk musculature.

Shoulder

The following routine of shoulder exercises is designed specifically for the rehabilitation of recurrent shoulder dislocations. The difference between the program of exercises for shoulder dislocations and other shoulder disabilities is that in exercises for the shoulder dislocations, *the upper limb should not be raised above shoulder level.* If the upper limb is raised above the level of the shoulder, there is a very high probability of dislocation while the exercise is being performed, particularly in such movements as raising a weight overhead in the standing position. Exercises in which the upper limb is raised above shoulder level are contraindicated. This routine of exercises is equally useful for other disabilities of the shoulder.

A passive circumduction exercise for the shoulder joint is shown in figure 8.58. This is used for loosening the structures around the joint during the early stages of rehabilitation. A large circle is described with the arm relaxed. The other hand rests on a firm surface in order to allow the limb to describe a circle. Muscle contraction around the shoulder joint should be kept to a minimum. This motion should be performed several times, depending upon the tolerance of

Figure 8.58. Shoulder passive circumduction.

the individual in terms of pain and range of movement. A clockwise as well as a counterclockwise circle should be described.

As the shoulder joint begins to increase in mobility and the tolerance for resistance exercise increases, an exercise for the abductors of the shoulder should be performed as indicated in figures 8.59 and 8.60. In the beginning stages of resistance exercise, only the weight of the upper limb should provide the resistance. The arm should be raised and lowered as shown. Progressive resistance exercise techniques described previously for strength development should be employed. A dumbbell or other object may be held in the hand to provide resistance. Once the weight to be lifted is equal to the amount that can be lifted in the unaffected shoulder joint, the exercise should be done bilaterally with a dumbbell in each hand. Bilateral exercise helps to maintain symmetry of the muscles. Again, it should be emphasized that the limb should not be raised beyond shoulder level.

An exercise for the shoulder flexors is shown in figures 8.61 and 8.62. The limb should not be raised beyond the height indicated, should be held momentarily, then lowered to the starting position. All movements should be executed without momentum.

Shown in figures 8.63 and 8.64 is an exercise for the muscles which hyperextend the upper limb at the shoulder joint. The limb should

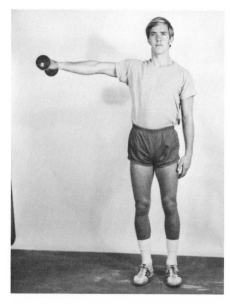

Figure 8.59. Shoulder abduction—Start.

Figure 8.60. Shoulder abduction—Finish

Figure 8.61. Shoulder flexion—Start.

Figure 8.62. Shoulder flexion—Finish.

Figure 8.63. Shoulder hyperextension—Start.

Figure 8.64. Shoulder hyperextension—Finish.

be moved as far back as possible while an erect posture is maintained.

An exercise for the muscles that elevate the shoulder girdle, called a shoulder shrug, is shown in figures 8.65 and 8.66. This is done by "hiking" the shoulder girdle against resistance. This exercise often requires greater resistance than the other exercises indicated in this routine.

Figure 8.65. Shoulder shrug—Start.

Figure 8.66. Shoulder shrug—Finish.

Shown in figure 8.67 is the finish position of an exercise for the horizontal adductor muscles at the shoulder. The start position is with the limbs horizontally abducted with the hands at about the level of the floor. From the starting position, the upper limbs are raised to the positions shown, held momentarily, then lowered to the starting position. Extensibility of the pectoral muscles is enhanced by allowing the weight to force the limbs as far toward the floor as possible. Some elbow flexion during the exercise may be necessary in order to stabilize that joint. Therefore, more resistance can be applied specifically to the shoulder joint.

The finish position of an exercise for the scapular adductors is shown in figure 8.68. The scapular adductor muscles are activated and muscles

Figure 8.67. Shoulder horizontal adduction—Finish.

Figure 8.68. Shoulder horizontal abduction—Finish.

which perform horizontal abduction of the shoulder joint will also be maximally contracted. The starting position for this exercise is with the hands near the floor. It is especially important for the individual to raise the limb as high as possible on each repetition. This is also an important postural exercise.

An exercise for the muscles which rotate the humerus medially and laterally is illustrated in figures 8.69, 8.70, and 8.71. The starting position for this exercise is indicated in figure 8.69. The elbow is flexed to ninety degrees. The shoulder is abducted to ninety degrees. The anterior aspect of the shoulder joint should be in contact with the edge of the table or bench. The humerus should be rotated medially while the shoulder remains in contact with the bench as shown

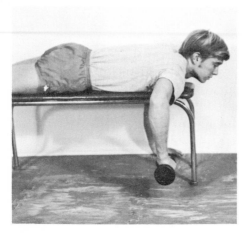

Figure 8.69. Shoulder rotation—Start.

Figure 8.70. Shoulder medial rotation—Finish.

Figure 8.71. Shoulder lateral rotation—Finish.

in figure 8.70. After performing medial rotation according to progressive resistance techniques, the arm should then be exercised through lateral rotation which is indicated in figure 8.71. It is particularly important that the humerus be rotated on its longitudinal axis. Adduction and abduction of this part should not be performed. In laterally rotating the upper arm as illustrated, it may *appear* that the restriction of not raising the weight above shoulder level is contraindicated; it should be remembered that the *upper* arm should not be raised above shoulder level. This type of exercise should not be executed in any other position than that illustrated here.

Elbow

Shown in figures 8.72 and 8.73 is an exercise for developing the strength of the elbow extensors. When strength of the involved limb reaches that of the uninvolved limb, the exercise should be done with both upper limbs. The "overhead press" exercise, described in the section on general conditioning, is recommended.

Figure 8.72. Elbow extension—Start.

Figure 8.73. Elbow extension—Finish.

An elbow flexor strengthening exercise (biceps curl) is shown in figures 8.74 and 8.75. Once the limbs are of equal strength, a barbell utilizing both upper limbs should be used. In performing the barbell exercise, it is suggested that the individual stand with his back against the wall. His heels should be approximately six inches from the wall to prevent him from using momentum of the trunk to aid in elbow flexion.

Figure 8.74. Elbow flexion—Start   **Figure 8.75.** Elbow flexion—Finish

Wrist

An exercise for the wrist flexors is shown in figures 8.76 and 8.77. If one wrist is weaker than the other, it is recommended that a dumbbell be used until the strength of the wrist flexors becomes equal. Thereafter, a barbell should be used as illustrated.

Illustrated in figures 8.78 and 8.79 is an exercise for the extensors of the wrist. The wrist extensors tend to be proportionately weaker than the wrist flexors. Adjustments should be made, therefore, in terms of the resistance applied. Progressive resistance procedures should be applied, increasing the weight as tolerance for further exercise permits.

Figure 8.76. Wrist flexion—Start

Figure 8.77. Wrist flexion—Finish

Figure 8.78. Wrist extension—Start

Figure 8.79. Wrist extension
—Finish.

199

Neck

Due to the increasing number of rear-end automobile collisions, injuries to the cervical and thoracic regions are on the increase. Once the acute symptoms have been relieved by other therapeutic measures, an exercise program is usually instituted. The following exercises consist of isometrically contracting the muscles of the neck in all planes of motion against resistance offered by the individual's own hand or hands (Randall, 1963). Most often, this form of exercise is used to relieve the pain of muscle "tension" and to develop strength. The individual often complains of severe headaches after such an injury. These headaches often interfere with his attention, particularly for the student in a classroom. The exercises can be performed inconspicuously because they are basically isometric in nature and can be repeated several times against the individual's own maximum resistance which is manually applied. Sitting at a classroom desk with the forehead resting in the hand, the forehead is pressed against the hand. Next, with the elbow resting on the desk and the hand against the side of the face, the individual should forcefully attempt to turn the head to the right and then to the left. The face is pressed alternately toward the hand which offers the resistance. There should be no visible movement of the head. The next exercise is with the fingers clasped together behind the head. The head should be forced back toward the hands without any movement. This should be repeated several times.

EXERCISE PROGRAM FOR GENERAL CONDITIONING

There are many disabling conditions and divergencies which require a program of development exercises. The following is a selected series of exercises which are recommended for the development of endurance, flexibility, and strength. Although other exercises may be utilized for general conditioning, those included are considered essential to such a program.

The order in which endurance, flexibility, and strength exercises are performed during the exercise session is important. General endurance exercises involving total body movement should be performed prior to other types of specific exercise. Increasing the rate and duration of gross movement results in an improvement of the cardiovascular mechanism. In addition, this form of exercise enhances total body warm-up.

Flexibility exercises should follow endurance or warm-up procedures. It is generally held that increased cardiovascular activity which increases bodily temperature helps to increase connective tissue pliability. The potential for improved flexibility, therefore, appears greater. It is also believed that a general elevation in body temperature tends to decrease the possibility of injury while stretching is being performed. Strength-development exercises should follow flexibility exercises which have been preceded by endurance exercises designed for general warm-up.

Although only two endurance warm-up exercises are suggested here, many other similar activities may suffice as well. It is important that the exercise involve total body movement which results in a rapid elevation of circulatory responses in a short period of time. Endurance warm-up exercises should be continued until a feeling of breathlessness or a state of mild fatigue is induced.

Illustrated in figure 8.80 is an individual "running in place." The knees should be lifted as high as possible, with the elbows held at approximately a ninety-degree angle. An attempt should be made to touch the knee to the hands on each step. Running, in this case running in place, is perhaps the best endurance or warm-up procedure.

An endurance warm-up exercise involving primarily the lower trunk and lower limbs is shown in figure 8.81. The knees and hips are alternately flexed and extended from a pushup position with the arms

Figure 8.80. Running in place   **Figure 8.81.** Alternate knee and hip flexion.

held straight. The hands should remain in the starting position throughout the exercise. The rate at which the exercise is performed should be increased as tolerance for further exercise increases.

Flexibility Development Exercises

Flexibility exercises are designed to increase the range of motion in the areas in which limitations of movement frequently occur because of inactivity. Although the exercises in the following series are designed to increase the flexibility of the connective tissue in areas which are most frequently limited by adapted shortening, not all of them need be executed during each session. The hamstrings, lower back and upper back, and neck stretching exercises should be performed during each exercise period. These exercises should be repeated slowly five to ten times. The stretch should be continued to the point of discomfort and slightly beyond on each repetition on each flexibility exercise.

Shown in figures 8.82 and 8.83 is a hamstring stretching exercise performed in the sitting position. With the trunk flexed as far as possible, the knees should be extended until they are as straight as

Figure 8.82. Hamstring stretch, sitting—Start.

Figure 8.83. Hamstring stretch, sitting—Finish.

possible. An alternate position for this exercise is illustrated in figures 8.84 and 8.85. The hands should remain in contact with the floor as the knees are extended as far as possible as shown in figure 8.85.

Figure 8.84. Hamstring stretch, standing—Start.

Figure 8.85. Hamstring stretch, standing—Finish.

An exercise for specific application of stretch to one hamstring muscle group (Billig) is illustrated in figures 8.86 and 8.87. The placement of the arms is merely for the maintenance of balance. The left leg should be held as straight as possible while the right leg is placed in front of it. The individual should bend slowly from the waist with the left elbow projecting diagonally downward. This exercise should be repeated to the opposite side.

Figure 8.86. Hamstring stretch (Billig)—Start.

Figure 8.87. Hamstring stretch (Billig)—Finish.

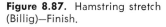

An exercise for stretching the adductor muscles of the hip joint is shown in figure 8.88. With the feet drawn as closely to the body as possible, the individual should press forcibly down on the knee joints as shown.

The flexibility exercise (Billig) shown in figures 8.89 and 8.90 is designed for increasing the extensibility of fascial ligamentous bands in the low back and anterior pelvis. This exercise is particularly beneficial for females with painful and/or difficult menstruation (dysmenorrhea). The forearm should be placed against a wall at shoulder

Figure 8.88. Adductor stretch.

level. The hand is placed just behind the opposite hip joint. With the knees straight and gluteal and abdominal muscles strongly contracted, the pelvis should be forced diagonally forward and to the opposite side.

Figure 8.89. Pelvic stretch (Billig)—Start.

Figure 8.90. Pelvic stretch (Billig)—Finish.

The lower-back stretching exercises are shown in figures 8.91 and 8.92. They may be done either sitting on the floor or on a chair. The exercise involves pulling the trunk forward and downward with the abdominal muscles. Flexing the knees in this position allows a more effective stretch in the region of the lumbar spine.

Figure 8.91. Lower-back stretch.

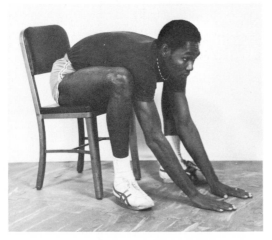

Figure 8.92. Lower-back stretch.

Illustrated in figure 8.93 is an upper-back and neck flexibility exercise. The upper extremities should be forced downward against the floor while an effort is made to touch the toes to the floor with the knees extended as shown. It is important that the pelvis be as far over the head as possible. An alternate procedure which involves almost the same movement is for the lower limbs to be held in the air, while being alternately flexed and extended with the pelvis supported by the hands.

Illustrated in figures 8.94 and 8.95 is a spinal rotation stretching exercise performed while in a sitting position. The pull of the hands

Figure 8.93. Upper-back and neck stretch

Figure 8.94. Spinal rotation stretch, sitting—Start.

Figure 8.95. Spinal rotation stretch, sitting—Finish.

Figure 8.96. Spinal rotation stretch, standing.

against the thigh adds the force necessary to cause rotation of the trunk. A special effort should be made to rotate the head during the stretch in order to increase the mobility in the cervical area.

Shown in figure 8.96 is an alternate exercise—spinal rotation stretching in the standing position. In the standing position, an attempt should be made to twist the spine in such a way that the individual may look over the shoulder toward the heel of the opposite foot. The motion should be continued as far as possible to both sides.

Strength-Development Exercises

The ten exercises which follow are designed for the development of strength. The exercises are sit-up, back raise, leg extension, heel raise, bench press, scapular adduction, biceps curl, erect row, overhead press, and latissimus pull. For each exercise, three methods of applying resistance are shown. The first illustration utilizes the application of weights, the second employs the Exer-Genie Exerciser, and the third involves the use of the Universal Gym. The progressive resistance exercise procedures outlined in chapter 7 should be used when performing these exercises.

The flexed-knee sit-up on the slant board with a five-pound weight held behind the head is shown in figure 8.97. This exercise for individuals with low tolerance should be started from a flexed-knee position on a horizontal surface with no resistance behind the head. As tolerance increases, the slant board may be increased in elevation in addition to resistance held behind the head. It should be noted that the trunk is "curled" up to the sitting position. This tends to exert more force on the abdominal muscles as compared to the hip flexors. Figure 8.98 illlustrates the same exercise using the Exer-Genie Exerciser attached to a door jamb. In figure 8.99, the flexed-knee sit-up

Figure 8.97. Flexed-knee sit-up on slant board with weight behind head.

Figure 8.98. Flexed knee sit-up.

Figure 8.99. Flexed-knee sit-up on slant board.

is being executed without resistance behind the head on the Universal Gym slant board.

The back-raise exercise is illustrated in figure 8.100. This is a strengthener for the back and hip extensor muscles. With the feet anchored as shown, the fingers should be clasped together behind the head. The trunk is then elevated to a horizontal position. A momentary hesitation should be made at the horizontal position in the range of motion. The trunk should then be lowered to the starting position. As tolerance for this exercise increases, a weight should be placed behind the head for additional resistance. Of all the exercises in the general conditioning program, the greatest improvement can be expected in the back raise. This phenomenon suggests that the strength of the back in most people is below that which may be required when maximum effort is desired. It may also explain the high incidence of back disabilities in unconditioned individuals. Shown in figure 8.101 is a back-extension exercise utilizing the Exer-Genie Exerciser with the device anchored in a door jamb. The individual extends at the hips until the body is in a horizontal position. The individual then returns to a sitting position and continues to execute the exercise with the other set of pulling handles as shown. In figure 8.102, the back raise is shown being performed on a slant board of the Universal Gym. The difficulty of the exercise is advanced by increasing the angle of the slant board in relation to the floor.

Leg-extension exercises are shown in figures 8.103, 8.104, and 8.105. Illustrated in figure 8.103 is an exercise for the extensors of the ankle, knees, and hips in which the individual straddles a barbell. The hands should be spread to permit balancing of the weight. The back should be held as straight as possible throughout the exercise. When the weight is lifted, the action should be at the ankles, knees, and hips only. Back movements should be held to a minimum. This exercise is less hazardous than the often used "squat" exercise in which the barbell is placed across the shoulders. Also, assistance is not required to place the weight on the shoulders at the beginning of the exercise and to remove it at the termination of the exercise. Figure 8.104 shows the use of the Exer-Genie Exerciser for the development of the ankle, knee, and hip extensors. Shown in figure 8.105 is leg extension utilizing the Universal Gym for resistance.

A heel-raise exercise for the development of the triceps surae muscle group is shown in figures 8.106, 8.107 and 8.108. In order to provide a greater range of motion for the ankle, a board should be placed under the balls of the feet as shown.

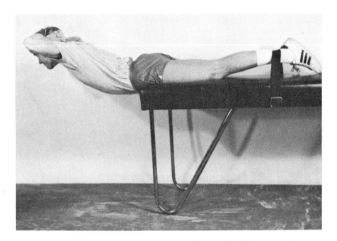

Figure 8.100. Back raise

Figure 8.101. Back extension

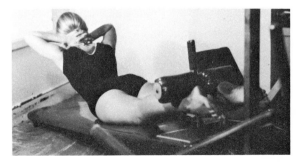

Figure 8.102. Back raise on slant board

Figure 8.103. Leg extension

Figure 8.104. Leg extension

Figure 8.105. Leg extension

Figure 8.106. Heel raise

Figure 8.107. Heel raise

Figure 8.108. Heel raise

An exercise primarily for the development of the elbow extensors is shown in figures 8.109, 8.110, and 8.111. An exercise done with a barbell or the Universal Gym is the traditional bench press. This exercise also includes development of the pectoralis major. The wider the hands are spread on the bar, the more stress will be placed on the pectoral muscles. A narrow grip places a greater stress on the triceps brachii muscles. Assistance may be required in order to place the barbells into the starting position. The exercise shown with the Exer-Genie Exerciser is primarily concentrated within the triceps brachii group.

A postural antigravity exercise involving the scapular adductors is illustrated in figures 8.112, 8.113, and 8.114. This exercise involves the application of resistance to the middle trapezius and rhomboid muscles.

An exercise for strengthening the elbow flexors is shown in figures 8.115, 8.116 and 8.117. The action included in this biceps curl may be performed also with the palms downward. This variation provides strengthening exercise for additional muscles involved in this area. There is little difference, however, between these two positions in regard to the action that takes place at the elbow joint. When a barbell is used for resistance, it is suggested that the individual stand with the heels approximately six inches from the wall and with his back to the wall. This position prevents backward swinging of the trunk as the movement of elbow flexion is performed.

An erect rowing exercise is illustrated in figures 8.118, 8.119, and 8.120. The finish position is shown in all three illustrations. An erect position should be maintained throughout the exercise. This exercise is designed primarily to strengthen the deltoid muscles. The abdominal muscles should be contracted in such a way as to maintain firm trunk stability throughout the motion.

An overhead press exercise which is designed to develop the strength in the shoulder area is shown in figures 8.121, 8.122, and 8.123. This exercise involves resistance from shoulder level to a position as far overhead as possible. Stability of the pelvis should be maintained throughout the exercise by a strong contraction of the abdominal and gluteal muscles. When using weight as resistance, the sitting position is preferred to standing, because it affords greater safety for those individuals who may have a tendency toward back disabilities.

An exercise for strengthening the latissimus dorsi muscle is illustrated in figures 8.124, 8.125, and 8.126. The exercise shown in the first of these illustrations is a bent-arm pullover. The start of the exercise is with the bar at about the level of the top of the head. The weight should then be drawn forward and upward in an arc-type motion while the elbows are simultaneously extended. The exercise

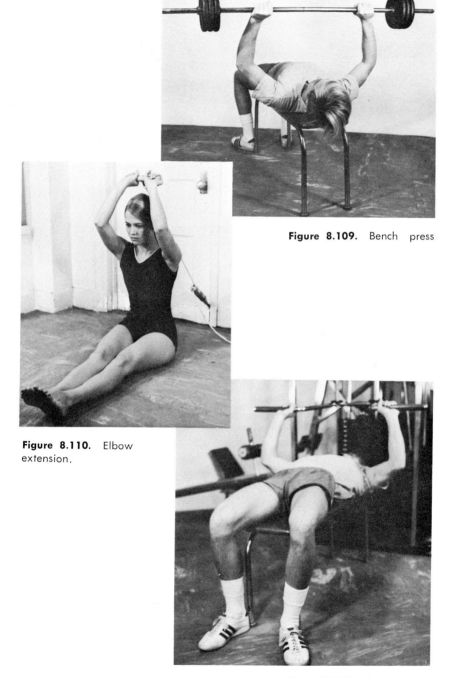

Figure 8.109. Bench press

Figure 8.110. Elbow extension.

Figure 8.111. Bench press

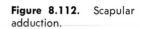

Figure 8.112. Scapular adduction.

Figure 8.113. Scapular adduction.

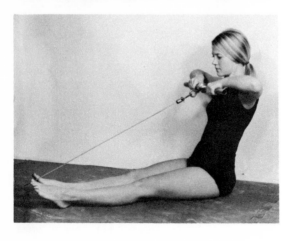

Figure 8.114. Scapular adduction.

Figure 8.115. Biceps curl

Figure 8.116. Biceps curl

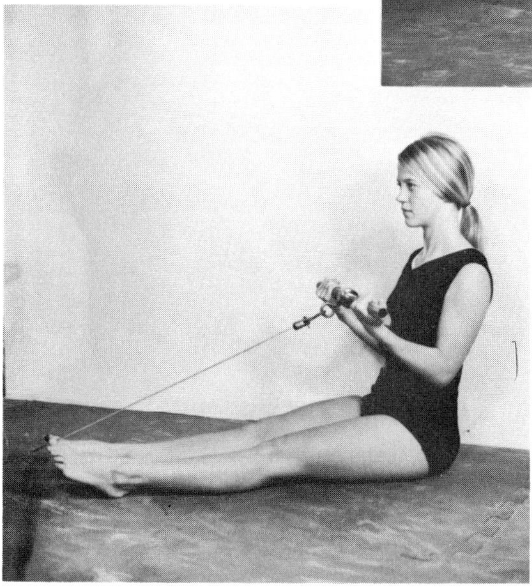

Figure 8.117. Biceps curl

Figure 8.118. Erect row

Figure 8.119. Erect row

Figure 8.120. Erect row

Figure 8.121. Overhead press

Figure 8.122. Overhead press

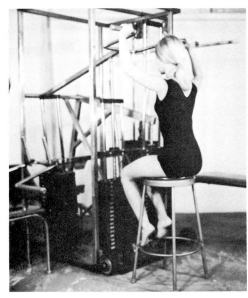

Figure 8.123. Overhead press

Figure 8.124. Pull-over

Figure 8.125. Latissimus pull.

Figure 8.126. Latissimus pull

should terminate when the weight has reached the highest point in the arc. An alternative to this exercise is to perform approximately the same motions with the elbows held in an extended position throughout the arc of motion. Excessive resistance should be avoided at the initiation of the exercise because the joint structures of the shoulder are in an unfavorable position to maintain joint integrity. The second illustration with the Exer-Genie Exerciser involves starting with the arms extended overhead. With the elbows straight, the arc of motion should continue until the hands are at approximately the level of the waist. When the Universal Gym is used, as shown in figure 8.126, the exercise is begun with the arms extended overhead and finished with the bar either behind or in front of the head. A variation of this exercise is with the bar being pulled through a full arc of motion in front of the body similar to the exercise illustrated in figure 8.125.

SELECTED REFERENCES

1. *Corrective Physical Education: Teaching Guide for Junior and Senior High Schools*. Pub. No. SC-566. Los Angeles City School, Division of Instructional Services.
2. DeLorme, Thomas L., and Watkins, Arthur L. *Progressive Resistance Exercise*. New York: Appleton-Century-Crofts Inc., 1951.
3. Falls, Harold B.; Wallis, Earl L.; and Logan, Gene A. *Foundations of Conditioning*. New York: Academic Press, Inc., 1970.
4. Flint, M. Marilyn, and Diehl, Bobbie. "Influence of Abdominal Strength, Back Extensor Strength and Trunk Strength Balance upon Antero-Posterior Alignment of Elementary School Girls." *Research Quarterly* 32 (December 1961): 490, 498.
5. Kraus, Hans. *Therapeutic Exercise*. Springfield, Ill.: Charles C Thomas, 1949.
6. Licht, Sidney, ed. *Therapeutic Exercise*. 2nd ed. New Haven, Conn.: Elizabeth Licht, 1965.
7. Logan, Gene A. *Adaptations of Muscular Activity*. Belmont, Calif.: Wadsworth Publishing Co., Inc., 1964.
8. ———. "Therapeutic Muscular Activity in the Adapted Physical Education Class." Paper presented at the National Convention, American Association for Health, Physical Education and Recreation, Chicago, Illinois, 1966.
9. Lowman, Charles LeRoy, and others. *Corrective Physical Education for Groups*. New York: A. S. Barnes and Co., 1928.
10. Metheny, Eleanor. *Body Dynamics*. New York: McGraw-Hill Book Co., Inc., 1952.
11. Randall, Leila C. Personal communication. University of Southern California, 1963.
12. Rasch, Philip J., and Burke, Roger K. *Kinesiology and Applied Anatomy*. 3rd ed. Philadelphia: Lea & Febiger, 1967.
13. Shelton, Robert E., and Logan Gene A. "Internal Derangements of the Knee and Common Back Disabilities." Paper presented to the

Midwest Convention, American Association for Health, Physical Education and Recreation, Cincinnati, Ohio, 1952.

14. ——–. "Therapeutic Exercise for Common Disabilities of the Back, Shoulder, Knee and Ankle." Paper presented to the National Convention, American Association for Health, Physical Education and Recreation, New York, New York, 1954.

15. WALLIS, EARL L., and LOGAN, GENE A. *Exercise for Children.* Englewood Cliffs, N. J.: Prentice-Hall, Inc., 1966.

16. ——–. *Figure Improvement and Body Conditioning through Exercise.* Englewood Cliffs, N. J.: Prentice-Hall, Inc., 1964.

sports in the adapted physical education program

The adapted physical education program consists primarily of therapeutic exercise and several activities falling under the heading of sports. The sports phase of the program may include sports, games, rhythms, and aquatic activities.

A student can benefit from his participation in the sports phase of the adapted physical education program regardless of the cause of his divergency. If he is attempting to adapt himself to a permanent disability or is participating in the program because of a recommendation for limited physical activity, the sports phase of the program may best serve his specific requirements.

The sports program should offer a wide variety of activities. These activities should be selected consistent with the skill level of the individual. Physical activities which provide the greatest carry-over value for leisure-time pursuits should be offered in this phase of adapted physical education.

SPORTS PROGRAMMING

The diagnosis and medical recommendation of the physician establish the boundaries within which the student's activities may be planned, directed, and supervised by the adapted physical education teacher. The important role played by the physician in establishing limits within which the instructor must function requires that a clear line of communication exist between the instructor and the physician. The complexity of the physical limitations of atypical students often necessitates a two-way interchange of information in order that the physician's recommendations be properly administered.

223

At the time of the student-instructor conference, the instructor should gain as much information and understanding of the student's previous experience as possible. This information is essential in order to be able to determine the skill level attained by the student. At the conference with the student, his interests in specific physical activities should be determined. Furthermore, it should be ascertained whether or not he has had an opportunity to participate with "normal" individuals of his own age.

The comparison of the types of activities offered in the sports phase of the adapted physical education program and those used in regular physical education should show little, if any, difference. *The aim of adapted physical education should be to prepare the student to return to participation in the regular physical education program.* Therefore, the sports phase of the adapted physical education program must make use of the activities of the regular physical education program. However, due to the lack of opportunity for skill development in many handicapped children, it is often necessary to provide activities within the adapted physical education program that are not generally offered in the regular program. The adapted physical education teacher must be truly interested in providing activities for specific motor development levels which are at the same time interesting, pleasurable, and challenging to the student.

In planning the adapted physical education program, the instructor must determine what the student can do within his particular physical limitations. The instructor must consider (1) the activities in which the student's peers are participating and (2) how he can best provide a program which will allow the student to participate in the same or similar activities.

In general, the task of the adapted physical education teacher involves studying each individual's interests, aptitudes, and abilities in order that the activities of the regular physical education program can be adapted to his requirements. The most difficult phase in the adaptation of physical activities to the individual centers around four limitations often imposed by the student's physical condition. These are (1) lack of strength, (2) lack of flexibility, (3) lack of endurance, and (4) lack of skill development.

Every effort should be made in planning the sports program to offer activities that are suited to the students enrolled at a particular time. In order to attempt to meet the individual and group objectives of the students, a large degree of latitude must be maintained to provide an effective program.

Because the handicapped individual has more failures with which to contend than do his peers, every opportunity should be provided for success. Although these successes may be small and gradual, they can provide encouragement and motivation. These are essential for optimum development of the student. On the other hand, it should not become obvious to the student that their "successes" are being handed to them without their genuine achievement. Progress must be made through the efforts of the individual. The teacher's role is to establish the proper setting and aid the student in this process.

SPORTS SELECTION CRITERIA

Sports included in the adapted physical education program should be selected on the basis of two general groups of criteria. The first is that all sports and activities should meet the criteria established for any sound physical education program. The second group include those criteria which should be followed for the specific adaptation of activities for physically handicapped students:

1. sports which are appropriate to the student's age and interests,
2. sports which are in accordance with the physician's diagnosis and recommendations,
3. sports which are within the limits of the student's physical disability,
4. *sports which do not require extensive adaptation of rules or major changes in the nature of the activity,* and
5. sports which are applicable to the greatest number of students with regard to their various physical disabilities.

The adapted physical education program should provide for gradual progression from the simplest level of performance that the individual's physical limitations and previous experience permit to the highest level of performance he is able to achieve. Basic skills should be stressed since most of these students will not have had an opportunity to develop skill previously. Sports should be offered that provide the most carry-over value. The students should be made aware of the value of sports participation during the rest of their lifetime.

An effort should be directed toward the goal of providing experiences in a variety of dual, group, or team games and sports. It is through participation in group activities that the student is given the opportunity for the development of desirable social characteristics. To that end, participation in coeducational adapted physical education is of great value. Handicapped individuals often are segregated because of their particular disability. Therefore, group participation provides an opportunity for identification, recognition, and approval by other individuals. Activities which provide an opportunity for socialization should receive major emphasis in the adapted physical education program.

Participation in carefully selected activities of the sports phase of the program can provide the handicapped student with an opportunity for relief of the "tension" of modern living. This may result, in part, from a momentary rearrangement of the student's emotional life. Satisfactions may be attained in sports participation which are often denied in other areas of the student's life.

The sports phase of the program must provide an opportunity for the student to develop and utilize those interests, understandings, and skills which will permit him to participate safely and successfully with his non-handicapped peers. It should be reemphasized that the ultimate goal of the adapted physical education program is to return the handicapped student to the regular physical education program.

SELECTED REFERENCES

1. *Corrective Physical Education: Teaching Guide for Junior and Senior High Schools.* Pub. No. SC-566. Los Angeles City Schools, Division of Instructional Services.
2. DANIELS, ARTHUR S., and DAVIES, EVELYN A. *Adapted Physical Education.* 2nd ed. New York: Harper & Row, Publishers, 1965.
3. FAIT, HOLLIS F. *Special Physical Education.* 2nd ed. Philadelphia: The W. B. Saunders Co., 1966.
4. HUNT, VALERIE V. *Recreation for the Handicapped.* Englewood Cliffs, N. J.: Prentice-Hall, Inc., 1955.
5. KLAFS, CARL E. "Rhythmic Activities for Handicapped Children." Paper presented to the Southwest District Convention, American Association for Health, Physical Education and Recreation, Long Beach, California, 1957.
6. LOGAN, GENE A. *Adaptations of Muscular Activity.* Belmont, Calif.: Wadsworth Publishing Co., Inc. 1964.
7. MATHEWS, DONALD K.; KRUSE, ROBERT; and SHAW, VIRGINIA. *The Science of Physical Education for Handicapped Children.* New York: Harper & Row, Publishers, 1962.
8. STAFFORD, GEORGE T. *Sports for the Handicapped.* 2nd ed. New York: Prentice-Hall, Inc., 1947.
9. STONE, ELEANOR B., and DEYTON, JOHN W. *Corrective Therapy for the Handicapped Child.* Englewood Cliffs, N. J.: Prentice-Hall, Inc., 1951.

organization and administration of the adapted physical education program

Organization concerns the phase of educational planning that attempts to discover and answer questions concerning the nature and scope of the proposed program. It considers such broad areas as (1) the need for the program, (2) the kinds of students to be served, and (3) the specialized services which may be needed in order to implement the program. Organization may be thought of as consisting of a series of information-finding steps that are prerequisite to administration.

Administration concerns that phase of educational planning that attempts to implement the instructional program proposed by the organizational process. It involves the development of policies and procedures which are designed to provide guides and rules for the conduct of the instructional program. It includes such functions as (1) scheduling of several classes, (2) selection and assignment of the instructional staff, (3) class organization, and (4) the utilization of the facilities and equipment provided for the program. Its effectiveness can be determined only by how well it assists in increasing or improving the service to the individual student.

ORGANIZATION

Adapted Physical Education and the Regular Physical Education Program

Adapted physical education is a phase of regular physical education. This means that the activities, equipment, and facilities provided for the regular physical education program are also used in the adapted physical education program. Both of these programs must be carefully planned and directed to provide a wide variety of physical activity. The regular physical education program is designed to serve those students who lack physical handicaps. Adapted physical education, on the other hand, is designed for those students who may not safely or successfully participate in the regular physical education program because of physical limitations.

The adapted physical education student may participate in many of the activities in which their non-handicapped peers participate. However, it is necessary that their activities be modified in most cases. Thus, the adapted physical education program is an individually prescribed program of physical education.

Determining the Requirements of Students

The first step in organizing an adapted physical education program is the determination of the requirement for such a program. This involves the determination of the types and frequencies of handicapping conditions which limit the students' physical activity. These students must be identified for possible assignment to the adapted physical education program.

Many schools excuse handicapped students from physical education altogether because the institution does not provide an adapted physical education program. Every school has students who are unable to participate in the regular physical education program. These students may require temporary or permanent exemption from physical education.

All possible sources must be used to gain information to determine the requirement for an adapted physical education program. Before such a survey is conducted to make this determination, administrative approval must be secured. Cooperation from the staff of the school health services division is essential to acquire such information.

In school districts that require periodic physical examinations, information may be gained from an accumulative health record which is maintained for each student. Such a record is essential for gathering information to determine which of those students may benefit from an adapted physical education program.

Unfortunately, some school districts do not require physical examinations. Furthermore, they do not maintain health records for their students. Occasionally, they may have records for those students who have recently had an examination in order to determine the possible existence of physical disability. In this situation, establishment of an adapted physical education program may be difficult.

Other efforts should be made to gain as much information as possible from the existing health records maintained by the school. Through a review of the available records, it is possible to determine which students may be assigned to the adapted physical education program. Also, it is possible to determine the kind and frequency of the physical handicaps of these students.

Another approach that may be used is to request the student guidance counselors to report the names of all students, whom they advise, who are not participating in physical education. This will provide a list which may be checked against the health records.

A personal interview or group meeting with those students who have been excused from regular physical education can provide some information. At the outset, the students should be informed as to the purpose of the survey. It is important to emphasize positive aspects of the survey. The student should be requested to give information concerning the nature and extent of his disability and the limitations it imposes on his physical activity. The students should be asked to identify their family physician in order that a more complete and accurate compilation of information may be attained. The student's physician may then be contacted and information attained through a questionnaire or checklist.

Such a survey will identify students who should not participate in regular physical education. It should also provide information concerning the kinds of conditions which limit or prohibit vigorous physical activity. These conditions may then be classified or grouped into various diagnoses and frequencies to reveal the physical limitations and requirements of those students for whom the proposed program is being provided.

Soliciting Medical Cooperation

It is essential to secure adequate medical cooperation because adapted physical education is a program of physical activities for students with physical limitations. The major weakness of most adapted physical education programs is due to lack of adequate medical supervision.

Too often the teacher is required to determine the physical status of the student. The teacher is requested to select students to be enrolled in the adapted physical education program and to decide the specific activities for each person. This requires the teacher of adapted physical education to assume responsibilities which are beyond the scope of his training and professional authority. He is forced into the situation to determine the individual's deviations. The teacher must also determine those activities which he feels will be beneficial to the students' disability.

Only the physician is professional and legally qualified to determine the cause and implication of the student's adaptations. It is true that the physical educator is trained to observe marked adaptations of posture and to determine the demands and benefits of physical activity; however, he must not be asked to go beyond his authority. The teacher should refer to a physician those students who, in his opinion, vary from the norm to such an extent that it is questionable whether they may participate safely or successfully in the regular physical education program. The physician then determines the nature and extent of the student's disability. It is the physician's diagnosis and his recommendations that provide the basis for a sound program of adapted physical education.

The physical educator must assume the initiative for securing the needed medical supervision for the adapted physical education program. The family physician frequently is not well informed concerning the physical education program that is offered in a specific school district. The process of submitting a list of activities and requesting the physician to check those activities in which the student may participate is questionable. The physician's recommendation is only as valid as his knowledge of the school program.

Physicians often provide broad exemptions from all physical education. This is due in many cases to a lack of knowledge of the activities which are offered in a given program. In order to prevent a situation such as this, a method should be established for informing physicians about the activities which comprise the program. Information should be made available which indicates the degree of intensity of physical demands of the activities as well as the nature and purposes of the proposed adapted physical education program. Such information will assist the physician in providing a more specific recommendation within which the physical educator can work.

Often the physician is also unaware of the training or interest of those physical educators who conduct physical education classes for the handicapped. Furthermore, he often believes that the program is rigidly constructed and that specific recommendations from him are beyond the scope of the program. It is imperative that the liaison personnel between the physical education program and the physician convey the concepts and offerings of the program. Emphasis must be placed upon the requirements for the physician's cooperation with the program. The physician's cooperation is basic in order that the student receive maximum benefits from participation in the program.

If the physical educator and the school cannot secure the cooperation of the private physician alone, incorporated into this effort may be the school nurse, school physician, or consulting physician. Securing the private physician's cooperation is not an attempt to minimize the valuable assistance of the school health personnel. Their aid is needed in planning the proposed program. It is, however, an attempt to point out that after medical assistance and development of the program have been completed, the school health personnel must provide the guidance and responsibility for informing their colleagues about the adapted physical education program.

In those schools where school physicians are provided, the physician's cooperation is essential to the organization of the adapted physical education program. The physician should be requested to assist in the formulation of the policies and procedures concerning the selection and assignment of students to classes in adapted physical education. These should include policies and procedures concerning the responsibility for the determination or diagnosis of the student's physical status. The physician should help determine whether the examination is to be conducted by him or by his associates or by the student's private physician. A policy clearly indicating his responsibility for the assignment of students to the program, as well as the procedure for handling recommendations for physical activity, should be developed. His guidance should also be requested for the kinds of activities and specific exercises which may be used in the adapted physical education program. The sports phase of the program to be included in the adapted physical education program should be developed by the physical educator and approved by the school physician. Ideally, the physician and the physical educator may design a program together.

The problem of securing medical direction and supervision of adapted physical education in those instances where there is no designated school physician is difficult. Fortunately, many schools do provide a school nurse. Although the nurse cannot provide the needed medical guidance for the program, she is often able to assist in providing the initial contact with the physicians in the community. If neither a school physician nor a school nurse is provided, the physical educator must assume the responsibility for contacting local physicians to secure a physician who is willing to serve as a consultant for the adapted physical education program. This may be on a voluntary basis.

Another approach to securing the needed medical direction is to contact the various medical associations and health departments at the local, county, or state levels. They frequently have established procedures for providing their services to schools. Regardless of the manner in which the needed guidance is provided, the individual physician should be one who is vitally interested in physical education.

Classifying Physical Status of the Student

As previously indicated, the physician's diagnosis and recommendations serve as a basis for adapted physical education. Once the prescribing physician has been informed of the purpose of the program, it is essential to provide some method by which the medical or physical status of the student may be classified. The need for the physican's recommendations concerning the nature of the limitations which his diagnosis imposes upon the student's physical activity program is of utmost importance. A classification code should be developed and utilized by the physician which will provide the physical educator with the basic information that is necessary to plan and direct an adapted physical education program. A classification code which indicates specific limitations imposed by every kind of divergency is of little value. It is too involved and too lengthy for practical application. Therefore, the medical classification code for physical education should consist of generalized limitations which could be imposed by any one of several divergencies.

The classification code categories should be based upon careful analysis of the various physical handicaps. Similarity of specific limitations imposed by each kind of divergency provides a basis upon which categories could be formed. Thus, the nature of the student's limitation serves as a basis for planning his individual program of physical activity. Such categories might include one that would indicate that the individual should limit his energy output; another category would indicate that the individual should not participate in any physical activity which by its nature would expose the individual to trauma; another category would be that in which the individual is to avoid those activities that would result in increasing his intra-abdominal pressure. However, the use of a classification code should not limit the physician's recommendation concerning the individual activity programs. Rather, it should encourage him to make some suggestions concerning exercises that should be included in the student's program.

Nature and Scope of the Program

The nature and scope of an adapted physical education program will be greatly influenced by the philosophy of the physical education department, the nature and extent of the requirements of the students assigned to the program, and the physician's diagnosis and recommendations. It is of questionable value, therefore, to list specific games, sports, and rhythms that might be included in the program. The requirement of specific equipment and facilities which must be provided in order to offer an adapted physical education program is also inconsistent with good educational planning. However, it is possible to make generalizations concerning what should characterize a good adapted physical education program.

As indicated in chapter 1, students recommended for adapted physical education classes belong to one or more of the following general groups: (1) those desiring to rehabilitate a physical disability, (2) those desiring to adapt to a permanent physical disability, (3) those requiring a limited physical activity program, and (4) those requiring a developmental program. The requirements of these students will help to determine the nature and scope of the program that is to be provided.

It must be remembered that adapted physical education is primarily an individualized program. A student, because of the complexity of his condition, may be assigned or classified into more than one of the groups in terms of his requirements. Therefore, it is necessary to decide whether the sports or the therapeutic exercise phase of the program will best satisfy his requirements. Even though he may receive greater benefits from participation in one phase of the program than in the other, it might be advisable to have him participate in both phases.

Adapted physical education teachers often complain that the major limiting factor which influences the nature and scope of their program is the provision of adequate facilities and equipment. In many instances, it is not the lack of appropriate equipment or facilities, but the improper utilization of existing materials. One problem concerning facilities and equipment for the adapted physical education program is that they are frequently planned or selected too early in the organizational process. Determination of facilities or equipment to be used in the adapted physical education program must be made only after careful consideration is given to the requirements of the students whom it is to serve.

It is not necessary to have special activities, equipment, and facilities prior to offering an adapted physical education program. This type of program may be provided by any school that offers a regular physical education program. An adequate program can be offered immediately through the utilization of carefully selected existing regular physical education facilities.

Although the facilities and equipment which are used in the regular program may be used in the adapted physical education program, certain specific facilities and equipment are useful. Provision should be made for an indoor room which may serve for therapeutic exercise. A sports area is also needed. It is advisable to have both indoor and outdoor facilities for both phases of the program.

ADMINISTRATION

It is beyond the scope of this book, or any book, to discuss specific administrative practices for all school situations. There are general principles that should serve as guidelines to the administration and conduct of any adapted physical education program. Therefore, it must be remembered that the specific practices and administrative forms discussed here are to be considered applications of the principle of policy. These practices should be evaluated and accepted *or* rejected in terms of one's local situation. The administrative planning which is common to adapted physical education programs at the junior high school and high school levels are discussed here.

Administrative Handbook

In order for the adapted physical education program to run efficiently and effectively, it is essential that policies and procedures be developed. Collecting these policies and procedures into an organized and written form results in the evolution of an administrative handbook.

Such a handbook should contain the basis for the establishment of procedures to be utilized in the conduct of the program. The handbook may serve the following functions:

1. An operational guide for administering the program.
2. A reference for the application of policy concerning the cooperation or coordination of the school health services, the student's personal physician, and/or the department of physical education.
3. A resource guide for the administration of the physical education department with regard to the adapted physical education pro-

gram, facilities, equipment, staff, intra- and interdepartmental relationships.
4. A reference for maintaining continuity and consistency in regard to policies and procedures within the adapted physical education program.

Guidelines for Adapted Physical Education Programming

The following procedures are recommended as a guide for adapted physical education programming: (1) Before engaging in any activity within the adapted physical education program, all students must have their physical status certified by their personal physicians or by the school physician; (2) As a phase of the physical examination, the student's medical status must be classified in relation to his ability to participate in the physical education program; (3) The examining physician shall complete a medical classification card for each student whose physical condition makes restriction or special supervision of physical activities desirable; and (4) The physical education department shall keep the medical classification cards on file for all students currently enrolled in physical education.

Medical Classification System

A medical classification system is suggested that permits the physician to communicate to the adapted physical education staff broad, general recommendations for the student. Such a procedure should convey not only contraindications, but should also give added information that will meet the requirements of each individual student. A recommended system which involves the use of letters and numbers is known as the "UCLA system." This system, reported by Rossi, provides an excellent guide for administering an adapted physical education program (Rossi, 1954).

Each student is classified into one of three main groups, A, B, or C by the examining physician. Those students who are classified C require a restricted program. The physician also indicates the nature of the limitation as well as the nature of the program which will best meet the requirements of each student by using the appropriate number or numbers listed in the following code:

A—Not Restricted.
B—No Swimming (sinusitis, allergy, ear infection, etc.).

C—Special or Restricted. (Student is to be placed under the supervision of the adapted physical education staff.)

1. Energy Output to Be Kept Down: Should avoid dyspnea and fatigue. Cases of heart disease, asthma, convalescence from infectious disease, etc., will fall under this classification. Specify degree of restriction.
2. Protect from Trauma: Students with atrophied limbs, recent fractures, cerebral concussions, high myopia, front teeth recently straightened, etc.
3. No Close Contact with Other Students or with Mats; Keep out of Pool: Cases of repulsive or mildly infectious skin disease, such as pustular acne.
4. Not to Use Legs More than Necessary: Students, otherwise normal, who suffer from mild foot strain, old leg injuries, healed thrombophlebitis, etc.
5. Keep out of Pool and off High Places: Persons subject to convulsive seizures or periods of disturbed consciousness.
6. Adapt Activity to Some Deformity: For students who are blind or deaf or have lost a limb, but who are not particularly fragile; and similar cases.
7. Avoid Increased Intra-Abdominal Pressure: Such as caused by heavy lifting or straining. For students with hernia. (Recent appendectomy or other abdominal surgery.)
8. Recommended for Certain Regular Physical Education Classes (Activities): To be used when the physician wishes to specify certain regular physical education activity which would be beneficial, such as swimming, for patients with muscle weakness following poliomyelitis.
9. Recommended for Special Corrective Physical Exercises: For students who do not need to have their activity limited but who would benefit in a positive way from special exercises designed to correct or alleviate some defective condition. Pronated feet, recurrent shoulder dislocations, muscular underdevelopment, some cases of dysmenorrhea, and unusually poor posture are a few examples.
10. No Physical Education: If the school's requirement in physical education is to remain unfulfilled because of physical defect, the approval of the director or assistant director of the Student Health Service is required on the special yellow exemption form provided by the Registrar's office.

Medical Recommendation Form

Some type of form is useful upon which the physician may indicate his recommendations. The form should contain a place for the name of the student, year in school, date, height, weight, age, and other such information. One area should indicate the letters, A, B, and C and also the numbers 1 through 10 which can be used to indicate the number recommended in the classification code. Another space may be provided for the medical diagnosis and special recommendations. There should also be space for the signature of the examining physician.

Record of Posture Examination

The utilization of a form similar to the one shown on figure 10.1 for recording the findings of a postural screening examination is beneficial. The adapted physical education teacher may use the form when conducting postural screening of students for possible referrals to a physician. The physician may utilize the form during the physical examination. A single form may be used for recording periodic examinations through the use of colored inks or pencils. The severity of the possible deviations may be checked by using the numbers indicated. There are no objectively determined criteria for the use of these numbers as they relate to the severity of the divergencies. However, the following standards may serve as a guide: (1) *noticeable or slight,* approximately 1/2-inch deviation; (2) *mild or moderate,* approximately 1- to 1 1/2-inch deviation; (3) *severe,* more than 1 1/2- or 2-inch deviation.

Medical Referral Procedure

Ideally, each student enrolled in physical education would have a physical examination and medical classification each year. This practice is seldom encountered; physical examinations are usually scheduled only when the student enters the first grade, seventh grade, and high school. However, there are some instances when the student requires medical reclassification. Some may require reclassification as a result of an injury received in the activity class of the regular physical education program, intramurals, and the athletic program. Others may require reevaluation of their classification in relation to the activity in which they are currently enrolled or participating. Finally, some may need reclassification because of a change in their medical status as

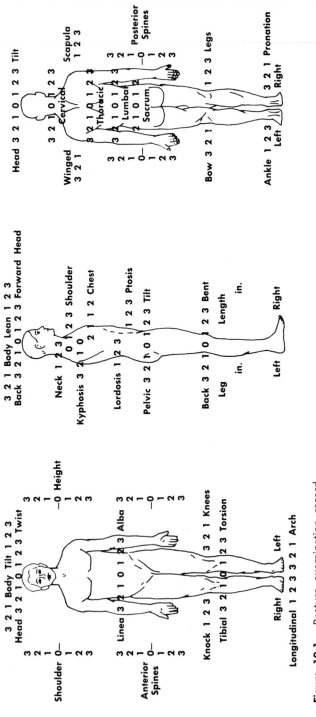

Figure 10.1. Posture examination record

a result of illness, disease, or operation, or as a consequence of their response to participation in rehabilitation activities in the adapted physical education program.

Regardless of the reason for the medical reclassification of his physical status, definite policies and procedures must be developed whereby the student is referred to the physician for reexamination. The adoption of a "referral slip" procedure is a valuable method of securing new information concerning the student's current physical condition. Such a method has the advantage of indicating to the physician that the adapted physical education staff is interested in the student's welfare. It also provides the physician a form upon which he can make his recommendations directly to the instructor of the student's adapted physical education class.

Recommendations from the Private Physician

Where medical supervision is provided by the school physician, the student with a medical recommendation from his private physician should be referred to the school physician. The school physician will then take appropriate action, and the private physician's recommendations are incorporated into the student's program by the adapted physical education teacher. The instructor should never assume the responsibility for changing the student's program on the basis of the recommendation from the student's private physician. Such changes must be made by the school physician who has been delegated the responsibility for the medical direction and supervision of the adapted physical education program.

Assignment to and Removal from the Adapted Physical Education Program

All those students whose physical condition prohibits their participation in the regular physical education program should be assigned or enrolled in adapted classes. Further, at no time should any student who requires such services be denied them because of class size. Since the adapted physical education program is concerned with providing physical education program experiences for students with physical limitations, it is essential that a physician certify the student's medical status before the student is considered for assignment to the program.

There should be definite policies and procedures established for the assignment of students to adapted physical education classes. There should also be policies and procedures for their reassignment to the regular physical education program. Such assignment or reassignment may be determined by the receipt of the medical classification and recommendation card by the instructor of the specific class. However, since the assignment of a student to adapted physical education may involve major changes in his total program, it may be more advantageous to establish an *admissions* and *dismissal committee*. This committee should consist of (1) the school physician, (2) the school nurse, (3) the instructor of adapted physical education, (4) the school guidance counselor, and/or (5) an administrative officer of the school. Periodic reevaluation of each student enrolled in the adapted physical education classes is essential. This reevaluation should be made by both the instructor and the prescribing physician.

Temporary Restrictions

A high frequency of joint injuries are received in the physical educational program. The majority of these injuries are sprains and strains which do not require extensive periods of time for recuperation. However, they may prohibit the student's participation for a day to three or four weeks. In addition, during the school year, several students may be expected to receive more serious injuries. Conditions to be expected are (1) fractures or dislocations, (2) serious illness involving long periods of convalescence, and (3) postsurgery rehabilitation. As a result, it is necessary to develop policies and procedures for those students who have temporary restrictions of their participation in the regular physical education program.

The following procedures are recommended for dealing with temporary restrictions:

1. When the student's disability is such that it is expected to limit or restrict his participation in the regular program for a semester or more, the student should be sent to the school physician or his personal physician so that his medical classification may be reclassified. The prescribing physician should include on the medical recommendation card the diagnosis, classification, recommendation, and the expected period for which the restriction is to apply. The student is then assigned to the adapted program. At the termination of the semester or of the period of time for the restriction, the instructor should send the student to the prescribing physician for reevaluation. This procedure will generally result in the reclassification of the student's medical status and the resultant reassignment to the regular physical education program.

2. When the student's disability is expected to limit or restrict his participation in the regular program for more than a week, the instructor of the regular physical education class should send the student to the instructor of the adapted physical education program. At this time, in conference with the student and depending upon the reason for restriction, the decision will be made whether or not the student should be referred to the prescribing physician for possible reclassification. Whether or not the student is referred to the physician, he should keep up his attendance and participation in some desirable activity in the adapted physical education program. If the student was sent to the physician for examination, he should be automatically reclassified by the adapted physical education staff at the end of the restriction period. This procedure would be followed unless the physician indicated that he would like to see the student again. Therefore, it is advisable for the prescribing physician to indicate on the medical recommendation card if the student is to be automatically reclassified at the end of the time for the restriction, or whether he wants to reevaluate the student's condition prior to reclassification. However, the instructor should never reclassify the student at the end of the restriction period unless he is sure that the student is able to participate in the regular program safely and successfully. Under no circumstances should he reclassify any student who evidences any complications of his original condition.

3. When the student's disability is such that it is expected to limit his participation in the regular physical education program for less than a week, the student's physical activity usually may be adjusted quite satisfactorily by the regular class instructor. The instructor may limit the individual's participation or modify his class activity in some other appropriate manner. However, when the instructor is in doubt as to what he should do concerning the student, he should send the student to the instructor of the adapted physical education program for advisement and possible program modification.

Scheduling of Classes

Scheduling of adapted physical education classes should be predicated upon the principle of serving the students most efficiently and effectively. Ideally, there should be an adapted physical education class whenever there is a regular physical education class scheduled. This helps to facilitate transfer of students from one program to another. Ease of transfer is important particularly for temporary restrictions.

However, it is impossible or even unnecessary to schedule that many classes in most schools; therefore, careful planning must guide the scheduling of the adapted physical education classes. If the school has an athletic program that holds its team practices during the last period of the day, it is recommended that an adapted physical education class be scheduled also during that period. This permits those student athletes who are injured in the program to receive guidance and supervision to facilitate the rehabilitation of their injuries.

Adequate supervision must be assured in order to provide an adapted physical education program which includes both a therapeutic exercise phase and a sports phase. The major problem in programming adapted physical education concerns the way in which the teacher may supervise both phases of the program at the same time. There is little question that the student may benefit from participating in both phases of the program. It is suggested, therefore, that the program be organized so that both phases are provided for each class. This may be accomplished by scheduling the therapeutic exercise phase on Monday, Wednesday, and Friday, and the sports phase on Tuesday and Thursday.

For those students whose conditions permit, provision must be made for their participation in the selected activities within the regular physical education program. For example, a student may be assigned to a regular physical education class for badminton instruction. At the termination of the instructional period of the activity, the student is reassigned or returned to the adapted physical education program. This procedure of assigning students on a limited basis to a regular physical education class is called a "farm-out." In implementing the farm-out procedure, a close relationship is necessary between the adapted physical education instructor and the teacher in the regular physical education program.

In order to meet the requirements of the students assigned to the adapted physical education classes, there must be periodic individual and group conferences between the students and the instructor. It is recommended that group and individual conferences be held during the first two or three meetings of the class.

The purpose of the initial group meeting is to orient all the students to the program. This orientation should include departmental rules and regulations, purposes, and objectives of the adapted physical education program, and its nature and scope. The latter would include a discussion of the therapeutic exercise and sports phases of the program.

Small group discussions and individual conferences are utilized to help each student establish his program. This assistance is basic to the achievement of the objectives of the program. The discussions and conferences are also concerned with determining the specific areas and exercises to be used for the rehabilitation or general conditioning of those students assigned to the therapeutic exercise phase of the program. They also assist in the selection of specific sports, games, and rhythms to be used by those students assigned to the sports phase of the program.

Following the discussions and conferences, the students are given instruction concerning their particular program of exercises or sports activities in which they will participate. Again, because of the commonality of limitations of physical activity and medical recommendations for various kinds of handicapping conditions, it is more efficient in terms of time to group the students by commonalities for the purposes of instruction and supervision. It is on the basis of commonalities of disabilities that the "exercise-routine method" concept discussed in chapter 8 was developed for use in administering exercises for most joint disabilities. The student assigned to the therapeutic exercise phase of the program, after having received instruction and learned his specific program, should be instructed to record his progress on cards provided for that purpose.

Students who are assigned to the sports phase of the program should be encouraged to participate in individual, dual, or team sports. Such activities as badminton, table tennis, paddle tennis, volleyball, basketball, and softball should comprise the sports phase of the adapted physical education program.

CONCLUSION

It is believed that the adapted physical education teacher's function is to (1) utilize existing knowledge of man in motion, (2) understand the effects of external and internal forces which affect motion, and (3) determine the demands of various physical activities on the organism. By applying principles of exercise, the professionally prepared physical educator should be able to provide physical activities which will aid in the alleviation or amelioration of negative adaptations of the body resulting from the forces of gravity, congenital defects, injury, illness, or disease. This is the major aim of adapted physical education.

SELECTED REFERENCES

1. AAHPER COMMITTEE ON ADAPTED PHYSICAL EDUCATION. "Guiding Principles for Adapted Physical Education." *The Journal of the American Association for Health, Physical Education and Recreation* 23 (April 1952):15, 28.

2. CLARKE, H. HARRISON, and CLARKE, DAVID H. *Developmental and Adapted Physical Education.* Englewood Cliffs, N. J.: Prentice-Hall, Inc., 1963.

3. *Corrective Physical Education: Teaching Guide for Junior and Senior High Schools.* Pub. No. SC-566. Los Angeles City Schools, Division of Instructional Services.

4. DANIELS, ARTHUR S., and DAVIES, EVELYN A. *Adapted Physical Education.* 2nd ed. New York: Harper & Row, Publishers, 1965.

5. FAIT, HOLLIS F. *Special Physical Education.* 2nd ed. Philadelphia: The W. E. Saunders Co., 1960.

6. KELLY, ELLEN DAVIS. *Adapted and Corrective Physical Education.* 4th ed. New York: Ronald Press Co., 1965.

7. LOGAN, GENE A. *Adaptations of Muscular Activity.* Belmont, Calif.: Wadsworth Publishing Co., Inc., 1964.

8. LOWMAN, CHARLES LeROY, and YOUNG, CARL HAVEN. *Postural Fitness.* Philadelphia: Lea & Febiger, 1960.

9. MATHEWS, DONALD K.; KRUSE, ROBERT; and SHAW, VIRGINIA. *The Science of Physical Education for Handicapped Children.* New York: Harper & Row, Publishers, 1962.

10. ROSSI, LORENZO J., JR. "Corrective Therapy in a School Environment." *Journal of the Association for Physical and Mental Rehabilitation* 8 (July-August 1954):115-116.

index

AAHPER Committee on Adapted Physical Education, 9, 243
Abramson, Arthur S., 72, 99
Achilles flare, 78
Achilles tendon, 33, 37
Adam's position, 96
Adamson, G. T., 145, 153
Adaptations:
  anteroposterior, compound, 88-90
  faulty weight-bearing, 76-79
  lateral, 90
  spinal, lateral, 95-100
Adapted physical education, 1-10
  bases for, 6
  definition of, 4-5
  objectives, 5
Adapted physical education program:
  administration of, 234-244
  administrative handbook, 234-235
  assignment to and removal from adapted physical education, 239-240
  classes, scheduling of, 241-243
  classifying physical status of student, 232
  medical classification system, 235-236
  medical recommendation form, 237
  medical referral procedure, 237-239
  nature and scope of program, 233-234
  organization, 227-234

  physician, private, recommendations from, 239
  posture examination, record of, 237
  programming guidelines, 235
  regular physical education program and, 227-228
  requirements of students, determining, 228-229
  restrictions, temporary, 240-241
  soliciting medical cooperation, 229-232
Adaptive shortening, 20
Administrative handbook, 234-235
Admissions and dismissal, committee for, 240
Agonist, 20
Albinism, 111
Amputation,
  congenital, 103, 110
  surgical, 110
  traumatic, 110
Anatomic movements, 27-28
Anatomic position, 26
Anatomic movements and positions, list of, 27-28
Anatomic "snuff-box," 137
Anatomic structures and relationships, 30-61
Anderson, Theresa W., 118
Ankle, the, 31-38, 122-126
Antagonist, 20
Anteroposterior postural adaptations, compound, 88-90

Antigravity musculature, 64-68
Anulus fibrosus, 129
Arch:
 longitudinal, 71
 medial longitudinal, 35
 metatarsal, transverse, 72
Arch-height test, functional, 76-77
Arnheim, Daniel D., 10
Asthma, 115-116
Atrophy, 141
Auditory handicaps,
 endogenous, 113
 exogenous, 113
Aural handicaps, 112-113
Auxter, David, 10
Axillary angle, 97

Back, the, 129-132
"Back head," 87
Ball, Jerry R., 144, 152, 154
Barham, Jerry N., 62
Basmajian, J. V., 62, 76, 100, 119
Billig, Harvey E., Jr., 117, 119
Billig stretch, 117, 204, 205
Blind, the, 112
Bone growth, normal, 14-15
Bones:
 calcaneus, 31, 34
 sustentaculum, tali of, 34
 clavicle, 50, 54
 cuboid, 31, 34
 cuneiforms, 34
 femur, 38
 greater trochanter of, 41
 lesser trochanter of, 41
 fibula, 32
 humerus, 50, 51, 52, 58
 metatarsals, 34
 navicular, 31, 34
 patella, 38
 pelvis, 41
 anterior inferior iliac spine of, 41
 anterior superior iliac spine of,
 41
 phalanges, 34
 radius, 58
 scapula, 50, 54
 acromion process of, 52, 54
 coracoid process of, 51, 52, 54

 glenoid fossa of, 54
 spine of, 51
 sesamoid, 80
 talus, 31, 32, 34
 tarsals, 34
 tibia, 32, 38
 tuberosity of, 38
 ulna, 58
Bones, brittle, 109
"Bowlegs," 94
Boyton, Dorothy A., 100
Braune, Christian Wilhelm, 70, 87
Breckenridge, Marian E., 17
Britten, Samuel D., 17
Bunion, 81
Burke, Roger K., 10, 94, 100, 148,
 154, 221
Bursa, 81
Bursitis, 81

Callus, 80
Calve-Perthes' disease, 107
Capsule, articular, 19
Cardiac anomalies,
 functional, 115
 organic, 115
Cardiovascular conditions, 103
Cardiovascular endurance, 138, 145,
 147
Carpal index, 13-14
Cartilage, articular, 20
Cataracts, 111
C curve, 97
Cerebral palsy, 103, 113-115
 ataxia, 114
 athetosis, 114
 rigidity, 114
 spasticity, 114
 tremor, 114
Cervical spine and head relationships,
 87-88
Chenoweth, Laurence B., 68, 69, 79,
 100
Circuit training, 145-147
Clarke, David H., 10, 99, 152, 244
Clarke, H. Harrison, 10, 99, 152, 244
Classes, scheduling of, 241-243
Clubfoot, 105
Colestock, Claire, 100

Committee on Adapted Physical Education of the AAHPER, 9, 243
Conference of Executives of American Schools for the Deaf, 113, 119
Congenital conditions, 102
Congenital and pathological conditions, 101-119
Contraction:
concentric, 22
eccentric, 22
isometric, 22
isotonic, 22
phasic, 22
Cooper, Hazel, 100
Cooper, John M., 62
Cooper, Kenneth H., 147, 152
Coordination,
general, 151
specific, 151
"Coordination exercises," 152
Corn, 81
Corrective physical education, 4
Corrective Physical Education Teaching Guide for Junior and Senior High Schools, 99, 221, 226, 244
Corrective therapy, 4
Cortex, areas of,
motor, 23
premotor, 23
sensory, 23
Coxa plana, 103, 107
Coxa valga, 106
Coxa vara, 106
Cozen, Lewis, 119
Crowe, Walter C., 10
Cruze, Wendell W., 18
Curriculum Committee for Health, Physical Education, and Safety in the Elementary Schools, 17
Cysts, bone, 103

Daniels, Arthur S., 10, 99, 226, 244
Davies, Evelyn A., 10, 17, 99, 226, 244
Davis, Elwood C., 62, 69, 100, 152
Deaf, the, 113

Deaver, G. G., 114, 119
Delagi, Edward F., 72, 99
DeLorme, Thomas L., 143, 152, 221
"Derotation" principle, 99
Development, 11
Developmental levels, postural patterns of, 15-17
Developmental physical education, 4
Deviation, 95
de Vries, Herbert A., 10, 23, 26, 62, 149, 150, 151, 153
Deyton, John W., 226
Diabetes mellitus, 116
Diagonal movements and planes, 26
Diaphysis, 14
Diehl, Bobbie, 157, 221
Disability grouping, 4
Discs,
interarticular, 20
intervertebral, compression herniations, 129
Dislocations, 124-125
ankle, 124-125
congenital, 103, 106
elbow, 135
hip, 129
shoulder, 133
Drew, Lillian Curtis, 100
Dunkelberg, James G., 10, 102, 103, 119
Dynamic stabilization, 48
"Dynamic tension," 144
Dysmenorrhea, 116
Dysplasia of the hip, 106
Dyspnea, 115

Egstrom, Glen H., 149, 153
Elbow, the, 58-61, 135-136
Emotional involvements and physical disabilities, 3
Endurance, 145-147
cardiovascular, 145
muscular, 145
Endurance development exercises, 201-202
Epilepsy, 117-118
grand mal, 118
petit mal, 118
psychomotor seizure, 118

Epiphyseal plate, 14
Epiphysis, 14
Erb's palsy, 103, 105-106
Exercise for congenital and patholog-
    ical conditions, 173
Exercise for general conditioning,
    200-222
  endurance development, 201-202
  flexibility development, 202-208
  strength-development, 208-222
Exercise for musculoskeletal injuries,
    173-200
Exercise for postural adaptations,
    157-173
Exercise programs, 155-222
  ankle, 174
  back, 184-191
  elbow, 197-198
  hip, 180-184
  knee, 175-180
  neck, 199
  shoulder, 191-197
  wrist, 198-199
Exercise-routine method of adminis-
    tering therapeutic exercise,
    156
Exercise, therapeutic, classifications
    of, 138
Exercise therapy, 4
Exer-Genie Exerciser, 146, 172, 180,
    208-221
Exostosis, 81

Fait, Hollis, F., 10, 100, 226, 244
Falls, Harold B., 10, 24, 62, 151, 153,
    221
"Fashion model slouch" posture, 90
"Fatigue slump" posture, 88-89
Feet, the, 71-82
Femoral epiphysis, slipped, 108
Fischer, Otto, 70, 87
Flat back, 86, 87
"Flat neck," 87
Flexibility, 137, 147-150
Flexibility development exercises,
    202-208
Flexibility development exercises for
    postural alignment, 158-162
Flint, M. Marilyn, 10, 157, 221

Foot-ankle postural adaptations, 92-
    93
Foot divergencies, other common, 79-
    82
Foot-leg alignment, 76, 83
Foot positions, 72-73
Foot test, functional, 79
Forces that affect man's movements,
    63-64
"Forward head," 87
"Forward shoulders," 86
"4" position, 131
Fractures,
  fibula, of the, 125
  hip, of the, 128
  navicular, of the, 136-137
  tibia, of the, 125
  vertebrae, of the, 131-132
Frederick, A. Bruce, 153
Fries, Corrine, 70, 100
Fuller, Dudley Dean, 72, 100
Fulton, John F., 10

Gallagher, J. Roswell, 119
Garrison, Karl C., 17
Genu recurvatum, 83
Genu valgum, 94
Genu varum, 94
Glassow, Ruth B., 62
Glycosuria, 116
Goff, Charles Weer, 68, 100
Grant, J. C. Boileau, 62, 76, 100, 119
Gravity:
  center of, determination of, 70
  effect of, 63-64
  effect of on upright posture, 68-70
Gray, Henry, 62
Green, Morris, 119
Grid screen, posture, 82
Grollman, S., 25
Growth and development, 11-18
"Guiding Principles for Adapted
    Physical Education," 5, 9

Hallux valgus, 81
Hammer toe, 80
Handbook, administrative, 234-235
Handicapping conditions:
  acquired, 102
  congenital, 102

Hathaway, Winifred, 111, 119
Health problems, special, 114-118
Helbing's sign, 78
Helfrich, H., 137
Hellebrandt, Frances A., 70, 100, 143, 153
Hemiplegia, 113
Hernia,
abdominal, 117
inguinal, 117
umbilical, 117
Hettinger, Theodor, 144, 154
Hip, the, 41-45, 128-129
Hirt, Susanne E., 70, 100
Holland, George, 148, 149, 153
Hollow back, 86
Hunt, Valerie V., 100, 154, 226
Hurlock, Elizabeth B., 17
Hyperglycemia, 116
Hyperopia, 111
Hypertrophy, 142
Hypoglycemia, 116

Individual physical education, 4
Injury:
acute, 120
chronic, 120
compression, 120
elongation, 120
traumatic, 120
Injury mechanism:
compression, 120
elongation, 120
Insulin, 116
Isometric strength-development exercises for postural alignment, 163-166
Isotonic strength-development exercises for postural alignment, 167-173

Jacobson, Edmund, 151, 153
Jensen, Clayne, 62
Joint and muscle interrelationships, 22-23
Joint structure, 19-21
Joints:
freely movable, 19
immovable, 19

integrity of, 20
movement of, 28-29
slightly movable, 19
Joints and their movements, list of, 28-29

Kasch, Fred W., 119
Keegan, Jay J., 130, 137
Kelly, Ellen Davis, 100, 244
Kendall, Florence P., 100
Kendall, Henry O., 100
Kerby, Edith, 112, 119
Kessler, J. W., 10
Kinzly, Hazel L., 100
Kirk, Samuel A., 112, 119
Klafs, Carl E., 226
Kleinberg, Samuel, 14
Knee, the, 38-41, 126-128
"Knock-knees," 94
Kraus, Hans, 129, 137, 153, 221
Kruse, Robert, 10, 18, 100, 153, 226, 244
Kypholordosis, 87
Kyphosis, 86
cervical, 87
dorsal, 86
lumbar, 86
thoracic, 86

Lacertus fibrosus, 60
Lamb, D. R., 14, 17
Langerhans, islands of, 116
Lee, Doris May, 17
Lee, J. Murray, 17
Leg-thigh alignment, 83, 93
Legg-Calve-Perthes' disease, 107
Legg's disease, 107
Lengthening-strengthening principle, 149
Licht, Sidney, 153, 221
Ligaments:
anterior cruciate, 38, 40, 127
anterior talofibular, 31
anterior tibiofibular, 31
calcaneofibular, 31
calcaneonavicular ("spring" ligament), 35
coracoacromial, 52
deltoid, 32

iliofemoral (Y-ligament), 41
inguinal, 42, 43
lateral collateral, 38
lateral talocalcaneal, 31
long plantar, 36
medial collateral, 38, 126
medial talocalcaneal, 32
patellar, 38
posterior cruciate, 38, 40, 127
posterior talocalcaneal, 32
posterior talofibular, 33
posterior talotibial, 32
posterior tibiofibular, 33
pubofemoral, 41
talonavicular, 32
teres, 129
Linea alba, 46
Logan, Gene A., 10, 17, 24, 48, 62,
    69, 100, 119, 137, 140, 149,
    151, 153, 154, 156, 221, 222,
    226, 244
Logan, Roland F., 137
Loofburrow, G. N., 149, 153
Lordosis, 86
cervical, 87
lumbar, 86
Lowendahl, Evelyn, 117, 119
Lowman, Charles LeRoy, 16, 100,
    221, 244
Lumbar spine, 86
Lumbar-thoracic relationships, 87

Mallet toe, 80
Mainland, D., 13-14, 17
Mathews, Donald K., 10, 18, 100,
    153, 226, 244
Maturation, 11
Mayer, D. McCullagh, 119
McKinney, Wayne C., 10, 48, 62, 69,
    100, 118, 119, 152
Medical classification system, 235-236
Medical cooperation, soliciting, 229-
    232
Medical diagnosis and recommenda-
    tion of the physician, 6
Medical gymnastics, 4
Medical referral procedure, 237-239
Medical recommendation form, 237
Meniscus, 38, 126

Menstruation, 116
Metaphysis, 14
Metatarsalgia, 80
Metheny, Eleanor, 10, 69, 100, 140,
    153, 221
Miller, Augustus T., 10
Monoplegia, 113
Moore, C. A., 10
Morehouse, Laurence E., 10, 137,
    143, 154
Morgan, R. E., 145, 153
Morrison, Whitelaw Reid, 68, 69, 79,
    100
Morton, Dudley J., 72, 80, 100
Morton's metatarsalgia, 80
Moseley, H. F., 62, 137
Müller, Erich A., 144, 154
Multiple sclerosis, 103
Murphy, Margaret N., 17
Muscle:
cardiac, 22
extrinsic, 37
intrinsic, 36
involuntary, 22
voluntary, 22
Muscle spindle, 24
Muscle tension, 22
Muscles:
abductor digiti minimi, 36
abductor hallucis, 36
adductor brevis, 43
adductor hallucis, 36
adductor longus, 43
adductor magnus, 43
anconeus, 61
biceps brachii, 59, 60
    long head of, 52
    short head of, 52
biceps femoris, 38
brachialis, 59
brachioradialis, 60
coracobrachialis, 52
deltoid, 50, 51
erector spinae, 49
extensor digitorum longus, 32
extensor hallucis longus, 32
external oblique abdominis, 46, 49
flexor carpi radialis, 60
flexor carpi ulnaris, 60

flexor digiti minimi, 36
flexor digitorum brevis, 36
flexor digitorum longus, 32, 33, 37
flexor hallucis brevis, 36
flexor hallucis longus, 32, 33, 36, 37
gastrocnemius, 33, 41
gemellus inferior, 45
gemellus superior, 45
gluteus maximus, 44
gluteus medius, 44
gluteus minimus, 45
gracilis, 43
hamstrings, 41, 45
iliacus, 43
infraspinatus, 51, 52, 53
internal oblique abdominis, 46, 49
latissimus dorsi, 49, 57
levator scapulae, 54
lumbricales, 36
obturator externus, 45
obturator internus, 45
palmaris longus, 60
pectineus, 43
pectoralis major, 57
pectoralis minor, 52, 55
peroneus brevis, 31, 33, 38
peroneus longus, 31, 33, 36, 38
peroneus tertius, 31
piriformis, 45
pronator teres, 60
psoas major, 43, 49
quadratus femoris, 45
quadratus lumborum, 49
quadriceps femoris, 38, 41
rectus abdominis, 46
rectus femoris, 42, 49
rhomboid major, 54
rhomboid minor, 54
sartorius, 42
serratus anterior, 54, 56
soleus, 33
subscapularis, 51, 52, 53
supraspinatus, 51, 52
tensor fasciae latae, 42, 44
teres major, 53
teres minor, 51, 53
tibialis anterior, 32, 37
tibialis posterior, 32, 33, 36, 37

transverse abdominis, 46, 49
trapezius, 51, 56
triceps brachii, 53, 61
long head of, 53
triceps surae, 33
Muscular contraction, 22
Muscular dystrophy, 103, 110
facioscapulohumeral, 110
juvenile form, 110
mixed types, 110
pseudohypertrophic, 110
Muscular endurance, 138
Musculature, 22-26
Musculoskeletal injuries, 120-137
Musculoskeletal interrelationships, 19-62
Musculoskeletal movement, 26-28
Musculoskeletal system, 19-22
Myopia, 111, 112

Neurological integration, 23-26
Neuron:
afferent, 24
efferent, 24
Nolen, Jewel, 119
Nucleus pulposus, 129
Nystagmus, 111

Organization and administration of the adapted physical education program, 227-244
administration, 234-244
organization, 227-234
Orthopedic handicaps, 103
Osgood-Schlatter disease, 103, 108
Osteochondritis, 106-107
deformans juvenilis, 107
deformans juvenilis dorsi, 108
Osteochondrosis, 103, 106
Osteogenesis imperfecta, 109
Osteomyelitis, 103, 109
Osteopsathyrosis, 109
Overload, 142

Paraplegia, 113
Partially seeing, 111-112
Pathological conditions, 101
Pedo-graph, 74
Pelvic girdle alignment, 83-84, 94-95

Pelvic inclination, 84
  decreased, 84
  increased, 84
Pelvic-lumbar relationships, 85-86
Perthes' disease, 107
Pes cavus, 77
Pes planus, 77
Physical development, principles of, 12-13
Physical fitness, 1
Pierson, William R., 144, 154
Plumb line, 82
Podiascope, 74
"Poke neck," 87
Poliomyelitis, 103, 109-110
Positions, traditional, 163
  cross-sitting, 165
  erect standing, 166
  front-lying, 164
  hook-lying, 164
  prone, 164
  supine, 163
  "tailor's sit," 165
Postural adaptations, 63-100
  anteroposterior, 82-90
  functional, 70, 96
  lateral, 90-100
  structural, 70, 97
Postural patterns of different developmental levels, 15-17
Postural screening, 70-71
Posture,
  of adolescent, 16-17
  "good," 68
    aesthetic value of, 69
    criteria of, 69
Posture examination, record of, 237
Postures, concept of, 68
Pott's disease, 109
Pott's fracture, 121, 125
Prescribed exercise, 4
Principles of exercise, 138-154
Program, planning of, 8
Programming guidelines, 235
Progressive relaxation, 151
Progressive resistance exercise, 143, 174
Pronation of foot, 73

Quadriplegia, 113

Raab, Wilhelm, 129, 137, 153
Randall, Leila C., 200, 221
Range of motion, limited, 148
Rarick, G. Lawrence, 18
Rasch, Philip J., 10, 94, 100, 137, 143, 144, 148, 154, 221
Rathbone, Josephine, 100, 154
Recreation, 1
Refractive errors, 111
Reflex:
  arc, 24-25
  crossed extensor, 26
  extensor, 25
  extensor thrust, 25
  flexion, 25
  myotatic, 24
  postural, 24
  spinal, 24
  stretch, 24
  withdrawal, 25
Relationship of foot position to weight-bearing, 72
Relaxation, 150-151
  conscious, 150
  natural, 150
  progressive, 151
Remedial gymnastics, 4
Remedial physical education, 4
Restrictions, temporary, 240-241
Retrolental fibroplasia, 112
"Reversed C" curve, 97
"Reversed S" curve, 98
Rheumatic fever, 115
Rich, George Q., 144, 152, 154
Richmond, Julius B., 119
Riedman, Sarah R., 62
Rossi, Lorenzo J., Jr., 235, 244
"Rotary cuff," 51-53
"Round hollow back," 87
"Round shoulders," 86
"Round sway back," 87
"Round upper back," 86
Rusk, Howard A., 114, 119
Ryan, A. J., 154, 161

"SAID" principle, 140
Scheuermann's disease, 108
Schultz, Gordon W., 62
Scoliosis, 95
Scott, M. Gladys, 62

S curve, 98
Seaman, Janet A., 10
Seeing, partially, 111
Semilunar cartilage, 38
Separation, shoulder, 133
"7" position, 131
Shaw, Virgina, 10, 18, 100, 153, 226, 244
Shelton back routine, 187
Shelton, Robert E., 149, 154, 156, 187, 221, 222
Shoulder, the, 50-58, 132-134
Shoulder point, 133
Sills, Frank D., 154
Skeletal growth, 13-15
Skill, neuromuscular, 137, 151-152
Slipped disc, 129
Spatial relationship of muscles to joints, 21-22
Special education, 102
Spina bifida, 103, 109
Spondylolisthesis, 108-109
Sports in the adapted physical education program, 223-226
Sports programming, 223-225
Sports selection criteria, 225-226
Sprain, 121
  eversion, 122
  inversion, 122
Stafford, George T., 226
Steindler, Arthur, 13, 18
Stone, Eleanor B., 226
Strabismus, 111
Strain, 121
Streng, Alice, 113, 119
Strength, 141
Strength development, 141-144
  isometric, 142
  isotonic, 142
  principles of, 142-143
  procedures, 143-144
Strength-development exercises for general conditioning, 208-222
Stresses, environmental, 101
Stretching, slow and fast, 149-150
Subluxation, 121
Subtalar joint, 31
Supination of foot, 73
Swanker, Wilson A., 119
Sweetnam, Rodney, 100, 137

Synapse, 24
Synovial fluid, 19

Talipes, 104
  calcaneus, 104
  calcaneovalgus, 105
  calcaneovarus, 105
  equinovalgus, 105
  equinovarus, 103
  equinus, 104
  valgus, 104
  varus, 105
Tendons, 20
Therapeutic exercise, 138
Thigh-pelvic relationships, 85
Thomas, William L., 62
Thoracic-cervical relationships, 88
Thorndike, Augustus, 137
Thorpe, Louis P., 18
Three "I" principle, 140-141
Toe, overlapping, 81
Tonus, muscle, 26
Torticollis, 103, 111
Tractus iliotibialis, 42
Transverse tarsal and subtalar joints, 31
Trauma, 120
Triplegia, 113
Trunk, the, 46-50
Tuberculosis, 103
  skeletal, 109
  spondylitis, 109
Tumors, bone, 103
12-minute field test, Cooper's, 147

"UCLA system" of medical classification, 235-236
Universal Gym, 146, 172, 208-221

Vertebrae, rotation of, 98-99
Visceral ptosis, 85
Visual acuity, 111
Visual handicaps, 111-112

"Waiter's tip" deformity, 106
Walker, S. M., 149, 154
Wallis, Earl L., 24, 62, 140, 144, 151, 152, 153, 154, 221, 222
Watkins, Arthur L., 143, 152, 221

Weight-bearing and foot position, 72
Wells, Katharine F., 62, 142, 154
Wiles, Philip, 100, 137
Williams, J. G. P., 129, 137
"Winged scapulae," 87
Wolff, Julius, 13, 18

Wolff's law, 13, 71, 72
Wrist, the, 136-137
Wry neck, 111

Yessis, Michael, 145, 154
Young, Carl Haven, 16, 244